MANAGING YOUR RENTAL HOUSE FOR INCREASED INCOME

Managing Your Rental House for Increased Income

A UNIQUE SYSTEM DESIGNED TO MAKE
MORE MONEY NO MATTER WHAT
HAPPENS TO THE ECONOMY

Doreen Bierbrier

McGraw-Hill Book Company
New York St. Louis San Francisco Bogotá Guatemala
Hamburg Lisbon Madrid Mexico Montreal Panama Paris
San Juan São Paulo Tokyo Toronto

This publication is designed to provide accurate and authoritative information in regard to the subject matter covered. It is sold with the understanding that neither the publisher nor the author is engaged in rendering legal or accounting services. If legal advice or other expert assistance is required, the services of a competent professional person should be sought.

Adapted from a Declaration of Principles jointly adopted by a Committee of the American Bar Association and a Committee of Publishers and Associations.

1 2 3 4 5 6 7 8 9 DOC DOC 8 7 6 5

ISBN 0-07-005232-8

LIBRARY OF CONGRESS CATALOGING IN PUBLICATION DATA

Bierbrier, Doreen.
  MANAGING YOUR RENTAL HOUSE FOR INCREASED INCOME
  1. Rental housing—Management. 2. Real estate management. I. Title.
HD1394.B435 1985   647'.92   84-17167
ISBN 0-07-005232-8

BOOK DESIGN BY PATRICE FODERO

*This book is dedicated
to the memory of my
mother, Fay Bierbrier,
and to her sense of values
and her sense of humor.*

CONTENTS

CONTENTS

CONTENTS

ACKNOWLEDGEMENTS

I am indebted to a good number of people who helped me put this book together.

Marcie Heidish and Jacques de Spoelberch for getting me started on the right foot in the publishing world.

Steve Berman of the Census Bureau who made major contributions to Chapter 1.

Bruce Harwood for providing innumerable valuable comments on how to shape the form and content of the book.

Gil Engler and Mike Lennon of HOMEPRO who guided me with their expertise on how to make home inspections.

Carl Jonson, CPA, who went over the chapter on record keeping with a fine tooth comb.

Staff from the Northern Virginia Board of Realtors—especially Wayne Howland, Joanna Tanner, Kay Schleuter, and Resi Strickler—who gave me their wholehearted cooperation.

Others who helped me with this book include Glenn Crellin, Peter Fronczek, Perry Gawen, Jr., Jon Kinney, Jack Melnick, Louise Porter, and Ralph Swope.

My tenants also enthusiastically helped me critique parts of the section on management. Thank you Anne Noto, Erin Dunn, Jackie Burcroff, Rene Raffini, Sue Gillettte, Laura Janis, Marcia Molde, Shannon Maher, Winnie Land, Loye Lockett, Dan Cooney, Cecelia Bold, and Nancy Schadler.

INTRODUCTION

I never had a dollhouse. I never had a treehouse. When my father tried to explain the advantages of investing in real estate to me after college, I told him I wasn't interested in money and went off to join the Peace Corps. In college I couldn't imagine a more terrible fate than being over 30, living in the suburbs, and making mortgage payments. And here I am now—over 30, living in the suburbs, paying off six mortgages, and loving it.

I own four houses and get very high rental incomes from them. *Managing Your Rental House for Increased Income* is a step-by-step manual which tells you how to get the same remarkable returns as I do from rental houses.

This book does not have a get-rich-quick scheme; it does not promise untold riches for minimal effort within a few months. Nonetheless, those of you who own or intend to buy a rental house may be able to pick up some suggestions to make your investment much more profitable than you could have imagined possible. If you own a certain kind of rental house and apply the principles in this book, you may be able to increase your rental income by as much as 50 percent. You will also probably never have another vacant house again.

Does my advice work? Well, for me it did. I came to Washington, D.C. with assets of about $10,000. Within 5 years I'd acquired assets of 40 times that initial sum, mostly in real estate.

It seems odd to be telling you this, because basically I'm still not a very materialistic person; nor for that matter am I a wheeler-dealer when it comes to buying houses. What I do seem to be able to do is to find and manage single-family houses for extraordinary income. More precisely, I don't really manage property at all. Rather, I manage to work with people—plumbers, carpenters, neighbors, and especially tenants—who help me get a very high rental income from the several houses I own.

I wrote this book for owners like me—for people who either have or want to buy one or more rental houses, and who want to get unusually high rent while maintaining their peace of mind. This book is for owners who care that their houses are well maintained, their tenants satisfied, and their neighbors pleased.

There is no secret to what I'm doing, but there is a system. I have developed some highly successful procedures for selecting an appropriate house, choosing responsible tenants, and providing good maintenance. Most important, though, to get the same high rental income I do, you'll have to put aside traditional theories about how to rent houses and to whom. You see, the key to my system is to rent certain kinds of houses not to a family, but to singles.

Many owners are afraid to rent their homes to singles because they believe the traditional stereotypes:

- Singles are transitory, and all sorts of people will be coming and going before the lease is up.
- Singles won't take the responsibility for mowing the lawn or making household repairs.
- Singles won't be able to coordinate all of the tenants in the house so that a collective rent check will be mailed to the owner on time each month.
- Singles are more likely than a family to vandalize and destroy a property.
- Singles will not become involved in the community, and neighbors will resent a group house nearby.

Stereotypes often contain some grain of truth, and the fears of owners have in many cases been justified. Yet I own four houses, all of which are shared by nonrelated singles, including my own. In 8 years:

- I have never had a vacant house after the first tenant moved in.
- I have never had any vandalism.

- No tenant has ever skipped out on a rent payment.
- Most tenants have stayed with me from 1 to 3 years.

The rental income from my houses is about 50 percent more than what those houses would bring if I rented them to families. Oh yes, one more point: I like my tenants and am on good terms with the neighbors near all of my houses.

Just luck? I don't think so.

The underlying reason why my rental system works is this: Although I receive substantial economic benefits from the arrangement, my tenants receive a good number of benefits in return. So do the neighbors. So does the community.

You have to take certain steps, though, to ensure that you will have these benefits to dispense. First, you need to determine if you are temperamentally suited to buy and manage rental houses. Then you need to find the right rental house—one that is structurally sound and can comfortably accommodate several singles. Next, you need to select compatible, responsible tenants who will work well together as a household. Then you have to be responsive to the needs of the tenants and attentive to the maintenance of the house. And last, you should keep relevant records.

This guide has been written to explain exactly how to do it.

One final note: I had the dickens of a time trying to make the text non-sexist, and finally gave up trying. Because practically all of my tenants, and most of the real estate agents I know are female, I usually refer to an individual tenant or agent as "she." Because most of the plumbers, electricians, and carpenters who work with me are men, I use "he" and "his" when I have to use a pronoun or an adjective to describe a tradesperson.

With that explanation, let us begin.

1

STARTLING CHANGES IN REAL ESTATE INVESTMENT

It's very difficult to make predictions, particularly about the future.

Attributed to Samuel Goldwyn

"Sell your home and find a home of comparable quality to rent. . . ." "As an investment, real estate is probably one of the poorest prospects for the future." "If you own income property now, this would be a good time to get rid of it."

Sound advice? In the last few years there has been a spate of doom and gloom books about investing in real estate. Some of the more popular of these books have been Douglas Casey's *Crisis Investing* (1980) and his later *Strategic Investing* (1982), Howard Ruff's *How to Prosper During the Coming Bad Years* (1979), and *The Coming Real Estate Crash* (1979) by John English and Gray Cardiff. The gist of the books is that we've been on a real estate bubble—particularly in and around many large metropolitan areas—and that the bubble is about to burst.

The doom and gloom argument certainly isn't new. The quotes in the first paragraph, for example, come from Harry Browne, who predicted an imminent real estate crash in 1970 in his book, *How You Can Profit from the Coming Devaluation*. He made a similar prediction in *You Can Profit from a Monetary Crisis* (1974). Yet, 1970 was the year that started the decade of the most spectacular house prices in the history of the United States. Between 1970 and 1979, median sales price of new, single-family houses increased from $23,400 to $62,900, or more than 168 percent.

The clear direction of house prices has been up over the past 90 years. And they have gone up dramatically for more than a decade. The median sales price of single-family homes in the United States even inched up between 1981 and 1982, at a time when interest rates for mortgages reached unprecedented heights; the median sales price for new homes went from $68,900 in 1981 to $69,300 in 1982. In 1983, when interest rates for home loans dropped, the median price surged again to $75,300. Despite some of the highest interest rates the United States has ever seen, housing prices didn't "crash."

To find out why real estate didn't crash, we have to consider the arguments made by those who thought it would:

WHY DIDN'T REAL ESTATE CRASH?

Argument 1

The reason that the price of houses is unrealistically high is because real estate can be purchased with just a small downpayment, and the rest on credit. The situation is reminiscent of the stock market prior to the Great Depression when speculators purchased stocks on margin. If real estate prices decline even slightly, it will trigger a panic and house prices will collapse.

Howard Ruff is right in his analysis that unlike stocks purchased on margin, there is no call in real estate if the owner has an amortized mortgage. Your mortgage lender, unlike your stockbroker, won't suddenly demand all the money due at once for a purchase you made with just a small downpayment.

In any event, it's more instructive to compare real estate investment now with real estate investment in the thirties rather than to compare real estate investment now with investment on the stock market then.

The reason that there were so many foreclosures during the depression of the thirties was that most people at that time had mortgages on which they only paid interest, with the principal due and payable after five years. Homeowners couldn't pay the lump sum of the princi-

2

pal when it was due, nor were the banks then in a position to finance the loans.

Today, however, most home loans are amortized. In other words, they are repaid in regular installments which consist of both principal and interest. Loans are completely paid off over a period of years, and no lump sum payment is ever called due.

Nor do most owners of single-family homes have much of a loan to pay off. Some 39 percent of all single-family houses in the United States had absolutely no existing mortgage on them in 1981—the identical percentage as in 1971. Of those owner-occupied houses with mortgages, half of the households reported their monthly payment to be $262 or less, according to the U.S. Bureau of the Census' *Annual Housing Survey: 1981.*

Argument 2

Real estate is not liquid like cash or gold or stocks. In times of economic disaster nobody will want to buy real estate, and owners will be stuck, unable to convert their property holdings to cash and to flee with their assets.

So where would people flee? If we are truly headed for a huge, economic disaster, what place would be safe?

In all probability, Americans would work together and muddle through, just as we've done throughout our history. The majority of us own our own houses and would probably stay right where we were until times improve. As for the renters, where would they go? Wherever they went they would have to rent, unless they decided to pitch their tents in the mountains for a few years.

The very safety of investing in single-family homes is that they are so illiquid. If a panic occurs in the stock market or the gold market, your fortune can be wiped out overnight. You can't sell a house overnight, though, and this ensures a certain stick-to-itiveness among owners. Most owners of single-family houses don't have to sell. They can hold on to their houses until they choose to sell.

Argument 3

Population is leveling off or actually declining, particularly in large metropolitan areas. Real estate prices will decline with a falling population.

3

Percent Growth in Value of Single–Family Houses in Selected Cities (1970–1980)

CITY (*SMSA**)	POPULATION IN 1970	POPULATION IN 1980	PERCENT GROWTH IN POP.	MEDIAN VALUE OF SINGLE-FAMILY HOME		PERCENT GROWTH IN VALUE
				1970	1980	
Boston	2,753,700	2,763,357	0.35	$23,800	$56,000	135
San Francisco	3,109,519	3,250,630	4.54	26,900	99,000	268
Washington, D.C.	2,861,123	3,060,922	6.98	28,200	79,900	183
Philadelphia	4,817,914	4,716,818	<2.10>	14,900	41,700	180
Detroit	4,199,931	4,353,413	3.65	19,600	42,500	117
Pittsburgh	2,401,245	2,263,894	<5.72>	15,300	42,700	179
Los Angeles	7,032,075	7,477,503	6.33	24,300	87,400	260
Chicago	6,978,947	7,103,624	1.79	24,300	65,000	167

* SMSA: Standard Metropolitan Statistical Area.
** *Sources:* U.S. Bureau of the Census, *Census of Housing: 1970*, vol. 1, *Housing Characteristics for States, Cities, and Counties*, pt. 1, *United States Summary* (issued December 1972). U.S. Bureau of the Census, *Census of Housing: 1980*, vol. 1, *Characteristics of Housing Units*, ch. A, *General Housing Characteristics*, p. 1, *United States Summary*, HC 80-1-A1 (issued May 1983).

Let's look at a few of the largest metropolitan areas that experienced either a decline or just a marginal increase in population between 1970 and 1980. (See chart on p. 4)

Clearly there is no correlation between a decline in population and a decline in the value of houses. In fact, the opposite may be true in some cases. If some city neighborhoods become gentrified places for the wealthy, one renovated townhouse, which may previously have housed two or three poor families with children, may now house a young couple with no children. The value of the property would have increased substantially rather than have declined.

Population growth or decline is just one factor of many that affect the price of real estate. Such other factors as the rate of inflation, tax incentives, and building construction costs may be even more significant.

Argument 4

One major reason that house prices are so high is that the prices reflect the tax benefits owners derive. Once the tax benefits of home ownership are reduced, house prices will drop sharply.

This argument was made in *Crisis Investing*, which was published in 1980, and prior to that in *The Coming Real Estate Crash*, published in 1979. However, it does not appear that Congress is in any hurry to reduce the tax benefits of home ownership.

In 1981 Congress gave real estate investors substantially more tax benefits when it passed the Economic Recovery Tax Act. The 1984 Tax Reform Act does not substantially reduce those benefits for the individual investor who buys a few rental houses.

But let's suppose, for the sake of argument, that a bill was passed which substantially reduces tax benefits for investing in real estate. Indeed, there probably would be a significant impact—not only for owners of rental property, but for renters, too, because one possible outcome would be that house prices would not come down, but that rents would go up in order to offset the elimination of the tax benefits.

Argument 5

House prices skyrocketed because low-interest, 30-year mortgages were available. Now that long-term low-interest money is drying up, house prices will fall.

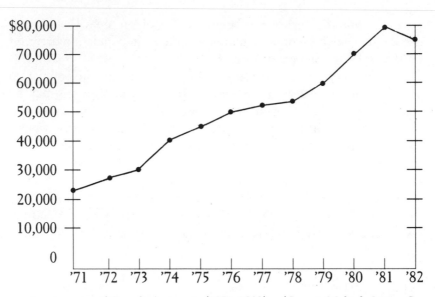

Average price of Canadian property (1971–1982). (*Source: Multiple Listing Service: 1982 Annual Report*, The Canadian Real Estate Association, Research and Publications Department. Don Mills, Ontario, Canada: April, 1983, p. 4.)

Canada has had 5-year variable rate mortgages since 1967. By 1969, long-term fixed-rate loans became virtually obsolete.

The accompanying chart shows the average price of properties processed through the Canadian Multiple Listing Service from 1971 to 1982.

There is clearly no evidence to date that short-term variable rate mortgages will cause real estate prices to collapse.

Argument 6

It is obvious that houses are overpriced. Only a small fraction of the American population can afford to buy a median-priced home when the interest rates on mortgages have been as high as they have been for the past few years. If people can't afford to buy houses at inflated prices, house prices must come down.

Why? When interest rates rose rapidly between 1979 and 1982, the number of houses put on the market declined sharply, but sales prices continued to climb, albeit slowly.

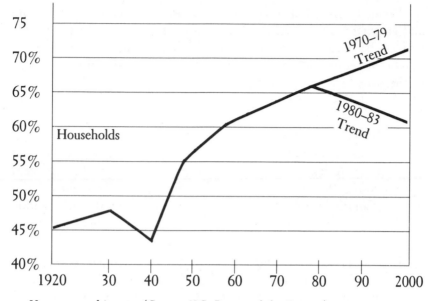

Home ownership rate. (*Source: U.S. Bureau of the Census.*)

Actually, this argument makes at least two other assumptions, both of which are questionable.

The first assumption is that massive inflation won't occur again and push salaries and house prices still higher.

The second assumption is that the majority of Americans will continue to be homeowners rather than renters. Before World War II, most Americans were renters: In 1940, only 43.6 percent of households were owner-occupied. That percentage steadily climbed to 65.4 percent in 1979. Then in 1980, for the first time since the Great Depression, homeownership rates fell to 64.4 percent, although house prices continued to climb. (See graph above.) It is possible that house prices may not come down even if the majority of people can't afford to buy houses. Rather, more of our population may be renters, and owners may decide to hold on to their properties rather than sell them.

Argument 7

"The price of housing is out of all proportion to rents" (*Casey*). *"The tip-off that real estate is now generally overpriced is that the prices of single-family houses have risen much faster than rents"* (*Browne*).

7

Right. I agree, but we come to opposite conclusions. The doom and gloomers say that house prices must fall, in order to get in line with rents. The opposite possibility is that we are on the verge of significant rent increases during this decade because rents have been in the bargain basement category.

Why do I say this?

- Between 1970 and 1980, median rent went up from $89 to $198 per month, an increase of 122.5 percent. The Consumer Price Index shows that prices in general rose 112.2 percent during that period. Rents, therefore rose only slightly faster than the overall inflation rate, and did not keep up with maintenance and repair costs of households which increased 130.4 percent.

- According to a study by the U.S. Department of Housing and Urban Development, the United States had the lowest annual rate of rent increase among nineteen industrialized nations during the seventies.

- Many owners of rental housing have the low-interest mortgage rates of 5 or 10 years ago. It is easier for them to generate a profit when their fixed mortgage expense is relatively low. When these buildings are sold in an era of high interest rates, or when owners need to refinance at higher interest rates, they will be forced to raise the rent to meet their costs. Tax-shelter benefits alone won't cover them.

If real estate will probably not crash and if we are in for significant rent increases, is it safe to assume that investors will continue to make profits using the same investment strategies that have worked in the seventies? The answer is a resounding, no.

HOW REAL ESTATE FORTUNES HAVE BEEN MADE

There are four basic ways to make money in real estate:

1. APPRECIATION
You buy a house, wait for it to go up in value, and then sell it for a profit.

2. TAX SHELTER

You buy a house and use tax write-offs—particularly depreciation—to reduce the tax you have to pay on other income you earn.

3. MORTGAGE REDUCTION

You slowly pay off the mortgage on the house, building up your equity—sort of like putting money in a bank account.

4. POSITIVE CASH FLOW

You receive an income from your property which exceeds your expenses. Conversely, "negative cash flow" means that you don't get enough income to offset expenses and you have to use additional funds to maintain your investment.

Classically, fortunes have been made when investors bought "cheap" and sold "dear." In the 1950s and 1960s many investors would buy a property, improve it by putting on a coat of paint and repairing a rotted porch, and sell the property for a few hundred dollars of profit. The investor would then use the profit from the sale as a downpayment to purchase a larger property. Typically, the investor would move up from a house to a duplex, and then to a fourplex, to a 12-unit apartment building, and to a larger apartment complex.

However, some unusual events occurred in real estate during the 1970s. House prices shot up dramatically—in some areas doubling and tripling in less than a year. There was a frenzy to buy. People looked on real estate as a marvelous hedge against inflation and as an excellent tax shelter.

Real estate speculators no longer even had to improve property in order to make a profit. Why bother putting time and energy into renovation and good management? All they needed to do was to buy a property for as little down as possible, get some tenant to sign a lease so the rental income would somewhat offset the mortgage payment, take a nice fat tax write-off, and sell in a year or so.

It was primarily through tax shelters and the appreciation resulting from inflation (or inflationary expectations) that investors expected to make profits. In the late 1970s, however, increasing numbers of astute investors realized they could also profit from positive cash flows—no, not positive cash flows gained from receiving rents, but income derived from structuring the terms in the buying and selling of real estate to their advantage.

Then, in 1979, the real estate market was shaken as interest rates on conventional mortgages started to rise, reaching a high of 18 percent in 1981. It was impossible for most would-be buyers to make home purchases. Those homeowners and investors who could afford to do so decided that this was not the time to sell. People who bought rental real estate absorbing large negative cash flows while anticipating a 10 or 15 percent annual rate of appreciation to bail them out when they sold the property in a year—these people were in trouble. They couldn't find buyers.

Even though the vast majority of owners of rental houses didn't go under, there has been a sober reassessment by real estate investors of how to make money in real estate, now that the halcyon days of the seventies are gone—at least for the time being.

A NEW STRATEGY FOR MAKING MONEY IN REAL ESTATE

If you read the current literature written by real estate investors, you will notice interesting changes from the advice given to the investors of the seventies. There is talk now about how to make money in real estate even at low levels of appreciation. And there are cautionary notes about how investors must make sure that a real estate investment is sound even when the tax benefits of a property are discounted.

Paying off the principal on your mortgage had been one of the most neglected ways to make money in real estate throughout the seventies. It's making a comeback in the eighties, now that interest rates on mortgages are no longer bargains. Some real estate authorities are now suggesting that people pay off high-interest mortgages as rapidly as possible in order to own their property free and clear.

General expectations for the residential real estate market are more somber than in the seventies:

- Money for housing will be in short supply during the eighties, and interest rates on mortgages will remain high.
- Barring a recurrence of rampant inflation, houses will appreciate much more slowly than they did in the previous decade.

- Owners will hold on to their houses for much longer periods of time than in the seventies.

Nonetheless, there is an underlying optimistic outlook for the real estate market because of demographic considerations. As has been noted by others, there are even more potential homebuyers for the decade of the eighties than there were during the past decade. Most Americans buy their first home at about the age of 30. Some 42 million Americans will become 30 between 1980 and 1990. That figure is 10 million more people than the number who reached the age of 30 between 1970 and 1980.

Ken Rosen, Chairman of the Center for Real Estate and Urban Economics at the University of California at Berkeley, reflected the view of many private investors when he predicted a strong growth in lower-priced single-family houses bought by first-time home buyers.

The problem which investors face is that if money remains tight and interest rates for mortgages are high, it will be difficult to resell investment houses quickly for a profit, despite the pent-up demand. At the same time, many young would-be buyers will be forced to remain renters longer than they had expected.

Real estate authorities have written about the implications of these trends, and investors are scrambling for new ways to make profits from the changing real estate market. Experts have written about equity sharing, about buying properties at foreclosure sales, and about structuring deals and manipulating trust notes to the investor's advantage. Few experts, though, talk about the most neglected way to make a profit in real estate—generating a positive cash flow from rental income through good management. Management has always been considered a hassle by real estate investors. Putting deals together is fun. Management is work.

Yet if investors will be forced to hold houses for longer periods of time, effective management of rental property will become increasingly important.

THE CHANGING RENTAL MARKET

Who will make the most returns on rental income during the eighties? Investors who understand the rental market and the enormous changes which are occurring in it.

Let me give you some facts, many of which come from *The Future of Rental Housing* (1981).

- *Traditional husband-wife households in the rental market are declining.*   Between 1970 and 1978, although renter households increased by 3.3 million, husband-wife households declined by 20.2 percent—a loss of 2.6 million households. Single-person households in the rental market, on the other hand, increased by 50 percent during the same period.
- *The fastest-growing number of all households in the United States is the single-person household.*   In 1790 only 3.7 percent of all households consisted of one person. By 1950 that figure had climbed to 10.9 percent. Approximately 25 percent of all U.S. households are now occupied by one person.
- *There is a small but rapidly growing number of households consisting of nonrelated people.*   In 1970 there were 1,094,000 nonfamily households which consisted of more than one person; by 1979 there were 2,630,000 such households, for an incredible growth rate of 140.4 percent. By comparison, family households increased by only 11.7 percent during the same period.
- *The trend toward nonrelated singles sharing a household with others is expected to increase.*   The trend toward house sharing will accelerate even more rapidly if, as anticipated, rents increase substantially and economic conditions are difficult. Between 1982 and 1983, for example, there was a swift and dramatic decline in new household formations. The Census Bureau had anticipated the formation of 1.7 million new households (for the previous 15 years, new household formations had averaged 1.5 to 1.6 million a year), but instead of the predicted 1.7 million households, only 391,000 were actually formed!

Where did all of the anticipated households go? At least in part, adult children moved back with their parents, and more nonrelated people, who may previously have rented one-bedroom apartments, began doubling and tripling up.

HOW TO PROFIT FROM THE NEW TRENDS

The best way to maximize your rental income, particularly during turbulent economic times, is to buy median-priced single-family houses and rent them to the fastest-growing segment of the rental market— singles. Your rental income will be particularly attractive if the house can be shared comfortably by several singles.

If you buy and manage your rental houses according to the suggestions in this book, you will profit no matter what happens to our economy—be it inflation, hyperinflation, recession, depression, or even economic stability.

Let's look at the following scenarios:

Inflation or Hyperinflation

With inflation or hyperinflation, the price of your house (at least on paper) will rise rapidly. You may, however, find it difficult to sell your house during this period because most people won't have access to the huge amount of money which would be required to make the purchase. In fact, you may not want to sell until the economy stabilizes, for fear that any profit you realized during this period would dissipate in value as rapid inflation continued.

Your costs for taxes, repairs, and improvements would also rise steeply. On the other hand, your rents would also increase, and the increased income would presumably cover your increased costs. You might even wind up with a large positive cash flow from your increased rents, particularly if you had a long-term low-interest fixed-rate mortgage.

Singles would not be able to afford to buy a house or to rent expensive apartments by themselves. More people would decide to move in with others in order to make housing costs more affordable.

Recession or Depression

Let's say the economy goes the other way and that we are plunged into a recession, or even a depression. On paper, the price of houses may stabilize or decline. Again, this may not be the best time to sell your investment houses if you want to make a profit. Money will be tight, buyers scarce, and prices lower.

On the other hand, your costs for taxes, repairs, and improvements would also decline. Again, many people would be forced to economize and singles would move in with others to reduce the money spent on the rent. Rents in general might fall somewhat, but the demand for low-cost rentals would be greater than ever and those rents would not come down significantly, if at all.

A Stable Economy

In a stable, healthy economy, the owner of investment houses rented to singles would still find a thriving market. Demographers agree that the trends toward later marriages, toward divorces, and toward an increasing formation of nontraditional households will continue, regardless of what happens to the economy.

IN SUM

You should be able to profit from the new trends in real estate by renting to singles. In a way, you will become like the smart, small farmer who makes a comfortable income by intensively working a specialty crop on a small plot of land. Your small holdings will produce a volume of rental income if you know how to manage it well.

You will be able to weather whatever the economy dishes out. You will be in a position to choose your own time to sell your investment, as you continue to harvest abundant rental income every month. And when the time comes to sell your investment, you will have an unusually large market for your investment house, because, as you will see in Chapter 3, the house you choose to buy will appeal to first-time home buyers, traditional families, senior citizens, people who work at home, and the growing number of singles who are buying homes.

POINTS TO REMEMBER

- It is unlikely that there will be a real estate crash, but the near future may prove to be a time of:
  - slow appreciation
  - fewer sales

- • tight money and high interest rates on loans for housing
- • increased rents

- • Effective management of rental property is becoming increasingly important to those investors who expect to make a profit from their real estate holdings.

- • Singles, whether they live alone or with nonrelated others, make up the most rapidly growing percentage of renters.

- • One way to increase your rental income, particularly in turbulent economic times, is to rent to singles who are willing to share a house with other singles.

FOR FURTHER INFORMATION

Gruen, Nina, Claude Gruen, and Wallace F. Smith: "Demographic Changes and Their Effects on Real Estate Markets in the 1980s," Development Component Series, Urban Land Institute, Washington, 1982.

This booklet provides an excellent analysis of broad demographic trends in the United States and what they mean for the real estate market.

Hall, Craig: *Craig Hall's Book of Real Estate Investing*, Holt, Rinehart and Winston, New York, 1982.

The chapter "The Outlook for the Eighties" is particularly useful in understanding why large rent increases are on the way.

Harney, Ken:

This syndicated real estate columnist is one of the best sources of current, accurate information on trends in the real estate market.

Sternlieb, George, and James W. Hughes: *The Future of Rental Housing*, Rutgers, Center for Urban Policy Research, New Jersey, 1981.

The statistical information about trends in rental housing in the United States is valuable.

U.S. Bureau of the Census: *Annual Housing Survey: 1981*, pt. A, *General Housing Characteristics*, ser. H-150, no. 81, *Current Housing Reports*, Washington, 1983.

The survey compiles such interesting housing statistics as vacancy rates, the percentage of households which are owner-occupied, and the amounts that people pay for rent.

U.S. League of Savings Institutions: "The Challenge of Homeownership in the 1980s" (Discussion Paper 1) and "Homeownership Affordability in the 1980s" (Discussion Paper 2), 1983.

Both of these papers discuss in simple terms such issues as the affordability gap, the decline in average new home sizes, and other changes impacting the real estate market.

2

MANAGEMENT: DO YOU HAVE WHAT IT TAKES?

A MOST UNLIKELY REAL ESTATE ENTREPRENEUR

Social science has a rule called the Law of the Instrument, which states that if you give a child a hammer, the child will soon discover that everything in the world can be fixed by hammering. The words may seem whimsical, but the thought is important. People see the world through their own unique perspectives. Everyone who has a special skill will be inclined to think that the best way to solve most problems in any field is with that skill.

Along the same lines, people's perceptions of reality are based on what they have actually experienced. A millionaire's perception of human nature and of how to accomplish something may well be different from that of a youngster raised in the ghetto. Both are convinced that their concept of reality is correct, because both base their premises on encounters they have had in their own lives.

I say this by way of cautioning you in this book; I can only vouch for what has worked for me. Let me tell you a little about my experiences with rental houses to help you decide for yourself whether the style of management which has worked for me will be suitable for you.

In the first place, money and houses have never been an overriding interest for me. How, then, did I get involved in real estate?

I suppose it started in 1976, when I bought my first house. At that time I was earning a modest salary (by Washington, D.C., standards) as a government worker. I decided that the only way I could afford to buy a house in a good neighborhood was to buy a house large enough to accommodate a couple of housemates who paid rent. If everything worked out, the rental income would cover more than half of my monthly house payment and two-thirds of the utilities. Adding in the tax advantages and the probable rate of appreciation, I figured I would actually be making money by buying a house. Further, when the loan on the house was paid off at some time in the future, I would own a valuable asset free and clear.

As you can see, although money has never been my overriding interest, I have always believed in utilizing it effectively. After all, there was no sense throwing away money by putting it in a bank account at 5¼ percent interest when the annual cost of living had gone up more than 8 percent over the previous couple of years. Nonmaterialistic, yes. Foolish, no.

I found my house. Settlement* was in November. That first month, while I was looking for housemates, my financial situation was very tight. Almost all of my life savings went toward the downpayment on the house. I turned the thermostat down to 55 and put on several layers of sweaters. I could see my breath in the living room many an afternoon.

I found my two renters within 6 weeks. Not only was the money crunch relieved, but I found that I actually enjoyed having housemates.†

Now that my housing was taken care of, I could go back to concentrating on my career. I had always worked in public service—with the Peace Corps, with a family planning program in rural California, and in 1976, with the U.S. Government.

Unfortunately, while I had a high regard for many of my colleagues in government, I felt increasingly irrelevant and frustrated in a large bureaucracy. So many decisions are beyond your control. The two songs that ran through my mind most often then were "Look What

---

* *Settlement* means the close of a real estate transaction; in some regions of the United States, it is better known as *the close of escrow*.

† Readers who are sharing their own house with tenants, or who are thinking about housesharing, may be interested in my first book, *Living with Tenants: How to Happily Share Your House with Renters for Profit and Security.*

They've Done to My Song, Ma" and "You Can Take This Job and Shove It."

People see what they want to see, and I began to see that a large number of my colleagues felt irrelevant and frustrated, too. Some of them could tell you to the day, 5 years hence, when they would retire. Many of them felt trapped by their salaries and their pension plans. I decided that I never wanted to feel trapped by the federal retirement system, or for that matter by any other company pension system.

I looked at my life and thought, Okay, Doreen, what have you done that you enjoy doing? Where have you gotten gratification?

My biggest accomplishment in Washington was buying a house and creating a management system for it that worked. That feat created a certain status for me among my co-workers, friends, and family. Although the fact that the house had appreciated considerably in value during the first year had little to do with my own efforts, people pegged me as a smart businessperson.

I thought about buying other houses for investment purposes. The problem was that rents simply weren't high enough to cover mortgage payments and expenses, and my salary couldn't cover much negative cash flow. So how could I rent houses to produce a much higher rental income than the market rate would suggest?

It dawned on me that there were a lot of singles in the Washington area who were in a living situation similar to mine. Many of us were doubling and tripling up to cut living expenses. Three singles, each having modest salaries, could comfortably pay the rent for an average single-family house. I calculated, though, that if a house were spacious enough to accommodate four singles instead of three, and if each tenant were charged an average rent for someone sharing a house, then the collective rent would be higher than if that same house were rented in a conventional manner to a family.

Let me show you what I mean: In the Washington area, a typical house may be rented for $750/month. If three singles pay an equal share of the rent, each would pay $250. If you have a house that can accommodate four tenants, and charge each tenant $250, your total rent would be $1,000 per month.

Generally, though, owners of rental houses were afraid to rent to singles, discriminating against them in favor of renting to a married couple or even to a family with children. Many of the existing group

19

houses had a reputation for being rundown and managed haphazardly. Yet my own household was working quite well, and I was sure that I could set up a system of renting to singles that would avoid many of the problems associated with group houses.

WHY GROUP HOUSES ARE OFTEN DISASTERS

Group houses have the reputation of having more vandalism, wild parties, evictions, and problems in general than do houses rented to families. Why? Because in most cases the owner treats the individual tenants as if they were members of a family group. Usually, each tenant in the house is required to sign a lease that holds each of them, collectively and individually, responsible for fulfilling the terms of the lease.

Consider a typical example:

Two friends pull in a couple of extra people to rent a house. The four of them sign a year's lease with the owner. One of the renters turns out to be exceedingly messy. There's now a large stain on the carpet. The tenants don't report it to the owner, though, because they know that they'll all be obligated to pay for the damage, and it was only the slob's fault.

Then, 4 months into the lease, one of the renters gets a job in another state. There are no terrific applicants to take the person's place immediately, but the household decides that it's best to get someone—anyone—in fast; otherwise, the remaining three tenants will have to cover an extra portion of the rent out of their own pockets. They only hope that the new person will turn out to be okay.

The new tenant decides to have her boyfriend visit for a few days, but he doesn't leave. One of the original tenants decides that she's not going to live with the slob and the boyfriend both. She moves out. Her replacement doesn't mind the slob and doesn't mind the boyfriend, because he doesn't mind the house. In fact, she literally doesn't "mind" the lease agreement: for fun, she'll use the living room wall as a dart board. Landlords are rich and exploit tenants by collecting rent. Why should she care what happens to a house owned by a Simon Legree? In fact, why bother paying her share of the rent for this rundown house?

Voilà. Problems.

PREPARING FUGU,* OR HOW TO DEVISE A MANAGEMENT SYSTEM FOR SINGLES

Why wasn't I having problems in my own household?

- Because I selected each housemate very carefully, in cooperation with the other housemate.
- Because my housemates each had a separate rental agreement, being responsible *individually* for their own rents and their own damages, if any.
- Because repairs, when needed, were made very quickly.
- And most importantly: *Because there was no sense of an adversarial landlord-tenant relationship.* Rather, there was a feeling in the household that "we are all in this together."

The trick, though, was to devise a management system that worked as well for houses in which I didn't live. Using language from conventional lease agreements and a little common sense, I put together a system which, it seemed, would be attractive to conscientious tenants while still protecting me.

Now all that I had to do was to find someone with the money to buy a house in which I could try my new management system.

THE UNEXPECTED PURCHASE OF MY FIRST RENTAL HOUSE

A year after buying my own house, I unexpectedly bought my first investment house. It was unexpected because I had never imagined buying another house, with so little of my own money left in savings. My first house purchase had almost wiped me out financially.

Steve, a doctor friend of mine, had agreed to buy a house when I found one I thought would be suitable to rent to singles. He was to provide the downpayment and offer his own credentials to a mortgage lender who would have laughed at mine. I was to find the house, manage it according to the new management system I had devised,

---

* Fugu, otherwise known as globefish, is highly poisonous. When carefully prepared by Japanese chefs, though, it becomes a delectable dish.

21

and make sure that the rental income would offset any expenses, so that Steve wouldn't have a negative cash flow.

After searching weekend after weekend for 6 months, I found a house with the right financing, the right location, and the right floor plan for rental to singles. I negotiated the contract, and Steve said to bring it over. He wasn't there. Then he said he would contact the owner directly. He never did. Then he said he would come to the owner's house to sign the contract. He didn't show up at the appointed time.

Feeling exceedingly frustrated and on the verge of tears, I phoned my father. He encouraged me to buy the house myself, because the existing loan on the house had been financed through the Veterans Administration, and VA loans can be assumed by practically anyone, regardless of qualifications. My father offered to loan me the downpayment, although I insisted on paying him back rapidly at a business rate of interest.

I went back to the seller, took a deep breath, signed the purchase contract myself, went home, burst into tears, and thought, What have I done?

At the time, I was earning $18,000 per year. Somehow I would have to come up with $780 per month to pay for the loan on the house and the loan to my father. Normally such a house would then have rented for about $450. Nonetheless, I figured I could get $165 from the person in the basement area, $145 each for the two tenants who would have the two bedrooms on the first floor, and $185 from the tenant who would have the whole second floor to herself. The grand total of the combined rents would be $630 per month. This meant that I would have to pay $150 per month out of my own pocket—but paying that sum would at least be possible. Most people would have been glad to buy a house with none of their own money down and with a regular cash outlay of only $150 per month. Actually, when you factored in the tax benefits and payment on the principle, I would practically be getting a free house, not even counting the probable appreciation. And in a few years, after paying off my father, I'd be getting a comfortable positive cash flow.

What scared me was the thought that the system might not work. What if I couldn't put together a household of four compatible people? What if the tenants would be coming and going, and every other month I'd have to try to find new ones? What if the tenants were irresponsible and didn't maintain the place?

As far as I was concerned, though, from the moment I signed the purchase contract there was no turning back. It is amazing how things fall into place when you have no choice.

I began advertising in the classifieds for tenants. It was the middle of winter. The phone did not ring off the hook. I screened potential tenants, scared that I'd have to pay next month's mortgage myself— out of my own meager savings. I kept pushing aside the thought, Take anyone, Doreen, anyone who can pay the rent. I got a grip on myself and remained firm about screening procedures, rejecting several applicants before finding my first tenant—Peggy.

Peggy was clean-cut, steadily employed, and came from a family with plenty of brothers and sisters. She was very accustomed to sharing a household and pitching in with the chores. Between the two of us, we got a second tenant, and together we selected a third. A few months later, after a bathroom was put into the basement, we got our fourth. The household was complete.

Much to my relief, the system worked. The tenants stayed with me; they kept the house up, helped me repair the garage roof, and invited me to their Christmas party at the end of the year.

The next year when my government salary increased considerably, I bought another rental house, filled it with singles, and everything worked out well again. Again, the high rental income I received covered practically all of my expenses.

After I bought my third house, people actually began to ask my advice on real estate matters. Even my supervisors at work wondered how a single, mid-level program analyst could afford to buy three houses in about as many years.

There really was no secret to it. My own living expenses were modest because I shared my house with renters, and the consistently high rental income sustained the houses I had bought.

When government layoffs hit our agency in January 1982, I was one of the few people to volunteer to be laid off. Friends said that I glowed during the last month of federal service. A few days before my employment was to be terminated, someone stopped me in the hallway to ask if I were in love. I left federal service throwing a wine and cheese party for my unfortunate colleagues who had to stay. Friends came from all parts of the building to wish me well.

A year and a half later, with no steady source of income, I bought my fourth house.

Why buy houses instead of other real estate investments?

I like buying and managing houses and have never been tempted to "graduate" to apartment complexes or commercial real estate.

When telling you about the advantages of owning houses as investments, I feel like I'm on a honeymoon as Mickey Rooney's eighth wife. I know what's expected of me, but I'm not sure I'll be able to do it any differently than how it's been done before. Oh well, here goes.

The Advantages of Houses

Ease of Purchase   Of all types of residential and commercial properties, the buying and managing of houses probably requires the least degree of sophistication. Purchase agreements are relatively simple. And the money you need to get started is usually less than that required for other real estate investments. In some cases you can buy houses for nothing down or 5 percent down. Even a conventional 20 percent downpayment, though, is often less than you would have to pay to buy other types of real estate.

Leverage   A relatively small downpayment will enable you to own an asset so valuable that you would have to save for 15 or 20 years if you had to pay the full purchase price up front; $10,000 may well tie up a $100,000 asset for you.

Assurance of an Almost Continuous Rental Income   If you buy land, you get no rental income while you hold it. Commercial property, on the other hand, can be leased for many years at relatively high rents. But vacancies in commercial properties may last for months or even years; you have to be in a position to withstand high expenses with no rental income to offset them.

In most areas, houses set at fair market rent will be leased within 1 or 2 months. If you follow my rental system, you are virtually assured of never having a vacant house after the first tenant has moved in.

Tax Shelter   In addition to a rental income, houses provide a means to shelter your income, just as do all residential and commercial properties. Unimproved land, though, won't provide you with important depreciation benefits.

Liquidity   Real estate in general is considered to be an illiquid investment. You can't sell your property in one day and get cash for it immediately. Single-family houses, though, are much more liquid than other types of real estate investments. You can wait years to sell land, apartment buildings, or commercial properties. But if you offer fair terms, you can usually find a buyer for a house within 60 days.

You don't need to sell your investment to get cash from it rapidly. Lenders look on houses as excellent collateral for loans, and, providing you have sufficient equity in a property, you should be able to get a loan within a few weeks.

Simplicity of Management   Most investment houses are managed by individuals rather than by companies or corporations. If you are the sole owner, you don't have to report to shareholders or work on forms for the Securities and Exchange Commission. You can manage your investments in your spare time while holding down a regular job.

Government restrictions, such as rent control, are less likely to apply to owners who have a few single-family houses. Most federal and state laws are designed to apply to multi-unit buildings.

Control   Many investments are passive. You buy stock, mutual funds, or gold and hope that the experts will invest your funds wisely, or that forces beyond your control will push the market up.

You have much more control over the profitability of rental houses that you own and manage. You can structure the terms of the purchase and sale of the properties to meet your own financial needs. You can decide what improvements should be made to increase the value of your properties. You alone are responsible for structuring your man-

25

agement system. And you also select the tenants and tradespeople who will help you make your investment profitable.

Financial Safety   During inflationary times, single-family houses have a track record of appreciating in value more than most other investments do. And even during a depression, having a house is like having money in the bank; it will always be worth something. As long as you can meet your house payments, the principal on your loan will slowly be paid off, and you will have an asset which will be valuable even in deflated dollars.

Diversification   The money you would spend to buy one apartment building could be used to buy several single-family houses. If you make a mistake in buying an apartment building—because it turns out that the building wasn't structurally sound, for example, or because you chose an apartment in a location that was on the downswing— you may be in big financial trouble.

If, on the other hand, you own several single-family houses in various locations, your risk is spread out. If one of your properties turns out to be a lemon, your loss, if any, will be minimized.

The Disadvantages of Houses

People who tout the advantages of owning real estate are less likely to tell you the disadvantages of owning and managing single-family houses.

Some investors just don't have the temperament for managing tenants in single-family houses. In fact, some of the best buys on the real estate market are available from frustrated owners who are willing practically to give their rental houses away because they never want to see another tenant again.

There are ways to minimize the disadvantages, but let me tell you the problems first.

Vacancies   If you manage your house in a conventional way, you will have absolutely no rental income when you have a vacancy. A house is either 100 percent rented or 100 percent vacant.

An apartment building, on the other hand, has many units, and the management is usually able to determine a predictable vacancy rate. Rental income from the occupied units pays the expenses while the vacant units are being shown to prospective tenants.

Maintenance   It takes more time per unit to maintain ten houses which are dispersed geographically than to manage twenty apartment units in the same building. With ten houses, potentially ten furnaces may need maintenance and ten roofs may need repair. The management personnel of an apartment building will of course have only one roof and one furnace to worry about.

Further, if three tenants in an apartment building have plumbing problems, you or a plumber might be able to fix all three problems in an hour or so. But if you have three plumbing problems in three different houses, you or the plumber may have to spend three times as much time traveling to each house to fix the problems. If it's the plumber and not you doing the work, your bill may be three times higher for the houses than for the apartment building.

Destruction and Neglect   My guess is that there is more vandalism and neglect in rented houses than in rented apartment units. If neighbors in an apartment building hear unusually loud noises coming from an adjoining unit, they are likely to report the disturbance to management.

Tenants of single-family houses have been known to trash a place, and none of the people in neighboring houses either knew about it or felt responsible to find out who owned the property in order to report the destruction.

Skipouts   "Skipouts" are those tenants who vacate the house without giving the owner any notice, usually after they have managed to evade paying rent for a few months.

Again, it's easier for tenants to skip out of a house unnoticed than out of an apartment building, especially one in which they would have to make arrangements to use a freight elevator.

Tenant-Owner Conflicts   Far and away the most overwhelming landlording problems are not things, but people. If a roof leaks, you get a roofer to repair it. If a pipe bursts, you call in the plumber. But how do you react when the rent is late, or your tenants have taken apart an engine and its parts are strewn all over the backyard,

27

or people in neighboring houses phone you at 1:00 A.M. to tell you that your tenants are having a loud party, and that unless you do something about it they are going to call the police?

Time   Once your house is rented, you will usually spend less than a half-hour a month on each rental house. Overall, though, management of rental houses is more time-consuming than are passive investments. You will have to spend some weekends screening phone calls from potential tenants. You will be called about the malfunctioning central air-conditioning during a 100° heat wave, and during a snowstorm about the furnace that suddenly went on the blink. And your tenants, legitimately, will expect you to drop everything to take care of their needs immediately.

Geographic Immobility   I am of the opinion that the number of problems you have in managing a household is directly proportional to your distance from the property. If you buy rental houses and intend to manage them yourself, you may want to live in the same geographic vicinity as your houses.

All of the above disadvantages can be minimized, as you will see. The first step to hassle-free management is to find a house that will be attractive to your renters and will be capable of generating a sufficiently high income to be attractive to you. That's what the next chapter is about.

POINTS TO REMEMBER

- The advantages of owning single-family houses are:
    - ease of purchase
    - leverage
    - assurance of an almost continuous rental income
    - tax shelter
    - relative liquidity
    - simplicity of management
    - control
    - financial safety
    - diversification

- The disadvantages of owning single-family houses are:
  - vacancies
  - maintenance
  - destruction and neglect
  - skipouts
  - tenant-owner conflicts
  - time commitment
  - geographic immobility
- The disadvantages of owning single-family houses can be minimized, and the first step is to find a suitable property.

FOR FURTHER INFORMATION

Glubetich, Dave: *Money Magic*, Impact Publishing, San Ramon, California, 1978.
The coming housing shortage in medium- and low-priced single-family homes is discussed, along with the advantages of owning investment houses.

Morris, Hal: *Crisis Real Estate Investing*, Harbor Publishing, San Francisco, 1982.
This explains the benefits of owning single-family houses and gives practical advice on getting positive cash flows from rental houses.

3

HOW TO FIND A HOUSE

THREE WAYS TO HIGH RENTAL INCOME

Managing a rental property is a little like the Japanese tea ceremony. It takes little time to drink the tea. Ninety percent of the work goes into the preparation.

Once the rental house has been purchased, made ready, and the tenants have been selected, managing the place should become relatively easy for the investor. The most time-consuming task the investor faces is finding and preparing the *appropriate* house for rental. Two major factors will help you determine whether or not a house will be an appropriate investment.

First, the terms of the purchase must be economically attractive. We'll discuss this more in Chapter 5, "How to Negotiate the Purchase." For our purposes now, I can summarize by advising you to look for a house with a price in the median range for your locality, which also has assumable long-term low-interest financing or the possibility of substantial owner-financing at below-market interest rates.

Second, the house you select must be capable of producing an exceptionally high rental income.

There are several ways to get a very high rental income from a house.

1. Buy a Mansion

One way, of course, is to buy an expensive house and charge a high rent for it. However, we are talking here not of high rent alone, but of high rent in relation to the market rate for comparable rentals in the area.

A $250,000 house may bring in $1,000 per month in rent. That's not difficult. The trick is to get a $100,000 house to bring in $1,000 per month in rent.

2. Run an Illicit Rooming House

Another way to make a lot of rental income is to buy a sprawling, run-down house with eight makeshift bedrooms and five jerry-built bathrooms and to jam it with tenants. You could get very high rent if you leased a house to twelve people even if you charged each tenant a modest amount.

You could undoubtedly make even more money if you rented your ramshackle house to forty-five illegal aliens who used it in eight-hour shifts, never letting the beds grow cold.

Such a system of cramming people into a house would assure you of a phenomenal rental income. It would also assure you of irate neighbors, phone calls at all hours of the day and night, law suits, vandalism, and an extremely low price when you tried to sell your cannibalized investment.

3. Find a House Suitable for Singles

A third way to get a high rental income is to find a modest single-family dwelling that is in a good location and that has a floor plan assuring maximum privacy to the few selected singles to whom you will rent.

That's what this chapter is about.

What is a "good" location?

The first rule of real estate investment, according to the popular axiom, is to buy a property in a good location.

Most real estate books will tell you that a good location for a rental house is one:

- in an area of well-maintained houses
- near good schools
- near shopping centers and jobs
- close to public transportation
- in a quiet residential neighborhood

Some of these features are important when you are looking for a house in which to put singles, but others are not as important as they would be if you were to rent to a family with children.

Put yourself in the place of your single tenants. All members of the household most likely have full-time jobs. Access to public transportation or proximity to a good highway system is important to them if they have to commute to work each day.

Singles tend to eat out more often than families do and want to be close to a little night life. Most singles do not want to live in a secluded suburban community. They want to be in easy range of restaurants, theaters, nightclubs, and recreational facilities.

On the other hand, your singles won't care if the school system is the best in the area, because they probably don't have children living with them.

Neither are singles as picky as a family with young children may be about living on a busy street or having a creek nearby.

Singles, like others, want to live in a safe, attractive environment. Nonetheless, younger singles may be more adventuresome than most families are able to be. Singles may willingly rent in marginal neighborhoods that are undergoing renovations.

One last point. When you are looking for a house in a good location, think of yourself. Look for a house that is no more than 10 or 15 minutes away from your own house. Managing houses is a lot easier when it takes you no more than a few minutes to drive to your rental house to show it to a prospective tenant or to fix a leaky faucet. It's only human nature to put off such duties when you have to spend a half hour driving to the property and a half hour back.

How many tenants will you have?

Local zoning ordinances may regulate the maximum number of unrelated tenants that may legally reside in a house. Many localities, though, officially allow four or more unrelated persons to share a house.

All of my rental houses have four tenants in them, and that seems to work well. If you have a household with fewer than four people, the combined rent of the tenants may be less than what you would get if you rented the house to a family.

On the other hand, if you go much beyond four tenants, the psychological and emotional atmosphere of the house may change. Unrelated people who live together can generally relate well to one other person in a house and be comfortable with two. Their emotional ties may stretch to a third person.

The atmosphere is different if seven or eight people are sharing a house. Not only may cliques form, increasing the chance of personal conflicts, but when many people are responsible for maintaining a house, it's easier for the responsibility of all to become the responsibility of none. Tenant turnover will be greater, too, and you will have to spend more of your time trying to fill vacancies.

My advice, then, is to stick with four people even if zoning ordinances permit more than that number in a house.

THE IDEAL FLOOR PLAN

You will be looking for a house, then, which will accommodate four people comfortably. This means that you will need to find a place with at least four bedrooms and two baths.

Sometimes houses have only three bedrooms, but there is another area of the house—a finished basement or an attic, for example—which could easily be converted into an additional bedroom or two.

Look for houses with bedrooms on different floors or at opposite ends of the house. A bedroom may be the one place where an individual has total privacy in a house shared with others. The more privacy you can offer a tenant, the higher the rent you can get.

Two-story houses with finished basements often have bathrooms as well as bedrooms on all floors. Such houses are ideally suited for renting to singles.

On the other hand, single-story rambler-style houses usually have three bedrooms clustered around one bathroom, and the same is true for many colonial-style houses. Worse, many older houses are designed so that one bedroom leads directly into another bedroom. Although singles may be willing to share these houses with other tenants, the people in the household may feel as though they were living on top of each other, and lack of privacy increases the potential for conflict.

Yet, single-story houses shouldn't be ruled out, particularly if they have bedrooms at different ends of the house or have finished basements in which you could put a bedroom and a bathroom.

A WORD ABOUT ACCESSORY DWELLING UNITS

When you're looking for a house to buy, I suggest that you look for an area of the house that could easily be converted into an accessory dwelling unit.

What is an accessory dwelling unit? It's an independent living area within a house which is subsidiary to the primary residence and has its own separate cooking facilities and bathroom. It usually has its own separate outside entrance, too. Other names for accessory units are "basement apartments" and "mother-in-law suites."

Currently, most local zoning ordinances prohibit accessory units. It is possible, though, that zoning ordinances will be liberalized within the next 10 years in response to the demographic, social, and economic changes occurring in our society.

Changes have already been taking place—if not in law, in fact. Despite current restrictive local ordinances, an estimated 2.5 million accessory dwelling units (most of them technically illegal) were created within single-family dwellings between 1970 and 1980. One expert estimates that 300,000 such units are being built yearly.

Zoning codes change slowly, but they do change eventually. When zoning restrictions are lifted, your house will be particularly attractive to the wide variety of people who find an accessory unit to be an appealing feature. These future buyers of your house will include:

- first-time home buyers who need a rent-paying housemate to help pay the mortgage
- partners, not romantically involved, who buy a house together but want their own living spaces
- senior citizens who value their privacy but would like some extra rental income

- people who work at home and want an area of the house for their business, an area separate from their living space
- traditional families who would like a separate guest suite for visitors or relatives who may stay with them awhile

In the meantime, if you pay close attention to your local zoning ordinance, you can usually stay within the law and still rent that area of the house which will one day be an accessory unit. Check with your zoning office. Often, the ordinance will say that a separate unit is defined as illegal if it has cooking facilities—or in other words, if there is more than one kitchen in the house. In many jurisdictions, you could legally have a renter in a finished basement. The renter could have her own bedroom, bathroom, cabinets, sink, and refrigerator as long as you have not also supplied a cooking facility.

ADDITIONS WHICH WILL MAKE YOU MONEY

If you are considering buying a rental house, or if you already own a house, analyze the rooms to determine what additions could be made to give singles maximum privacy.

You can put additional walls, toilets, or a kitchenette, if permitted, into the house. An addition which is practical and well-placed could increase your rental income, possibly by several hundred dollars per month. For example, the installation of a bathroom in a recreation room may enable you to rent a downstairs area that you wouldn't otherwise have been able to rent. That bathroom will give you an extra tax write-off, as well, and provide an additional feature to increase the value of your house when you sell it.

ADDITIONS WHICH WILL COST YOU MONEY

Beware, however, of trying to make additions which are inappropriate to the residence. Putting a toilet in a kitchen, for example, may enable you to rent an area of the house that you couldn't have previously. Nonetheless, if an addition makes the room look ugly, if it violates health codes, or if the work is amateurish, you may not be able to attract a high-quality tenant, and the resale value of your house may actually diminish rather than increase.

How to determine how much rent YOU CAN GET

There is no magic formula for determining the amount of rent that a house will bring. You have to study the market, and even then you'll come up with an estimated range of rent rather than an exact figure.

How Much Rent Could You Get by Renting to a Family?

First calculate how much rent a house would bring if it were rented to a family. Start by looking in the classified section of a newspaper under "Houses for Rent." Check those rentals which are in the same geographic location as the rental house you own, or where you would like to buy a rental house. Look for the advertised houses having the same number of bedrooms and bathrooms as your house and see how much rent is being asked.

Another method is to ask a real estate agent. A friendly agent can provide you with a wealth of information about rentals. Many real estate offices have access to detailed information about rental houses. A real estate agent can usually tell you not only how much rent is being asked for all the houses currently listed with real estate offices in the area, but also the rates at which houses have been rented within the past year. The agent may be able to tell you the exact features of each house, down to the dimensions of each room. Generally, though, you won't need to know such specific information when making your preliminary rental estimates.

You can also ask people in the neighborhood how much houses are renting for. But be wary of their answers. Residents who don't actually rent themselves may grossly exaggerate or underestimate house rentals in the area. It is not uncommon for a neighbor to say, "Why, I've heard that owner's making a fortune—maybe $900 a month— for that rental house over there." The actual rental income may be a more modest $600 per month. On the other hand, owners who have been in the neighborhood a long time, and have a relatively low monthly mortgage payment, may not be able to conceive that a house could rent for more than $300 or $400 per month, even if house rentals are well beyond that.

Unless they have just moved in and begun paying rent, be wary, as well, of information you get from renters. Sometimes owners will accept a modest rent from long-time tenants either because the tenants have taken excellent care of the property or because the owners have not kept track of rent increases. The rents they are charging may be less than the fair market rate.

Now write down, for comparison purposes, the amount of rent you think you could get if you rented to a family.

How Much Rent Could You Get by Renting to Singles?

Take the rental figure you have jotted down and add 40 percent to it. Rented to singles, your house should bring in 40 to 50 percent more than you would ordinarily receive if you rented it to a family, to make it worth your while.

Let me explain how to determine whether a house will indeed bring in that extra income.

Go back to the classified section of the newspaper. This time, though, look under "Roommates" or "Houses, Apartments to Share" or whatever other heading your local newspaper uses. Again, look first for location and find out the general range of rent being asked of individuals who will share a house in a particular area.

Let's say that you find the average rent is $175. Keep this figure in mind.

When you have walked through enough houses in a neighborhood, you will be able mentally to calculate approximately how much rent you could charge each of four tenants. For a bedroom smaller than the average size, you may only ask $165 from the tenant, while you may charge another tenant $215 for a master bedroom and private bathroom. Each rent should reflect the amount of privacy and amenities that each individual tenant will enjoy.

Unless all rooms and all amenities are indeed approximately identical, do not simply take an average rent and charge each tenant the same amount. By varying the rents, your tenants will be more likely to feel that the amounts are fair and that each person is paying for value received. There will be less chance of jealous bickering over who has the largest bedroom or the most private bathroom.

One last point about rents. Most of my tenants pay rent in digits ending in 5. Psychologically, a person who will pay $160 a month in rent will also pay $165, even though she may be more reluctant to pay $170. Hundred figures are also big psychological barriers. It is easier to find tenants who will pay $195 per month than $200 per month.

Okay, now walk through the house and add up the amount of rent you think you could get from each area of the house. You will need that total to figure out how much you can carry in the way of mortgage payments.

How much should your rental house cost?

Once again, there is no pat formula. Prices vary so much around the country that it's impossible even to come up with a range of figures that would be useful to you. My general advice is similar to that of many other authors: Look for a house in the lower end of the median-price range for your locality. Ideally, the house will be a relatively less expensive dwelling set either in one of the better sections of town or in an area undergoing rapid improvements and renovations.

You can work backwards to find out how expensive a house you can afford to buy. First, calculate your anticipated rental income. To be conservative in your calculations, reduce the amount of rent you expect to receive from each tenant by $10 or so. Then make sure that your estimated rental income will about cover your fixed monthly expenses for taxes, insurance, and the payment on the principal and interest of your mortgage.

We can see how this works by looking at an example. Let's say you think you can take in rent of $965 per month from four tenants. You find out that the property tax for this particular house is $900 per year and that the insurance will be $200 per year. You then can determine that you can afford a mortgage of up to $80,000 at 12 percent interest if the loan were amortized over 30 years. (You could, of course, change the amount of money you could afford to borrow by changing the interest rates or the time period over which the loan will be amortized.) Here is how the calculations were made:

	Monthly payment
Taxes ($900/year) divided by 12 months	$ 75
Insurance ($200/year) divided by 12 months	17
Mortgage payment on $80,000 @ 12% interest over 30 years	823
Total monthly payment	$915
Anticipated rent ($965) minus $10 each for 4 tenants ($40)	$925

Where do you get information about property taxes, insurance rates, and mortgage payments? If a house is listed for sale through a real estate office, the listing agent can give you all of the above information. You can also get the information on your own without too much difficulty. Your local government office has public records you can check to find out how much tax the county or municipality requires for that property. Your insurance agent will let you know approximately how much the insurance premium will cost, once you have described the rental house. And there are inexpensive books available which consist of amortization tables; these list the figures which tell you how much your monthly payment will be for a loan of any amount at different rates of interest over varying numbers of years. I recommend that you either buy a book of amortization tables or use a pocket calculator programmed to calculate amortization schedules.

How to search for your rental house

Work with Real Estate Agents

Close to 90 percent of all houses are sold through real estate brokers, so it behooves you either to find an agent or broker whom you can trust or to become a real estate agent yourself.

Agents who are knowledgeable and conscientious will save you a great deal of time in finding an appropriate house. Some are expert negotiators, able to present your offer in the best light to sellers too. In addition, real estate agents can provide you with up-to-date financing information that may save you thousands of dollars. Find one or two good agents, tell them your exact requirements, and then work with them exclusively.

If you are a serious real estate investor and have the time, you may want to become a licensed agent yourself. That way you'll be able to find out what houses are available by looking at the office's listing books. Many real estate offices belong to computerized multiple listing services. If you attach yourself to such an office, you will be allowed to use the office computer. You can then comb neighborhoods in minutes, looking for exactly what you want while sitting at a desk. For example, you could search for all houses which are listed between $65,000 and $85,000 in the Podunk subdivision and which have three or more bedrooms, two or more bathrooms, and a full, finished basement with an outside entrance. All such houses that have been listed with real estate firms using multiple listings will appear on your printout.

As an agent, you will be in a better position to negotiate directly with the seller, if you choose to. Some buyers prefer to leave the negotiations in the hands of a third party—an agent. Like me, however, you may find that you would prefer to negotiate directly with the seller, so that you can tailor an offer to suit both of your needs.

Another important advantage of becoming an agent is that you will get a commission when you buy or sell most properties listed through a real estate broker—even if the property is your own. You should be able to save hundreds if not thousands of dollars by being the listing or selling agent and representing yourself.

If you become an agent, you will also benefit by having constant access to information about financing, current sales, and real estate courses, all of which will help you buy and manage rental property better.

Read Classified Ads and Cruise Selected Areas

You should be reading classified ads for house sales and cruising selected areas on your own, even if real estate agents are also looking for houses for you. As you pass houses with a "For Sale" sign, observe how many floors each house has. Are there dormers, which may indicate bedrooms on the upper level? Are there windows on the lower level, which may indicate an accessory dwelling unit in the basement? Is there a side or back entrance that is easily accessible from the street or driveway? If you think that your tenants may have cars, is there sufficient parking?

If you find a house that interests you, tell your agent about it. Have her research the details for you.

Check Other Sources of Information If You Wish

Other sources of information about houses available for sale include:

- attorneys who handle estate settlements and divorces
- foreclosure departments of savings and loan associations
- neighbors and friends
- bulletin boards

I'm listing these leads without much discussion, because most of them will turn up the wrong type of house in the wrong neighborhood and in the wrong price range. You can usually use your time more effectively by working with a real estate agent, checking classified ads, and cruising selected areas.

RECAPPING IMPORTANT POINTS

Before we go shopping for your rental house, let's recap a few key points to keep in mind:

- Find a median-priced house in a good location.
- Look for a house with an assumable low-interest mortgage and/or with the possibility of substantial owner-financing at below-market interest rates.
- Find a house that can accommodate four singles.
- Make sure that the house is at most 15 minutes away from your own residence.

- Look for a house with at least four bedrooms and two bathrooms, or for a house in which you could easily add an additional bedroom or bathroom.
- Look within the house for an area that could readily be converted into an accessory dwelling unit.
- At a minimum, make sure that your rental income will offset your monthly mortgage, tax, and insurance payments.

WHAT TO LOOK FOR AND WHAT TO AVOID

Okay, now that you know what you are looking for and how to find it, let's go out and look at some houses.

House 1

You read the following advertisement in the classified section of your newspaper:

Elysium Fields. Beautiful, spac colonial; 4 bdrms, 2 baths, mother-in-law apt; assum fin @ 10%. $85,000. 123–4567

You phone the owner and learn that the house is only a few years old and has been maintained meticulously. You also learn that the 10% assumption mentioned in the ad applies only to $23,000 left on the first trust. The owner tells you that he is not in a position to hold a second trust note himself, so you will have to find a way to secure an additional $62,000 on your own.

You listen to what the owner has to say, knowing full well that what people say they will accept and what they actually will accept can be quite different. You say nothing at this point about financing, but ask to see the house.

The drive takes you 20 minutes because the house is located at the farther end of Elysium Fields at the outer edges of town.

The house indeed is beautiful. It is priced slightly higher than other houses in the neighborhood, but it has extra amenities—plush wall-to-wall carpeting and a picture window overlooking a semirural landscape.

Three of the four bedrooms are on the top floor. There is one bathroom upstairs. The fourth bedroom and second bathroom are in the mother-in-law suite in a separate wing of the house.

After walking through the place, you compliment the owners on their lovely residence and scratch the house off your list of possibilities. Why?

1. The house is in a quiet, secluded area—perfect for a family— dull for many singles. You may have to spend months to find four singles who would be willing to live in a semirural area if they had to commute long distances to work, to visit friends, or to go to the movies.
2. Although you could rent the bedrooms to four singles, it would be easier to rent if there were at most two bedrooms on one floor.
3. The price of the house and the financing terms, as stated, are not particularly outstanding.
4. The 20-minute drive is starting to push the outer limits of your distance requirements.

House 2

Your real estate agent phones to tell you that she has found a house which would be perfect—absolutely perfect—to rent to singles. It has five bedrooms and three bathrooms, and the owner is willing to hold financing at a below market rate. Further, the house is bordering an area that is rapidly increasing in value. You'll have to move fast, though, because the house is such a good buy at $72,950 that it may be gone within a few days.

You jump in your car and arrive at the house 15 minutes later. You see that perhaps 75 years ago the house was an elegant and comfortable home for an affluent businessman and his family and servants.

There are three fireplaces—one with an ornately carved mahogany mantel. The floors are discolored, but they are oak and would look gorgeous again when stripped and refinished.

The home has been turned into a rooming house. Your agent

was too modest in describing the house. There are actually seven bedrooms, not five. Rough partitions have been thrown up in a sitting room in order to make it into two additional bedrooms.

One of the bedrooms is in a basement with no windows. As you descend, you smell a faint, musty odor. A makeshift bathroom has been installed at an odd angle in the room and there is no exhaust for the moisture from the shower.

You look at the rest of the house and notice that the water pressure is weak when you turn on the faucets, that the electrical system hasn't been updated to provide sufficient amperage for modern electrical appliances, and that the furnace is an ancient oil burner. The kitchen is old and tiny, and the closets were designed for the days when people only owned a few clothes.

You estimate that someone could renovate the house for an additional $35,000 and perhaps make a decent profit by selling it in a year or two. Unfortunately, renovation is not your specialty; management is. It would be very difficult for you to rent the house to four singles who would put up with the renovation work, which might take months to complete. Nor would you ever consider renting that basement to anyone.

You leave the house for someone whose specialty is renovation. It's not for you.

You also decide to have a chat with your real estate agent to explain, once more, what kind of house you want.

House 3

On your way to work one day, you take a different route. On a side street you discover a small, older house with a "For Sale" sign out front. The house is in one of the better neighborhoods of town, but this particular house looks rundown. Further, just beyond the backyard there is a 20-foot high electrical substation. The sign on the dilapidated fence facing the backyard says, "DANGER, KEEP OUT."

The house has obviously been vacant for a while. The front yard is littered with leaves mixed with wrappings from fast-food chains. A gate, broken from its hinges, hangs open.

You think about the house all day. The location is excellent—2 blocks from a small shopping center, 1 block to public transportation, 15 minutes by car to the downtown metropolis, and 5 minutes from your own house. The neighborhood is upper middle-class. On the other hand, the house really looks too small to accommodate four singles. And that electrical substation is truly ugly.

You decide to pass by the house again on your way home. You notice that upstairs there are dormers, which may indicate bedrooms. There are windows on the basement level, too, and an outside entrance to the basement.

You call the telephone number of the "For Sale" sign and speak with the husband of the couple that owns the house.

He tells you that the house has three bedrooms and two bathrooms and that the basement is finished. The house has been on the market a few months, he says, and just last week they brought the price down from $95,000 to $89,500. The $89,500, he insists, is firm. He tells you that you can assume an existing loan of $35,000 at 8 percent interest. The owners are willing to hold a note for $34,500 at 11 percent interest—several percentage points below conventional financing rates—amortized over 30 years but due and payable in 5 years. They would, however, expect the buyer to make a downpayment of $20,000.

The owner tells you that the house is 35 years old, but that it has been well maintained and is in perfect condition. They are sure that the house will sell immediately, now that they have lowered their price. Other houses in the area, after all, are selling for over $100,000.

Having already researched the area, you know that at least the last piece of information is correct. The house is one of the lowest priced listings in that neighborhood. You ask to see the house. The owner tells you to get the key from a neighbor.

You get the key, open the door, and come face to face with a charming little fireplace in the living room. The rest of the house is barren. There is no furniture in the place, no carpeting, no curtains, and no blinds. The owners have stripped the house of all accouterments, leaving it starkly naked. All of its flaws can be seen.

As your eyes sweep the living room and dining room, you look out the window at the rear of the house. With no curtains or blinds, you clearly see the electrical substation looming over you.

You decide to focus your attention first on the house, not on the backyard. Actually, the floors are in good shape, and the walls

46

are solid plaster. The rooms have been freshly painted. In addition to the living room and dining room, the first floor has an old but functional kitchen, a bedroom, a bathroom, and a study adjoining the bedroom.

Upstairs there are two bedrooms and a bathroom. You turn on two faucets at once, flush the toilet and watch the faucets. The stream of water from the faucets doesn't diminish. The water pressure is strong.

The basement consists of two finished rooms, one of which has an outside entrance. The basement also has a utility room with a refrigerator, a very old dryer (but no washer), a relatively new gas furnace, and an old water heater. The basement is dry—no musty smell. You look for evidence of flooding on the lower walls, but find none.

You make a few calculations. It will cost perhaps $3,000 to install a full bathroom in the basement and about $600 for a new washer and dryer. The water heater will have to be replaced soon, but you would plan to wait until it starts leaking before replacing it. The plumbing looks okay and the electrical system has been updated.

You walk out the back door into the yard. It would probably cost you a few hundred dollars to install an attractive fence to hide the "DANGER KEEP OUT" sign and the dilapidated fence around the substation. Although you would have a professional landscaper sketch a design for the backyard, you can already visualize a modified oriental garden. A pine tree nestled among bamboo could be planted just in front of the electrical substation. You could never completely camouflage the structure, but a 40-foot pine would certainly help.

Okay, so far you estimate that your total outlay for the bathroom, the washer and dryer, and the landscaping and fence should be under $5,000.

Now you go back into the house once more, this time calculating the rent you anticipate:

- $235 for the person who has the bedroom, bathroom, and study on the first floor
- $195 each for the two people who have similar bedrooms and share a bathroom on the second floor

- $275 for the person in the basement who will have a private bathroom, the exclusive use of a refrigerator, and a private entrance

The house should bring you about $900 in rental income.

You go out the front door, lock it, and look at the house again from the outside. As you try to put the gate back on its hinges, a neighbor comes over.

"You thinking of buying this house?"

"Mmm. Thinking about it. I like the neighborhood a lot. The house can use some work, but I think it's structurally sound."

"That's what you think. The roof leaks. The owners did a quick patch job, but they've had a problem with the roof leaking for a few years."

"Really? It's a good thing you came along. Are there any other problems you know about?"

"No, not structurally, but the place sure is an eyesore for the neighborhood. I hope you take care of it better than Bob and Jane."

"Do you know the current owners?"

"Sure, they lived here for years before renting it out. They're basically good people, but they never kept the place up after it was rented. They've had this house on the market for over a year now. They started out by asking $105,000, but there were no takers. They dropped the price a few times and started to offer owner-financing. Now they really want to sell so they can leave the area and retire in Florida. They already bought a condominium down there and are supposed to move into it in a couple of months."

You thank the neighbor very much and find out her name and where she lives. She has given you important information, and she may well help you again in the future.

Now it's time for you to make more calculations. You find out how much property tax and insurance you would have to pay for that property. The property tax is $890 per year, and the insurance would be about $290 per year. If you assume the existing loan of $35,000 at 8 percent interest, your payment per month would be $257.

Okay, let's see what your fixed expenses would be each month and compare them with your anticipated rental income:

	Monthly payment
Taxes ($890/year) divided by 12 months	$ 74
Insurance ($290/year) divided by 12 months	24
Existing mortgage payment	257
Current total monthly expense	$355
Anticipated rent ($900) minus $10 each for 4 tenants ($40)	$860
Amount you could pay per month for an additional loan ($860 minus $355)	$505

What loan amount can you borrow for payments of about $505 per month? If you look at your amortization tables, you will find that one possible amount would be $45,000 at 11 percent amortized over 15 years. The payment per month would be $511.

The owners said that they would be willing to hold a note for $34,500 at 11 percent interest. That will be no problem. But they also want you to come up with a $20,000 downpayment and to pay them off completely in 5 years; you're not prepared to meet either of these conditions. Still, you and the owners' negotiating positions are not that far apart.

Bingo! You may have hit the jackpot!

Before you present your offer, though, you may want to make a thorough structural inspection of the house. You can use any defects you find to negotiate a better price and better terms with the seller. I'll show you what I look for in the next chapter.

Don't waste time, though. If you feel you may have a good deal, go for it as quickly as possible after making rough cost estimates of what you'll need to do. If you have put an escape clause in your purchase contract, which I'll explain later, you will be able to negotiate further if you find major defects.

POINTS TO REMEMBER

- Work with one or two competent real estate agents to find a suitable house, or become an agent yourself.
- To find a house on your own, read the classified ads and cruise selected areas.
- Look for a house with an assumable low-interest mortgage and/or with the possibility of substantial owner financing.
- Find a median-priced house in a good location.
- Find a house that can accommodate four singles.
- Make sure that the house is at most 15 minutes away from your own residence.
- Look for a house with at least four bedrooms and two bathrooms, or for a house in which you could easily add an additional bedroom or bathroom.
- Look within the house for an area that could readily be converted into an accessory dwelling unit.
- Make sure that your rental income will approximately cover your monthly mortgage, tax, and insurance payments.
- It's useful to make a careful inspection of the house before presenting an offer, but don't waste time.

FOR FURTHER INFORMATION

Allen, Robert G.: *Creating Wealth*, Simon and Schuster, New York, 1983.
  Among other topics, it discusses the many ways to find bargain properties and to structure terms which make them profitable.
Lowry, Albert J.: *How You Can Become Financially Independent by Investing in Real Estate*, Simon and Schuster, New York, 1977.
  Comprehensive and clear in its presentation, this explains how to find, negotiate, and finance real estate.
Nelson, Robert H.: *Zoning and Property Rights: An Analysis of the American System of Land Use Regulation*. MIT Press, Cambridge, Massachusetts, 1977.
  The author provides a very readable and informative analysis of American zoning regulations, of the precepts on which they are based, and of how they are likely to change.
Nickerson, William: *How I Turned $1,000 into Three Million in Real Estate in My Spare Time*, Simon and Schuster, New York, 1980.
  This real estate classic describes what the author looked for when buying the properties that turned him into a multimillionaire.

4

How to make a house INSPECTION

The difference between buying a house for a quick turnover and buying a house as a long-term investment is like the difference between a short-term fling and getting married. If you are going to be living with your investment for a long time, it's going to be more important to you that the roof won't have to be replaced than that the living room wallpaper is cute.

Before making an offer, you should make a preliminary assessment that the house is structurally sound. You will also want to note any improvements that have to be made, and their approximate cost. As mentioned previously, you can use some of your findings to negotiate with the seller. Your assessment will also enable you to weigh the cost of the improvements with the likelihood that those improvements would increase the value of the house.

Essentially, anything that makes the house look prettier or noticeably increases the comfort of its occupants will increase the market value of the house. Anything required simply to make the house habitable will not increase its market value significantly.

Improvements That Will Not Increase Market Value

- replacing a roof
- replacing a water heater

51

- replacing the plumbing
- replacing one gas furnace with another gas furnace
- upgrading the electrical service

Improvements That Will Increase Market Value

- painting it inside and outside
- adding a bathroom
- adding attractive landscaping
- replacing an old oil furnace with a more energy-efficient gas furnace
- installing central air-conditioning
- adding a washer and dryer

You can take it for granted that an older house will have problems and defects and that its value will not necessarily be increased by every improvement you ever have to make. There is no such thing as a perfect house.

Don't let the problems you discover scare you. Some investors get excellent buys by locating properties with obvious but easily fixable defects. The house that no one else wants because the basement floods, for example, might be bought on excellent terms. The problem can often be remedied simply by regrading around the house, cleaning the gutters, and making sure that the water from the downspouts drains a few feet away from the house.

Just make certain that you really can fix the defects for a relatively small investment of time and money.

WHAT TO TAKE WITH YOU

You can perform a fairly decent inspection yourself. You'll need a flashlight with a strong beam, an ice pick or jack knife, a screwdriver, a circuit tester or small lamp, and, if the house has a fireplace, a few sheets of newspaper and matches. Sounds like you're going on a treasure hunt, doesn't it? But each item has a purpose when you're making a house inspection.

You may want to make the inspection with a chart in hand so

you'll prompt yourself to be thorough. Write down your observations on the spot; otherwise, you may forget the problems you see.

Here's an example of a simple do-it-yourself inspection sheet, along with a corresponding evaluation sheet. Following these sheets, I will explain each item in more detail.

INSPECTION SHEET

Outside

			Comments
Size of lot			
Suitable for renters?	Yes	No	
Sufficient off-street parking?	Yes	No	
Grading			
Ground slopes away from house?	Yes	No	
Gutters and downspouts			
Clean?	Yes	No	
Firmly attached to house?	Yes	No	
Free of rust spots?	Yes	No	
Carry water at least 3 feet from house?	Yes	No	
Roof			
Few or no signs of disrepair or age?	Yes	No	
Foundation			
Absence of significant cracks or of soft mortar?	Yes	No	
Siding			
Appears to require no immediate repair or painting?	Yes	No	
Steps, railings, gates, and fences			
Firm and steady?	Yes	No	
Painting or repair not needed?	Yes	No	
If wooden steps, on a concrete slab?	Yes	No	
Gates in working order?	Yes	No	

INSPECTION SHEET (*Continued*)

Comments

Landscaping

Attractively landscaped?	Yes	No
Absence of overhanging branches or tree roots close to house	Yes	No
Existing trees and shrubs can remain?	Yes	No

Inside

	Walls	Floor	Ceiling	Window	Doors	Plumbing	Electrical	Other
Living room								
Dining room								
Kitchen								
Bedroom 1								
Bedroom 2								
Bedroom 3								
Bedroom 4								
Bathroom 1								
Bathroom 2								
Bathroom 3								
Family room								
Basement								
Utility room								

INSPECTION SHEET (*Continued*)

Inside

	Walls	Floor	Ceiling	Window	Doors	Plumbing	Electrical	Other
Hallway								
Attic								
Garage								

Comments: _____

_____

_____

_____

Appliances and Other

Comments

1. Does the house have insulation which is not UFFI (urea-formaldehyde foam insulation)?   Yes   No

2. How much amperage service is there? _____
How much voltage service is there? _____
Adequate amperage and voltage?   Yes   No

3. Does the water pressure seem adequate?   Yes   No

4. Have I probed wooden structures for rot or damage, and is the wood firm?   Yes   No

5. Is heat available in all rooms which will be occupied by tenants?   Yes   No

INSPECTION SHEET (*Continued*)

Comments

6. Is there adequate security in
   the house?   Yes   No

7. Are there sufficient phone
   jacks in convenient locations?   Yes   No

8. Do all of the following work
   appear to be problem-free?

Furnace or boiler	Yes	No	Absent
Air-conditioner(s)	Yes	No	Absent
Heat pump	Yes	No	Absent
Water heater	Yes	No	Absent
Is the bottom rust-free?	Yes	No	Absent
Refrigerator(s)	Yes	No	Absent
Stove(s)	Yes	No	Absent
Washer	Yes	No	Absent
Dryer	Yes	No	Absent
Dishwasher(s)	Yes	No	Absent
Garbage disposer	Yes	No	Absent
Compactor	Yes	No	Absent
Venetian blinds and drapery mechanism	Yes	No	Absent
Locks	Yes	No	Absent
Fireplace(s)	Yes	No	Absent
Doorbell	Yes	No	Absent
Smoke detector(s)	Yes	No	Absent

Comments: _____

_____

_____

_____

_____

_____

_____

_____

_____

_____

_____

EVALUATION SHEET

Points for Negotiation

Area of House	Nature of Problem, or Improvement Needed	Approx. Cost
Total estimated cost		

Other Problems Noted

Area of House	Nature of Problem, or Improvement Needed	Approx. Cost
Total estimate cost		

Estimated current market value of house $ _____

Total estimated cost of repairs
  and improvements $ _____
  Total $ _____

Estimated value of property,
  once improved $ _____

WHAT TO LOOK FOR

Outside

1. SIZE OF LOT

Unless the land in the area is unusually valuable, it is best for the lot to be relatively small when you buy a house for rental purposes. Most tenants, particularly singles, would prefer not to have to tend to a large lawn. Further, the smaller the lot, the more of the sales price you can attribute to the house rather than to the land; this will give you a larger depreciation deduction come tax time.

While you are looking at the size of the lot, also check to see that the property has offstreet parking, as well as sufficient room on the street for other tenant cars if you think your renters will have cars.

2. GRADING

Ideally, your house should sit on a gentle rise, so that rain hitting the side of the house will run off away from the house. If the earth around the foundations slopes down toward the house, you risk a damp or flooded basement, and the house will also be more likely to have moisture in the crawl space. Over a period of time, moisture will cause structures to rot and decay and will attract wood boring insects.

3. GUTTERS AND DOWNSPOUTS

See if the gutters are clogged with leaves and debris. You can tell by looking out of a top story window into the gutters below. Even looking up at the gutters from below, you can spot overflow marks from runoff that has spilled over the sides. Often you can actually see from the ground the tops of plants growing in gutters that haven't been cleaned.

See that each gutter is firmly attached to the house; otherwise, the water coming off of the roof will spill from the eaves before reaching the gutter.

You could be facing a more serious problem if you find rust spots along the bottom of a gutter. Rust means that the gutter is deteriorating and may soon have to be replaced.

Also check the downspouts. They should empty directly over a concrete slab, and the slab should be tilted away from the house, so that the water will ultimately drain at least 3 or 4 feet away from the foundation. Or, better still, the downspouts should empty into drain pipe which will carry the water even farther from the house.

4. ROOF

It's important to make a careful assessment of the roof's condition, because replacing a roof is a major expense. You'll also need to look at the flashing—that metal on the roof around chimneys, valleys, and plumbing vents—to make sure that it's not rusted or bent out of shape.

Roofs can be made of many different materials, each having its own advantages and disadvantages.

Asphalt shingle is a relatively inexpensive material with a lifespan of more than 15 or 20 years. After the first set of shingles is worn, it is possible to put on a second set without removing the first. After the second set goes, though, you need to have both it and the first set removed before you can put on another set of shingles. Of course the cost of removing the two sets of old shingles adds to the cost of the job. You can tell that the roof will need to be replaced soon if the shingles look thick and are starting to cup along the front edges; another indication is that large amounts of granules have been washing off the shingles and collecting in the gutters. Also check for missing shingles and shingles with slots between them.

Fiberglass shingle is a relatively new roofing material which is being used today in much current construction. Its expected life is 15 to 30 years depending on its weight. Heavier shingles last longer.

Asbestos and slate can last 50 years or more. Actually, some slate roofs in Europe are over 600 years old and are still going strong. Most American slates have a life expectancy of 50 to 250 years. Check to see whether any of the pieces have been broken and need to be replaced. Replacing a few pieces of slate is expensive, and replacing an entire slate roof is more costly than replacing practically any other type of roofing material.

Cedar shake can last 30 or 40 years if the butt is thick and rough and they have been installed properly. Roofs with thin, smooth shakes may last 15–25 years. Again, make sure that the shakes are in place when you look at the roof.

Built-up ply slag consists of several layers of tar paper and tar, with a top layer of gravel or slag, that normally lasts about 20 years. If bubbles form when you walk on the roof, you'll know it's deteriorating.

5. FOUNDATION
Check the foundation for cracks and for crumbling mortar. Cracks are usually nothing to worry about; they occur as a house settles, and almost all older houses are likely to have a few. Some cracks, however, can be a danger signal, indicating water damage or substantial structural problems. A professional housing inspector should take a look.

6. SIDING
Observe the construction materials of the outside walls. Brick, vinyl siding, and aluminum siding are good, if they were installed correctly. These materials are relatively maintenance free. Asbestos shingles, stucco and wood, need periodic painting.

What is the condition of the outside walls? Is the paint peeling or flaking? A paint job is expensive. Is some siding material missing? Will it have to be replaced?

7. STEPS, RAILINGS, GATES, AND FENCES
Are all of these structures firm when you apply pressure to them, or do you feel some wobbling? Shaky railings and stairs can be dangerous and may have to be fixed at once.

If the outdoor steps are wood, see if they are set on a concrete slab. If so, there will be less chance that the steps and adjacent structures of the house will have wood rot or termite damage. Wood in direct contact with the earth should at least be pressure treated.

8. LANDSCAPING
Like me, you may hope that the house you decide to buy is not well landscaped, because attractive landscaping usually adds to its price. I would prefer to buy a house at a bargain price, add a few hundred dollars worth of landscaping, and thus increase the value of the house myself by a couple of thousand dollars.

When you first inspect the property, check its trees to see if any have dead or rotting limbs that will have to be removed, and especially make a note of any trees that will have to come down because they are growing too close to the house. Tree removal can cost several hundred dollars per tree.

Inside

Inspect every room for the condition of its walls, floor, ceiling, windows, and doors. Look into the attic. In applicable rooms, check all of the plumbing and all of the electrical fixtures, outlets, switches, and major appliances. Let's take these in order:

1. WALLS

Are there any stains or crumbling spots on the walls? Such damage may indicate a leak in the roof, in its flashing materials, or in the plumbing in the room above you. Are the basement walls buckling? Poor outside drainage may be the cause.

Will the interior walls have to be painted? If so, this may be a major expense on the one hand, but a bargaining point on the other.

2. FLOORS

If there is furniture in the house, move it aside to inspect the floors. If there is carpeting on the floors, is it in good condition or will it have to be replaced? If new carpeting is needed, you may be able to save the existing padding and reduce your installation costs. If an existing carpet is discolored, it may merely be dirty, and you may be able to save money by cleaning it rather than replacing it.

Look for dark spots on wood floors. These could be urine stains from pets. If so, they may be impossible to remove. If the dark spots are near steam radiators, this may indicate a leak in the radiator's plumbing.

When you are inspecting the floor in the basement, check to see if there are any water marks or loose tiles, either of which may indicate that the basement floods. It is reassuring if the owner has carpeting in the basement, or has cartons stored on the floor near the walls.

When you return upstairs to the main level, jump hard on the floors. Do you feel vibrations, and do the windows rattle? These signs could mean that the house has inadequate supporting beams or that the underlying wood beams have serious damage.

3. Ceilings

Check the ceilings for peeling paint, cracked plaster, and stains. Any of these usually indicates a moisture problem—either from plumbing which needs to be repaired in the room above the ceiling, from caulking that needs to be replaced in the bathroom above the ceiling, or from a leak in the roof.

4. Windows and Doors

Try opening and closing all of the windows and doors. Do the windows slide up and down easily? Do any cords in old-fashioned windows need to be replaced? Are there storm windows and screens? Are any windows cracked or any screens torn that you will have to repair? If you intend to rent a basement area, is there adequate light and ventilation?

Do all of the doors close properly, including the sliding closet doors?

5. Attic

Ideally on a rainy day, go up into the attic, flashlight in hand. Do you see any water or water marks that could have been caused by a leaky roof? If there are ventilation openings at both ends of the attic, so much the better for the house. Houses need to "breathe," and the openings for ventilation should never be obstructed, even in the coldest winter. A well insulated, well ventilated attic will increase comfort, save energy, and prolong the life of the roof and of the heating and cooling systems in the house.

6. Plumbing

Check the water pressure in the house. Go to the bathroom on the top floor, turn on one faucet in the sink and one in the bathtub, and then flush the toilet. If there is a significant diminution of the water coming out of the faucets, the house has poor water pressure, which may indicate that the pipes carrying the water will soon have to be replaced. After 30 to 50 years, it is possible for corrosion to have built up inside a galvanized pipe narrowing its inside diameter and restricting the water flow. In time, such corroded pipes will need to be replaced.

When you check the plumbing in the basement, find out the type of pipe material used. Copper and some plastic materials are excellent. They can last virtually forever. If the pipes are galvanized, see if there are rust spots on the outside. Such spots indicate that the pipe may soon have to be replaced, and replacing plumbing can be a major expense.

Locate the main water shutoff for the house and the shutoff to outside water spigots, and see if there are shutoffs at each plumbing fixture. Then make sure that they all work.

Check all plumbing fixtures for drips and leaks. Flush the toilets to see that they are working properly—that the water goes down as it's supposed to and that it doesn't keep running.

While you are looking at the plumbing fixtures, note any caulking that will have to be done in the bathrooms.

7. ELECTRICAL SYSTEM

Most houses have 150 amp service, which is usually quite adequate. Certainly houses should have a minimum of 100-amp service. Unfortunately, some older homes still have 60-amp service; these houses may require additional wiring, which can be expensive. Modern houses also need 240-volt service.

If you check the circuit breaker or fuse box, you might find listed there the amperage and voltage that are servicing the house. The information written on the electrical box is not always accurate, however. To make sure, go to the outside of the house and look for the electrical lines coming into the house; you should see three lines if the house has 240-volt service, and only two lines if the house has 120-volt service. Then measure the wire on the outside of the house. These are estimates of what the measurements mean:

¾" or less	— 60 amps or less
1"	— 100 amps
1¼"	— up to 150 amps
1½"	— 200 amps

If the house was built or remodeled between 1960 and 1973, find out if it has aluminum wiring. Aluminum wiring can be a fire hazard unless the house has special switches and receptacles designed for use with aluminum wiring. You can sometimes find exposed wiring in the basement or in the attic. Aluminum wiring may be marked by the words "Aluminum" or by "AL" along the jacket of the wiring.

While you are looking at the wiring, note any wire that is deteriorating or crumbling. It will have to be taped or replaced.

Check all electrical fixtures, switches, and outlets to make sure that they work. Don't assume that a fixture without a light bulb would work if it had a light bulb. There could be a problem with the switch, the wiring, or the fixture itself. Unscrew a working bulb and screw it into the fixtures without bulbs to see if they work. Take your circuit tester or lamp, and plug it into every single electrical outlet to make sure that they all work. While you are doing this, note any rooms that lack outlets. There should be at least two outlets in every room; otherwise, your tenants will have no place to plug in their radios, televisions, and alarm clocks.

Appliances and Other

1. INSULATION

Check the insulation while you are in the attic. Many older homes built before 1940 had no insulation installed when they were first built.

Ideally, there should be adequate insulation. Your tenants will be much happier if they have low utility bills, and when you sell the house you will get a better price for it if the house is well insulated.

At a minimum, though, see if the insulating material is urea-formaldehyde foam insulation (UFFI). A foam with thermal qualities, UFFI is injected into walls and attic floors, where it hardens. Although little is clear, it is thought to pose a health hazard if it has been incorrectly installed. You can often detect UFFI by unscrewing a cover plate from a wall outlet or a switch and looking in around the outlet or switch box for a white, hard material. If UFFI is present, you'll need to have professional tests made to determine whether it is hazardous.

2. HEATING AND COOLING SYSTEMS

Check the heating and cooling systems of the house.

The primary source of heat for a house may be either a furnace, a boiler, or a heat pump. You can test a furnace or a boiler at any time of the year by putting the setting on a thermostat higher than the room temperature. For a forced air system, heat should come out of the registers in a few minutes. Radiators should become warm to the touch within 15 minutes if the boiler is working properly.

Heat pumps, on the other hand, control both heating and cooling. Only if it's cool outside should you test the heat pump by raising the thermostat setting to see if heat comes out of the registers. If it is warm outside, don't check for heat, rather turn the thermostat down and see if cool air comes out.

Central air conditioning systems and window units can only be checked if the temperature outside is 65° or warmer. If it is, turn the thermostat setting down, or turn the controls on the window units on, and see if cold air comes out.

Some central heating and cooling units are self-lubricating, while others must be oiled twice a year to be kept in good working order. You may want to ask the owner if the system has been regularly serviced. Ask, too, whether the owner would mind letting you see the receipts showing how often the unit has been professionally serviced. If the owner says he took care of the maintenance himself, ask him to show you where to put the oil to lubricate the motor. If he doesn't know where the oil holes are, this tells you something.

3. WATER HEATER

The water heater will have to heat enough water for the household. A 40-gallon gas fueled water heater should handle the needs of four to six people. (The equivalent for an electric heater would be a 66-gallon tank.) Open the little door leading to the pilot light and look for rust at the bottom of the tank. The water heater may have to be replaced in a few years if there is obvious deterioration on the bottom. You don't need to replace a water heater, though, until it actually starts to leak.

4. REFRIGERATOR(S) AND STOVE(S)

If the refrigerator is not plugged in, plug it in, and wait to see that it works properly. Don't forget to check the freezer compartment, too. Make sure that the seal around the refrigerator door is soft, not brittle, and that when the door closes, it closes tightly.

Turn on all of the top burners or heating elements on the stove, making sure that they work properly. Then turn on the oven and the broiler, to make sure that they also work.

5. WASHER AND DRYER

A washer and dryer are very attractive appliances to singles renting a house. You will get tenants faster and be able to charge more rent if the house is equipped with a washer and dryer.

Check to see that they work. Run the washer through all cycles.

6. DISHWASHER, GARBAGE DISPOSER, AND COMPACTOR

It's best if you don't have too many extra appliances in the household. Dishwashers, garbage disposers, and compactors won't bring you extra rent. The only thing they will bring you are additional repair bills.

7. FIREPLACE

Make sure that the damper can be opened and closed. Open the damper and start a fire in the fireplace with the newspaper you have brought. Is the smoke venting properly, or is it coming into the room? Inspect the smoke chamber and flue with your flashlight. Are there heavy creosote deposits? You may need to get it cleaned.

8. BLINDS AND CURTAIN PULLERS

Do they work?

9. DOORBELL

Ring it.

10. SMOKE DETECTORS

If the house has them, so much the better; otherwise, you will want to install them yourself. Push the test button to see if they work. If there is no button, check with cigarette smoke.

11. PHONE JACKS

There should be at least one phone jack in a convenient location on every floor used by your tenants.

This is what your completed inspection sheets might look like:

INSPECTION SHEET

Outside

			Comments
1. *Size of Lot* —suitable for renters?	[Yes]	No	
—sufficient off-street parking?	[Yes]	No	
2. *Grading* —ground slopes away from house?	[Yes]	No	
3. *Gutters and Downspouts* —clean?	Yes	[No]	
—firmly attached to house?	[Yes]	No	
—free of rust spots?	[Yes]	No	
—carries water at least 3 feet from house?	Yes	[No]	in back, 2 downspouts empty within inches of house
4. *Roof* —few or no signs of disrepair or age?	[Yes]	No	
5. *Foundation* —absence of significant cracks or soft mortar?	[Yes]	No	
6. *Siding* —appears to require no immediate repair or painting?	[Yes]	No	
7. *Steps/Railing/Gates/ Fences* —firm? steady?	[Yes]	No	
—painting or repair not needed?	Yes	[No]	back steps badly in need of paint
—if wood steps, on concrete slab?	[Yes]	No	
—gates in working order?	Yes	[No]	

INSPECTION SHEET (*Continued*)

Comments

8. *Landscaping*
   —attractively landscaped?　　Yes　[No]　rubbish and leaves in yard; needs extensive landscaping

   —absence of overhanging branches or tree roots close to house　[Yes]　No
   —existing trees and shrubs can remain?　[Yes]　No

INSPECTION SHEET (*Continued*)

Inside

	Walls	Floor	Ceiling	Windows	Doors	Plumbing	Electrical	Other
Living room			(1)					
Dining room								
Kitchen								
Bedroom 1				(2)	(3)			
Bedroom 2								
Bedroom 3								
Bedroom 4								
Bathroom 1								
Bathroom 2						(4)		
Bathroom 3								
Family room								

INSPECTION SHEET (*Continued*)

	Walls	Floor	Ceiling	Windows	Doors	Plumbing	Electrical	Other
Basement								
Utility room		(5)						
Hallway								(6)
Attic			(7)					
Garage								

COMMENTS: (1) Uneven plastering on ceiling near fireplace. (2) Window cords missing; window won't stay open. (3) Closet door won't slide shut. (4) Leak in sink faucet; tub badly needs caulking. (5) Water-stain mark in rear corner. (6) Loose banister. (7) Evidence of water marks on attic ceiling near chimney.

Appliances and Other

1. Does the house have insulation which is not UFFI? [Yes] No

2. How much amperage service is there? <u>150</u>
   How much voltage service is there? <u>240</u>
   —Adequate [Yes] No

3. Does the water pressure seem adequate? [Yes] No

4. Have you probed wooden structures for rot or damage, and is the wood firm? [Yes] No

5. Is heat available in all rooms which will be occupied by tenants? [Yes] No

6. Is there adequate security in the house? [Yes] No

INSPECTION SHEET (*Continued*)

7. Are there sufficient phone jacks in convenient locations? Yes [No]

8. Do all of the following work, and appear to be problem-free:

—furnace/boiler	[Yes]	No	Absent
—air conditioner(s)	[Yes]	No	Absent
—heat pump	Yes	No	[Absent]
—water heater	[Yes]	No	Absent
—is the bottom rust-free?	Yes	[No]	
—refrigerator(s)	[Yes]	No	Absent
—stove(s)	[Yes]	No	Absent
—washer	Yes	No	[Absent]
—dryer	Yes	[No]	Absent
—dishwasher(s)	Yes	No	[Absent]
—garbage disposal	Yes	No	[Absent]
—compactor	Yes	No	[Absent]
—Venetian blinds/drapery mechanism	Yes	No	[Absent]
—locks	[Yes]	No	Absent
—fireplace(s)	[Yes]	No	Absent
—doorbell	[Yes]	No	Absent
—smoke detector(s)	Yes	No	[Absent]

COMMENTS: Will need (1) a telephone jack installed in basement, (2) a water heater within a few years, (3) a washer, (4) a dryer within a few years, and (5) 3 smoke detectors.

WHAT TO DO WITH THE INFORMATION YOU HAVE COLLECTED?

After you have gone through the entire house, look at your inspection sheet. Some problems or potential problems may cost a lot of time and money to remedy and will be major points for negotiation. Others, like cleaning a gutter, are relatively trivial.

It is up to you how many points you will bring to the attention of the seller. It's silly to haggle over who will repair a leaky faucet if the terms for the purchase are otherwise attractive to you. Besides, if your purchase contract has clauses which state, "All appliances must be in working order at the time of settlement (close of escrow)" and "The yard must be clear of leaves and debris at the time of settlement," the seller is going to have to take care of these problems anyway. You don't necessarily need to bargain over these matters when you make your offer. Nonetheless, you may earn a bargaining chip if you sum up a number of trivial problems and say that you will take care of these if the seller will concede on another point.

Separate those problems of major and of minor concern to you. Estimate how much it would cost to remedy the problems and how expensive it would be to make improvements. Just make some ballpark figures. They don't have to be exact.

If you have absolutely no idea what the costs would be, phone a roofer, a plumber, an electrician, or other specialists. Describe the problems within their respective areas of expertise, and ask them for rough estimates. To be conservative in your estimates, use the high figures when they give you a range of prices.

As the last step, total the cost of the repairs and improvements, add that to the highest price you would be willing to pay for the house as it is now, and then estimate what the value of the house could be, once it's been improved. You will then see whether or not the costs of the repairs and improvements might be offset by the increased value of the house.

This is what your completed evaluation sheet might look like:

EVALUATION SHEET

Points for Negotiation

Area of House	Nature of Problem, or Improvement Needed	Approx. Cost
Basement	Install bathroom.	$3,000–$5,000
Utility room	No washer here; buy one immediately.	$ 300–$500
"	Dryer very old; buy new one.	$ 300–$500
"	Water heater rusty; buy one soon.	$ 300

EVALUATION SHEET (*Continued*)

Area of House	Nature of Problem, or Improvement Needed	Approx. Cost
Yard	Install fence and landscaping.	$600–$1,000
Attic and living room ceilings	Evidence of water leak near chimney— a problem with flashing?	$ 100 (?)
Total estimated cost		$7,400

Other Problems Noted

Area of House	Nature of Problem, or Improvement Needed	Approx. Cost
Gutters	Need to be cleaned.	$ 50
Downspouts	Need to drain water farther away from house.	$ 20
Steps	Need to be painted	$ 20
Yard	Needs debris cleaned up and dumped.	$ 50
Basement	Needs telephone jack installed.	$ 50
All floors	Need to install 3 smoke detectors.	$ 50
Bedroom #1	Fix window and closet door.	$ 50
Bathroom #2	Fix leaky faucet and caulk bathtub.	$ 30
Hallway	Fix loose banister.	$ 30
Total estimated cost		$350

Estimated current market value of house	$ 89,500
Total estimated cost of repairs and improvements	$ 7,750
Total	$ 97,250
Estimated value of property, once improved	$ 105,000

A WORD TO THE "UNHANDY"

Don't worry if you don't feel competent to make a thorough or accurate house inspection. It is difficult even for seasoned real estate investors to judge the age of a roof or to tell what a crack in a foundation means.

Just do what you can. Go ahead and make an offer on a house that interests you, using your best judgment. As you will see in the next chapter, you will protect yourself by putting a clause in your purchase contract permitting you to have a professional make a complete house inspection at no risk to yourself, if you decide not to go through with the purchase.

POINTS TO REMEMBER

- Expect older houses to have problems that will have to be remedied.

- Improvements which make a house look more attractive or which noticeably increase the comfort of the occupants will increase the market value of the house.

- Improvements or repairs that are required simply to make the house habitable will usually not increase the market value of the house.

- Inspect a house with a chart in hand, or you will forget what problems you see.

- Analyze your inspection sheet, estimate the costs to improve and repair the house, and use that information to negotiate the purchase of the house with the seller.

FOR FURTHER INFORMATION

Fairfax County Department of Consumer Affairs: *Something to Dwell on: Homebuyer's Shopping Guide*, 2d ed., Fairfax, Virginia, 1979.
    The booklet contains many useful suggestions about what to look for when you buy a house. (You may want to ask at your local government office about their publications for consumers interested in buying a house.)

Lennon, Michael: *The Homebook*, Homepro Systems, Inc. 110 W. Great Falls St., Falls Church, Virginia 22046, 1984.
    This loose-leaf notebook provides house inspection checklists and suggested remedies for over 475 common problems, as well as other useful information.

Roe, Thomas: "How to Inspect a House," in *Impact Report*, November–December 1982, Impact Publishing, San Ramon, California.

The author explains with charts and cost estimates how to inspect houses and small apartment buildings.

Schram, Joseph F.: *Finding and Fixing the Older Home*, Structures Publishing, Farmington, Michigan, 1976.

This presents detailed information on how to inspect and remodel older houses.

5

How to Negotiate the Purchase

Buying a house used to be a pretty straightforward process. The major focus of negotiation was usually the price, because the terms of the purchase followed a fairly conventional pattern. Most of the purchasers would put 10 to 20 percent down and find a mortgage for a 30-year period. The main concern of the sellers was how much cash they would walk away with after the deal closed. Such techniques as options, wraparound mortgages, equity-sharing, and seller-financing were generally used only by sophisticated buyers and sellers.

When the interest rates on conventional and government-backed financing became prohibitively high, however, a large array of creative financing methods came into widespread use.

As a result, the price of a property may no longer be the most important negotiating point. Astute real estate investors may now care less about the actual price of a purchase than about its terms. To give you a farfetched example, let's say that the owner of the house that you want to buy is asking $75,000 when comparable houses in the same neighborhood are selling for $65,000. Would you pay $75,000? You might, if the terms were no money down, 5 percent interest, and 30 years to pay off the mortgage.

Many books have been written about the various ways to finance the purchase of real estate; you'll find some of the best ones listed at the end of this chapter. Here, I'll just introduce you to some basic negotiating strategies and the major points to look for in purchase contracts to protect your own interests. So please don't look for any fancy footwork in this chapter, okay?

Let's assume that you'll be negotiating directly with the seller. In reality, most transactions are handled by real estate agents who will conduct the negotiations. Go through the process in this chapter anyway. The following pages may help you improve the way you explain your required and desired terms to the agent who does the negotiating for you.

Seven key steps in negotiating

Step 1: Analyze Your Own Position

Before you negotiate to buy a house, you must know very clearly which points in the negotiation will be crucial to you and which will be less consequential. To determine this, you need to decide how you intend to profit from the purchase, and to figure out how much of your money you intend to tie up in the house. Your analysis will in large part determine how you will structure your purchase offer.

For example, if you want to buy a house in order to resell it for a quick profit, it would obviously be crucial for you to negotiate an unusually low price, regardless of many other terms, so that you could immediately put the house back on the market at a higher price.

If you follow the tenets of this book, however, you will expect your profits to build over a period of 5 to 10 years or more. You will make money by getting much higher rent than usual, by slow appreciation in the value of the house, through tax savings, and by a gradual reduction of the principal balance on the mortgage. A major concern would be that you could meet your monthly payments comfortably for years to come. In this case, a low interest rate on the loan for the house may be more important to you than saving a few thousand dollars on the price.

If you buy a house, and plan to sell it within a year, you may not care if the lender is going to call the loan due in five years. You may anticipate paying off the loan when you sell the house. If, though, you expect to own the house for many years, you may never want to risk having a large lump sum payment due on the property.

Your purchase offer will also depend on the resources you have.

If you have access to only a limited amount of cash, you are obviously not going to be able to offer the seller a hefty downpayment. You'll have to find other terms to satisfy the seller.

Before you make an offer, you would, of course, have done your homework, and will know the answers to the following questions:

- Compared with similar houses in the neighborhood, how much is the house worth?
- Approximately how much would it cost to make necessary improvements and repairs?
- Once the house is fixed up, what would the new market value of the house be?
- How easy would the house be to rent?
- How much rent could the house be expected to generate?
- What monthly payments could you afford given the rental income you expect to receive?

Analyze the answers. You'll be using them not only to decide what terms to offer, but also to explain convincingly these terms to the owner.

Step 2: Know the Seller's Motivation for Selling the House

Find out why the house is being sold. It is important to learn why the seller is putting the house on the market at this particular time; you can find out from neighbors, tenants, real estate agents, and the owners themselves. Curiously, it is not primarily for financial reasons that many owners want to sell their houses. Many view their houses as obstacles in the way of achieving other goals:

- They may want to retire to another state.
- Their employers may have transferred them to other states.
- They may have gotten divorced and want a quick division of their property.
- They may have rented out the house for a while and become frustrated by management problems.

77

- They may have signed a contract to purchase another house and may need to sell their current house in order for the other transaction to go through.

Find out what time constraints the seller has. For whatever reason, the seller is often up against some deadline to sell the house. Conversely, another owner may prefer a delayed settlement, perhaps because a new house won't be ready for another 5 months. You can use the time factor as a negotiating point.

Find out what the seller will do with the money. You should find out what the owner plans to do with the money gained from the sale. If the owner has to pay off a loan and absolutely needs cash, you might offer a large cash downpayment in return for other concessions, such as a greatly reduced price. On the other hand, if the owner intends to turn around and invest the money elsewhere, you may be able to offer a small downpayment, along with monthly payments that have interest rates attractive enough to give the owner at least as big a return as could be obtained from the other investment.

Step 3: Establish Common Objectives for Yourself and the Seller

Before negotiating anything, both parties must have a common objective. In the case of consummating the sale of a house, simplistic as this sounds, a seller must want to sell the house and a buyer must want to buy it. The overall goal of the seller and of the buyer are the same—the consummation of the sale. Thus, the seller need not be your adversary.

It's helpful if you both adopt the attitude that you are on the same side of the fence, viewing a common problem—how to arrange the sale of the house in a way that is acceptable, and even advantageous, to both of you.

Step 4: Expect Some Misrepresentation from the Seller and Use It to Your Advantage

Children play marbles. The object of the game is to take as many marbles as you can away from the other guy to increase your own supply of marbles. Most sellers initially assume that they're in a marble game and that buyers are out to take advantage of them. As a result, few sellers are completely honest about the flaws and defects in the house.

Why can't somebody say, "Look, this house is worth $100,000, but I'm offering it for $98,000 because the roof needs to be replaced"? Instead, sellers offer the house for $100,000. You make them an offer of $95,000, explaining that the roof needs to be replaced. They counter at $98,500, and you settle on $97,500.

If the sellers had explained initially what the problems were, and then had told you that they had taken these problems into consideration when they offered the house at a certain price, you would have had less to bargain with. As it is, owners give you more negotiating power with each defect they hide which you discover before you buy the place.

A seller's deception may also place him under a time constraint. If a roof leaks, for example, the seller knows that water will come through the living room ceiling after the first good rain. So the seller is under pressure to sell the house before the rainy season.

You therefore have to play a game of hide-and-seek with many sellers. If you find the defects, you'll have more bargaining power. If you don't find the defects until after settlement, you'll probably have to pay to correct them, and I suppose the seller will feel triumphant in having won some extra marbles from you. This is a tiresome business if you don't enjoy playing the marble game.

Step 5: Establish Your Credibility by Explaining Your Own Position Honestly

Mark Twain once said, "Always do right. This will gratify some people, and astonish the rest."

I've found it helpful to explain exactly why I want to buy a house, how much rent I expect to get, and what I think I need to do to the house to fix it up. I let the owner know not only the terms on which I would consider buying the house, but also my reasons for having structured the offer the way I have.

Let me say that some respected real estate authorities disagree with this philosophy. Some would advise you to make sure that you know as much as possible about the seller and to try to make sure that the seller knows as little as possible about your motives. "Create pressure," they say. "Let the sellers know you're considering other properties, and that you're not overly enthusiastic about theirs."

My negotiating style is more relaxed. I try to let the seller know that if need be I'll walk away from a deal, but that I really do want to buy the property and that I will try very hard to come up with a reasonable offer, one that will meet both of our needs. Be warned: with my style of negotiation, you should be able to get reasonably good terms, but you won't make a killing.

I find it important to establish myself as a reasonable person who is not interested in playing marbles, thus trying to allay the seller's fears that this is a marble game. The best way I know how to do this is to level with the sellers.

Don't go after their marbles. Make a fair offer and explain why you have structured it the way you have. Point out how you have tried to take the seller's needs into consideration. Explain your own position, too. You are an investor. The seller should realize that you are not investing for your health. You will only be interested in a transaction that will make you a fair profit.

If the offer is fairly structured, the seller should realize that there is only some small flexibility for further negotiation, and then only if it involves give and take on both sides.

Step 6: Listen Very Carefully to Any Counteroffers from the Seller

If you are honest and reasonable, most sellers will usually try to be fair in return. Any counteroffer should be pretty close to your original offer. As much as possible, try to accommodate the terms of a reasonable counteroffer, particularly if you can trade some terms for others. Be accommodating on one request, and the seller will accommodate you on another.

Some sellers, though, will still think they're in a marble game and will try to push you to the wall. There is a saying in the stock market that "Bears make money (bear markets), bulls make money (bull markets), and pigs get slaughtered." Don't be greedy. But don't let the other guy be greedy either. Never want a deal so badly that you'd do anything to go through with it.

Step 7: Use Either Your Own Contract or a Contract with Which You Are Thoroughly Familiar

There is no such thing as a "standard purchase contract." When a real estate agent advises you that her firm's purchase contract is standard for the area, and when an owner assures you that his contract is a generally accepted one, be sure to know that there is no such thing as a standard contract.

You should also be aware that the contracts used by many real estate firms are written in favor of their clients, who are almost invariably the sellers. Most real estate firms, though, make it a practice to include clauses that protect both the buyer and the seller.

Often, even while there is no standard contract, there are local customs about who pays for what in the settlement costs. Learn the local customs and recognize that any deviation from them may entail negotiation.

You should also be aware that in certain areas of the country such major appliances as washers, dryers, and refrigerators are routinely included in the purchase price, whereas in other localities these items may stay with the seller. Your contract should specify clearly whether major appliances are included, whether fireplace screens stay or go, and whether the draperies remain with the house.

Investors who buy a lot of houses often make up "standard contracts" to meet their own specifications. They may even have these printed, making the contracts appear to be professional and inviolable. Some investors purposely title their own contracts "Standard Purchase Agreement" to fool sellers into believing that any deviation the seller wants is a deviation from the norm. In reality, of course, a requested change is merely a deviation from the exact terms the buyer wants.

If you buy just a few houses, the chances are good that you will be using a purchase agreement designed by a real estate company. If you do, scrutinize the form carefully, and understand every one of its terms before you fill in the blanks. Don't let the printed form intimidate you:

- You can line through clauses with which you disagree.
- You can add clauses which you believe to be essential.

Understand, though, that the more marked up a purchase agreement appears to be, the more likely it is for the other party to be suspicious about signing it.

Regardless of the purchase contract you use, there are certain useful clauses that you may want to insert if your contract doesn't already have them. I've included suggested clauses toward the end of this chapter.

Right now let's go over some of the terms that you may want to consider for in your purchase offer.

POINTERS FOR YOUR PURCHASE AGREEMENT

Price

Check the prices of comparable houses in the neighborhood before making your offer. Try to be sure that the price you offer is at least 10 percent less than that of comparable houses. In calculating your price, don't forget to take into account how much it will cost you for the repairs and improvements needed to make the condition of the house indeed comparable to that of others in the neighborhood.

Downpayment

Generally, the smaller the downpayment you can make, the better, because this increases your leverage. Just be sure that your rental income will come close to covering your regular monthly payments and expenses. A downpayment of 10, 15, or even 20 percent may not be unreasonable if the price and the other terms of the purchase contract are favorable.

Interest Rate on Loan

Try to find houses with existing VA or FHA (Federal Housing Administration) financing. These loans are assumable by virtually any potential buyer and can be passed along to subsequent buyers. Most older VA and FHA loans are very attractive because they usually carry a below-market rate of interest.

Owner-financing is also attractive if you can negotiate below-market long-term financing. If the owner would agree to make this financing assumable, you would have an additional bonus. That way you will be able to pass along attractive financing to potential buyers when you decide to sell your house.

Assumptions and "Subject To" Purchases

When an existing loan is assumable, you can either buy the house and assume the responsibility for the existing loan, or you can buy the house "subject to" the existing loan. In the latter case, you agree to make payments on the existing loan, but you don't assume any further responsibility for that loan. The previous owner remains legally responsible for the debt.

In most cases (unless you default), it doesn't matter how you take over the old loan, because you will be making the same payments on it. What does matter is that you can avoid paying the lender an assumption fee (or in some cases expensive points) if, rather than assume the loan, you buy the house "subject to" the existing loan.

Length of Loan Amortization

If the interest rate on the loan is relatively low—say 10 percent or less—try to have as long a payback period as possible, such as 20 or 30 years. On the other hand, long-term financing becomes less attractive, the higher the interest rate.

Prepayment Penalty

You should be able to pay off the loan whenever you want without being penalized. Make sure that there is no prepayment penalty in your loan agreement with any seller.

Balloon Payments

A balloon payment on a loan is a final payment that is larger than the previous payments. Creative financing techniques often call for relatively modest monthly payments for several years, terminating in an exceedingly large balloon payment. Some investors say that it's okay to have a balloon payment as long as it's not due within 5 years. I tend to be conservative. I advise you either to avoid large balloon payments entirely or to know in advance exactly how you intend to pay off your balloon note when it comes due.

Major Appliances and Personal Property

Try to purchase all of the major appliances in the house that are in working order. These include the washer, dryer, refrigerator, stove, air conditioner, and dehumidifier. You will want them for your tenants. It would also be helpful to you if the seller threw in garbage cans, a lawn mower, garden tools, and a snow shovel, if this equipment is already in the house.

Renting Prior to Settlement

You will save several hundred dollars if your house is rented as of the day you go to settlement. Otherwise, if you start looking for tenants after the close of escrow, your house may be empty for a month or two before you find all of your tenants and they have moved in. At a minimum, you want to be able to advertise and show the house to potential renters prior to settlement. In fact, some buyers state in their purchase contract that settlement will not take place until the purchaser has found renters who have signed a rental agreement. The ultimate approach is to have a clause in your contract permitting renters to actually move in before settlement occurs. That way you can have your renters in place with no downtime at all.

If your tenants will in fact occupy the house before you own it, the current owner will have to sign a simple rental agreement with each of the tenants you have chosen, and this agreement will be in effect until you become the official owner. The following is an example of such an agreement:*

INTERIM RENTAL AGREEMENT

This agreement has been entered into on   (date)   by and between   (Tenant)   and   (Owner)   and   (Purchaser)   for the property located at   (address) .

The following are mutually agreed upon points:

* State laws regulating real estate differ. Before using any of the suggested legal language in this chapter verbatim, you may want to consult a real estate attorney in your state.

1. Tenant will pay Owner a weekly rent of __(amount)__ in advance for occupancy starting on __(date)__ , and shall pay this amount in advance each week to Owner. Utilities are/are not included in the rent.
2. Tenant agrees to vacate the premises within 5 days if Owner makes such request in writing. If this occurs, Tenant shall be refunded any amount of rent paid for the days he or she does not occupy the house.
3. During the week that settlement occurs, rent will be prorated on a daily basis until the property is transferred to the new owner.
4. Unless caused by Owner's negligence or misrepresentation, Tenant waives all claims against Owner for any damage or injury occuring to any person or persons on the premises for the duration of this agreement; nor shall Owner be liable for any personal property which is stolen or damaged due to flooding, leaks, fire, malfunction of equipment, structural problems, or for any reason whatever.

(Tenant)	(date)	(Owner)	(date)
		(Purchaser)	(date)

Why would the owner let your tenants move into the house before settlement risking possible destruction of the house, injury to tenants, or an awkward situation should settlement not occur? There are several good reasons:

1. You let the current owner keep all of the rent that is collected prior to settlement, an amount that could run to several hundred dollars.
2. You make sure that the owner is aware that most insurance policies do not cover owners whose houses are left unoccupied for more than 30 days for vandalism and malicious mischief and glass breakage.
3. You have instilled confidence in the owner that you will select excellent tenants. You may offer to give the owners the opportunity to meet and approve each tenant you select.
4. You point out that the presettlement rental agreement has a clause requiring the tenants to vacate the premises within 5 days at the owner's request, assuring ultimate owner control.

If you are showing the house to prospective tenants before settlement but no tenant will move in until after settlement, they don't need to sign a rental agreement with the seller. You should, however, put the following point into your own rental agreement:

> Tenant understands that this agreement is immediately null and void if settlement does not occur by _(date)_ between _(You)_ and _(Seller)_ .

Why would renters accept such an ambiguous term of rental? They also must have absolute confidence that 100 percent of your effort will go into making sure that settlement occurs, and feel that this clause is a mere formality.

The main drawback to renting prior to settlement is that it locks you in more firmly to buying the house. Some investors like to wheel and deal until the day of settlement, and they can do this more effectively when the seller knows that they can easily walk away from the transaction.

For me it is quite different. I'm usually so relieved that I found the right house—the right location, financing, and floor plan for rental—that I focus all my attention on a smooth settlement, rather than on wringing any last minute concessions from the seller. And if you have a tight purchase contract, the seller shouldn't be able to pull any last minute surprises on you, either. If the seller does spring an unfair surprise on you at the last minute, you can still walk away from the purchase, albeit having wasted a lot of your time. I have never, however, had a situation in which settlement didn't occur.

Amount of Earnest Money Deposit

Most purchase agreements have a provision requiring a buyer to put up some amount of good faith money, to be held in escrow, that will be forfeit if the buyer decides not to go through with the purchase agreement. Some real estate agents say that the deposit should be about 5 percent of the purchase price, although there are no firm rules or requirements. Investors, of course, would say to put as little of your money at risk as you can get away with. On the other hand, the buyer may decide to offer a large earnest money deposit, if sellers are willing to negotiate more favorable terms on other points.

Timing of Settlement

As mentioned previously, the timing of the date of closing can also be used as a bargaining point. If the seller wants a quick settlement, you may agree to be accommodating in this regard if the seller will be more flexible on terms important to you.

Contingency Clauses

Every purchase contract should have at least one contingency clause, a clause to release you from the purchase agreement at no penalty to yourself.

Make your offer subject to a structural inspection within a certain time (say 5 working days) which meets your satisfaction. If for some reason you decide to back out of the contract within that time, you can say that you were not satisfied with the inspection. You will then be released from the contract with no penalty.

SUMMARY OF USEFUL CLAUSES FOR YOUR PURCHASE CONTRACT

Contingent on Home Inspection

"This contract is contingent until (time) , (date) upon a home inspection that is satisfactory to Purchaser. Cost of the inspection to be borne by Purchaser."

Contingent on Financing

"This contract shall be contingent upon Purchaser successfully obtaining financing for a loan of $_____, at _____% interest over _____ years with _____ point(s). Purchaser must be approved for such financing within _____ days. In the event that Purchaser, having made application for financing, and exercised due diligence in the pursuit thereof, requires further time to obtain such financing, this term shall be extended by _____ days."

Owner Financing

"Purchaser at settlement shall give and Seller agrees to hold a Deferred Purchase Money Deed of Trust and note secured on said premises in the original sum of $_____ due _____ years from date and bearing interest at the rate of _____ % per annum, payable in _____ (monthly, semiannual, quarterly) installments, consisting of principal and interest in the sum of $_____ commencing thirty (30) days from date of settlement.

Said deed of trust and note shall provide for prepayment in whole or in part without penalty, and may be assumed by any qualified purchaser/assignee."

Fixtures

"All improvements, fixtures, wall-to-wall carpeting, draperies including hardware, shades, blinds, window and door screens, awnings, stove, refrigerator, washer, dryer, dishwasher, disposer, and other items permanently attached to the real property, including built-in heating plant and air conditioning system, all plumbing and lighting fixtures, and all trees and shrubs, are included in the purchase price unless specifically excluded."

Personal Property

"The following personal property is included in the purchase price and is warranted by Seller to be in normal working condition: _____

_____."

Leakage and Seepage

"Seller warrants that there are no leaks or defects in the roof or basement and that the crawl space, if any, does not impound water. Any damage therefrom is to be repaired to the satisfaction of a professional building inspector at Seller's expense."

Appliances and Other Systems in Operable Condition

"Appliances, heating and cooling equipment, and plumbing and electrical systems, including all fixtures, will be in proper working condition at the time of settlement. Seller agrees to deliver the property free of trash and in broom-clean condition, and grants to Purchaser or Purchaser's representative the right to make a presettlement inspection."

Renting Prior to Settlement

1. "Purchaser has the right to enter the premises at any time prior to settlement for the purpose of showing the house to prospective renters."

2. "Seller agrees to enter into rental agreements with qualified applicants selected by Purchaser prior to settlement, and allow such tenants to move into the premises prior to settlement, according to the terms of the rental agreements."

3. "Settlement will occur on or about __(date)__ , but in no event prior to Purchaser having signed rental agreements from __(number)__ tenants."

Decoration and Cleaning

"Seller agrees to permit Purchaser to enter the premises prior to settlement in order to clean and decorate as necessary. However, in the event that settlement does not occur, permanently affixed improvements will remain on the premises and become the property of the Seller."

LET'S MAKE AN OFFER

Now let's practice using our negotiating principles. Remember Bob and Jane's house? It's the one with the electrical substation out back and the sign that reads "DANGER, KEEP OUT" (Chapter 3, House

3). Despite it's problems, the house has a number of very attractive features:

- Its location would be appealing to single renters.
- Below-market financing is available.
- Its floor-plan is ideal to get a very high rental income from four singles.
- The cost of the improvements would not be excessive, and many would add to the value of the house.
- Its a low-median priced house for the area, in a neighborhood of higher-priced houses.

Further, it appears that you are dealing with highly motivated sellers:

- The owners, who started off asking an excessively high price, have dropped the price considerably to its fair market value.
- They are under some time pressure. According to the neighbor, the sellers are scheduled to move into a condominium in Florida in a couple of months. In addition, they may realize that the roof leaks, in which case they'll be eager to sell before the next good rainfall, to avoid having to repair the roof, replaster the ceiling where it leaks, and repaint again.
- They are neglecting the house. They haven't spruced it up to sell it. It would appear that, psychologically, they have given up trying to get a top dollar for it.

Formulating Your Offer

After reflecting on what you think the house will bring in the way of income, how much you can afford in the way of monthly payments, and how much money you are willing to offer as a downpayment, you decide that the following points will form the basis of your offer:

What You Require

1. Your monthly payments for principal, interest, taxes, and insurance should be no greater than your projected rental income.

2. There must be no balloon payment at any time.

3. The downpayment should be no greater than 15 percent of the sales price.

4. Long-term low-interest owner-financing must be available.

What You Desire

1. The price of the house, already set at fair market value, would be even more attractive if you could shave off an additional 5 to 10 percent.

2. It would be very useful to you if the below-market owner-financing could be assumed by another buyer when the time comes for you to sell the house.

3. You would like to rent the place before settlement.

Think Like the Sellers Before Making Your Offer

Now, view your offer through the eyes of the sellers. Although your downpayment will be less than what the sellers wanted, and although they will not get all of their money in 5 years, they will nonetheless find you prepared to offer them other terms that should be quite attractive:

- You are prepared to go to settlement in a short time, so that the sale will be consummated before the sellers go to Florida.

- The sale is virtually assured, once the offer is accepted, because it will not be contingent on the sale of another house. (Many purchasers who buy a house as their own primary residence have to sell the house that they are currently in first.)

- Your offer on the purchase price is not unreasonably low.

- You are willing and able to relieve the sellers of the responsibility of making some necessary repairs and cleanup.

A Phone Call to the Sellers

Strategy firmly in mind, you call the sellers to set an appointment.
  "Hello, Mrs. Kane? This is Doreen Bierbrier. I spoke with your

husband earlier about the house you have for sale. I'm interested in buying it."

"Terrific! Just come on over and sign our contract."

"Before signing, I'd like to make sure that what I'll put in the contract will be acceptable to you."

"Well, the price and the terms are pretty much what my husband told you this morning."

"I'd still like to talk with you, if you don't mind, just to make sure that the terms are written to our mutual advantage."

"Okay. My husband and I will be home this evening. Could you come over about seven o'clock?"

"Yes. Fine."

You arrive at the sellers' luxury condominium exactly at 7 P.M. They invite you in and offer you a cup of tea, which you accept.

"So," Mr. Kane begins, "you want to buy our house, huh? It's a great buy—great location—a steal at the price. And the house is in excellent shape. The only reason it's on the market on such good terms is because we're planning to retire soon. Mind you, we're under no pressure to sell. No siree. We can always hold on to the property as a rental if we can't find someone to meet our terms."

"I agree with you, Mr. Kane. I like the house, and it is in a great location."

"Oh, please call me Bob."

"Okay, Bob. May I explain my exact position to you and your wife, so we can see if we can't work out some agreement that will satisfy your terms and still permit me to buy your house?"

"Shoot."

"I am very interested in buying your house and in going to settlement as soon as possible. The house is in a fine neighborhood, but what really attracts me to your house is that it's laid out perfectly for the type of renting I do. I think I can get $860 a month in rent from your house," I say, quoting a more conservative estimate than the $900 I'm hoping to receive.

I see Bob look at his wife and his wife look at him. They have probably been getting about $600 a month in rent.

"Why, sure you can, Doreen," says Bob, smiling ingratiatingly. "Once the house is fixed up a little, I'm sure you could get that type of rent."

"Bob, listen. Your house would normally rent for about $650

per month. I think I'll be able to get $860, because I intend to rent the house to four singles. I'd rent the top two bedrooms for $185 apiece, the bedroom on the first floor for $225, and after fixing up the basement, I'd rent that for $265."

You see from the look in Bob's eyes that he has a new respect for you. He is listening carefully to what you have to say now.

"I'm buying your house as an investment, and my objective, of course, is to make a profit. The offer I'm going to make may or may not be attractive to you. But just as you don't really have to sell, I don't really have to buy—although I really would like to buy your house, if at all possible.

"Now, I'm not an expert at buying houses," I continue, "but I am pretty good at management. My main concern is to make sure that the rents will cover any monthly payments I agree to make, with a little left over for repairs and vacancies. That way I could get your payments to you every month without any worry.

"As I understand it, your asking price is $89,500 with a $20,000 downpayment. You said that the $35,000 VA loan on the house could be assumed at 8 percent interest, and that you'd be willing to hold a note for $34,500 at 11% interest amortized over 30 years, but due and payable in 5 years.

"Bob, I want to accommodate your terms as much as possible. There are a few points, though, that I think we'll have to talk about.

"To begin with, you asked for a downpayment of $20,000. That's a lot of money. Particularly, because to rent the house as I intend to, I'm going to have to put a bathroom in the basement, put in a washer, and will probably have to replace the dryer and water heater pretty soon. I'd also like to put up a fence in the backyard and do a little landscaping. I figure that for starters it's going to cost me close to $8,000 to make those necessary improvements.

"There are two other major points of concern to me. First, even though I intend to hold your house for awhile, what if I had to sell it in a year or two? As an investor, I have to ask myself how easy it would be for me to sell the house, recoup my expenses, and make some profit. So I need to buy your house below the market price and make sure I can offer good financing terms to someone who is willing to buy from me. In other words, I need to be able to pass along any terms we negotiate to some future buyer.

"The other thing that scares me is that you want all of your money due and payable in 5 years. I have no idea how I could come up with that kind of money at that time.

"So, the offer that I've put together—which seems close to meeting your terms while making economic sense to me—is this: $84,000 with $8,000 as a downpayment. I would take over the payments on your existing mortgage and pay the rest to you at 11 percent interest not over 30 years, but much faster, over 15 years. Here are the figures I've worked out."

Existing loan of $35,000 @ 8% interest: monthly payment (principal + interest) =	$257
New loan of $41,000 @ 11% interest over 15 years, from sellers: monthly payment (principal + interest) =	466
Taxes @ $890/year: monthly payment =	74
Insurance @ $290/year: monthly payment =	24
Total monthly payment	$821

"If all goes well," I explain, "my rental income will be $860 a month. As you can see, after you factor in vacancies, repairs, and maintenance, I'm cutting it pretty close, but I really do want to buy your house."

There is a moment of silence as Bob and his wife look at each other. Bob responds.

"Let's think about this now. Your offer is not exactly what we had in mind, but it's not completely out of the ballpark. You seem sincere. I'll be honest with you. We're offering an attractive price and attractive terms as it is, because we'd really like to sell the house to someone who could go to settlement as soon as possible with no contingencies in the contract. If we could, we'd sell the house outright and not be bothered with it again. We figured, though, that if we had to go another route, we'd get as much money down now as possible, and then we could wait 5 years to cash out. We don't want to be tied up with this place for the next 15 years."

"Bob," I reply, "let's say that you got all of your money in one lump sum now. What would you do with it?"

"I guess we'd put it into something safe, like a treasury note, and use the interest as part of our retirement income."

"Well, basically, I'm offering you the same thing. You'll be getting principal and interest from me every month on a regular basis. Plus, you'll have the additional security that if I were ever to default, which is highly unlikely, you would get to keep my downpayment and any improvements I've made, as well as all of the monthly payments that you've received, in addition to getting your house back. It seems to me that you're in the driver's seat in this deal."

"Let me talk this over with my wife."

"Would you like me to leave?"

"No, we can just step into the bedroom, if you don't mind."

Fifteen minutes later, when Mr. and Mrs. Kane step out of the bedroom, they present me with this counteroffer: "Doreen, my wife and I want you to have the house. We think our price of $89,500 is fair, but because we'd like to make a quick sale, we'll bring it down to $86,000 for you. We're also willing to compromise on the downpayment. Do you think you could come up with $15,000? The rest would be amortized over 15 years at 11 percent interest, but instead of being due and payable in 5 years, we can make it due and payable in 7 years. That way you'll have a little more leeway for your balloon payment."

You mentally note that the sellers have not objected to your request that the terms of the loan be passed along to another buyer.

"I suppose I can meet your price," I sigh, "but I can't come up with $15,000. The most I can do is add another $2,000 to the downpayment, which would make it $10,000 total. And about the balloon note, Bob—if I were in your position, I too would want to get my money out of the property. Your counteroffer of 7 years before a balloon payment is due is considerate. Nonetheless, I really am scared about having a balloon payment at any time. You could imagine what it would feel like if you were in my shoes, with a balloon note coming due, and you didn't have the funds at the time. You could get wiped out. Can you think of a solution to this impasse?"

"Hmmm, I see your point, Doreen. Well, ah, let's see. Maybe after 7 years we could readjust the interest rate to whatever the interest rate on a treasury note would be at the time. How about that? Would that work?"

"I think you may have hit on the solution. Yes. That should work."

"Okay," Bob says, "we'll go with your $10,000 downpayment, since you're meeting our price of $86,000."

I look at Bob and his wife and say, "I'm also going to need your help on one other matter. It would help me enormously if I could rent the house before settlement. That way I'd have rent coming in right away. You and your wife would have to sign a simple rental agreement with the tenants for those few weeks we have until settlement."

She and Bob frown slightly at this.

"Of course," I assure them, "I'd pay for the advertising and I'd screen the tenants, and any rent we get before settlement would be yours. It would probably amount to a few hundred dollars." This catches their interest. "If you'd let me do that, I'd like to start cleaning up the yard and make a few repairs. I'd like to fix the broken hinge on your gate and tighten the loose banister in the hallway."

"We can let her do that, can't we, dear?" says Mrs. Kane.

"Yes," her husband says, "it's fine with us."

"There is only one final matter," I continue. "I always make my offers contingent on a structural inspection that meets my satisfaction."

"How long will it take to get it done?"

"Just to be sure, let's say five working days."

I conclude by saying, "Let me draw up a contract with all the points we've covered and see if it reflects exactly what we discussed."

"Oh, I have a contract form I can give you," Bob says.

"Don't worry, I have one of my own. I'll fill it out right now."

POINTS TO REMEMBER

When negotiating the purchase of an investment house, you need to:

- Analyze your own position.
- Know the seller's motivation for selling: Why is the house being sold? What time constraints does the seller have? What will the seller do with the money from the sale?
- Establish common objectives for yourself and the seller.
- Expect some misrepresentations from the seller, and use these to your advantage.
- Establish your credibility by explaining your position honestly.

- Listen carefully to any counteroffers.
- Use either your own contract or a contract with which you are familiar.

Try to include the following points in your purchase contract:

- The price is at least 10 percent below market value.
- A substantial amount of low-interest owner-financing is available, as well as assumable by a future buyer, and/or there is an assumable low-interest VA or FHA loan.
- There is no prepayment penalty.
- There is no balloon payment.
- Major appliances and essential personal property are included in the purchase.
- The buyer has the right to rent out the house prior to the close of escrow.
- The purchase is contingent on a satisfactory structural inspection.

FOR FURTHER INFORMATION

Here are a few of the many useful sources on buying houses:

Allen, Robert G.: *Creating Wealth*, Simon and Schuster, New York, 1983.

————: *Nothing Down: How to Buy Real Estate with Little or No Money Down*, Simon and Schuster, New York, 1980.

Bruss, Robert: *The Smart Investor's Guide to Real Estate*, Crown, New York, 1983.

Glubetich, Dave: *How to Grow a Money Tree*, Impact Publishing, San Ramon, California, 1977.

————: *The Monopoly Game*, Impact Publishing, San Ramon, California, 1978.

Lowry, Albert J.: *How You Can Become Financially Successful by Investing in Real Estate*, Simon and Schuster, New York, 1982.

————: *Hidden Fortunes*, Simon and Schuster, New York, 1983.

Morris, Hal: *Crisis Real Estate Investing*, Harbor Publishing, San Francisco, 1982.

Nickerson, William: *How I Turned $1,000 into Three Million in Real Estate in My Spare Time*, Simon and Schuster, New York, 1980.

There are two other sources of information that I'd like to mention:

1. The reports put out by Impact Publishing are short, clearly written pamphlets on many aspects of real estate investment. Many of the reports provide information that is practical and innovative. Others suggest tactics which will make you blush. No matter—many *Impact Reports* are stimulating. You can order copies by writing to:

Impact Publishing
2110 Omega Rd., Suite A
San Ramon, CA 94583

2. Though not dealing specifically with real estate, *Getting to Yes* by Roger Fisher and William Ury (Penguin Books, New York, 1983), is the best book I've ever read on how to negotiate to everyone's advantage.

6

HOW TO PREPARE
FOR RENTAL

According to the example in the last chapter, you have 5 working days to have a professional house inspection that meets your approval. A contingency clause for a structural inspection is important. It gives you a final chance to back out of your agreement to purchase the house without penalty. For some investors, the structural inspection also provides an opportunity to negotiate further with the seller.

One investor routinely offers to buy houses at full price subject to a structural inspection. The inspection he performs, however, invariably turns up thousands of dollars of needed repairs and improvements. He then renegotiates with sellers, forcing them to reduce the price of the house by several thousand of dollars.

My insistence on a contingency for a structural inspection is more a defensive tactic. I want to make sure that the house has no hidden surprises for me or my tenants.

WHY HIRE A PROFESSIONAL HOUSE INSPECTOR?

What can a professional inspector do for you that you can't do for yourself? Well, I for one don't go into crawl spaces, or climb on roofs, or take apart electrical boxes. Nor do I know whether some cracks I see are structurally insignificant or indicate serious problems.

A professional inspection may cost $100 to $250, but the inspection may also save you more money than it costs. How? A professional inspector may:

- Help you negotiate further with the seller to reduce the price. Sellers and settlement attorneys may argue with you, calling your judgment faulty, but they are less likely to argue with an official report from a home inspector.

- Ensure that your house is structurally safe for your tenants— or make you aware of problems that could put your tenants in jeopardy.

- Allow you to plan when certain repairs may be needed, or replacements made, and to estimate how much they may cost.

- Advise you of simple remedies for problems which you can do yourself, or suggest competent contractors to fix other problems.

You can find a home inspection service by looking in the yellow pages under "Building Inspection Services," "Inspection Bureaus," "Real Estate Inspectors," or similar categories. Better yet, ask real estate agents or other investors whom they would recommend.

Many reputable inspectors belong to the American Society of Home Inspectors (ASHI). Fees are usually set on a sliding scale and may, in part, be based on the sales price of the house.

The best inspectors prefer to have the purchaser (and possibly the seller) right there while the inspection is being made. The inspector can then verbally explain the problem areas of the house, as well as its positive features. Bring your own list of problems and questions developed from your own inspection of the house, and ask the inspector about them.

I've included an example of an inspection report prepared by a professional home inspection service in the appendix, so that you can see what one looks like.

WHAT TO DO IF YOUR STRUCTURAL INSPECTION TURNS UP UNANTICIPATED PROBLEMS

If your structural inspection turns up unanticipated problems, you have one of several choices:

1. Reread your purchase contract. The seller may be legally obligated to remedy the problem according to the terms of the existing

contract. Many purchase contracts, for example, require the seller to have all appliances in operating condition.

2. Decide if the problem is great enough to warrant bringing it to the attention of the seller. If the problem is relatively minor, you may decide to remedy it yourself.

3. If the structural inspection reveals serious problems, you have two alternatives. You can choose to back out of the contract entirely if you have put into it the contingency clause for a structural inspection, as I have recommended, and if you have reached your decision before the agreed deadline. Otherwise, you can outline the problem in an addendum to your contract and give the seller a chance to remedy the deficiencies. The seller then has the choice either to accept or to reject the new conditions you have made for the purchase.

SEVEN STEPS TO TAKE BEFORE SETTLEMENT

When the structural inspection has been completed, other contingencies in the contract have been removed, and it seems reasonably certain that you will be going to settlement, there are seven tasks you may want to perform before settlement.

1. TAKE AN INVENTORY OF ALL MAJOR APPLIANCES AND FIXTURES IN THE HOUSE

Write down the make and model number of all major appliances in the house. If anything goes wrong with any of the appliances, you'll need this information when you phone for repairs. You'll also have a precise inventory of the contents of the house. Though it rarely happens, it's possible for an owner to take a newer appliance and switch it for an older one just before settlement takes place. Tenants are also less likely to claim that a dehumidifier or an air conditioner belongs to them if they know that you have a complete inventory of the contents of the house.

The accompanying Inventory of Owner's Appliances and Equipment shows you what a completed inventory might look like.

INVENTORY OF OWNER'S APPLIANCES AND EQUIPMENT

456 Adam Street

Address

APPLIANCE/ EQUIPMENT	DESCRIPTION
Hot Water Heater (Capacity, 40 gal)	SEARS Power Miser 60 Mod. 153.337311, Ser. B79739211 Warranty until 2/84
Heating/Cooling System	CAC-FEDDERS Ser. CFA030A0-KD143401
Humidifier (Capacity:)	FEDDERS furnace Mod. CUG100A3A, Ser. HD148036 SEARS Mod. 303.938000
Dehumidifier (Capacity:)	NA
A/C Unit(s) BTU's: (Voltage:)	NA
(BTU's) (Voltage:)	NA
(BTU's) (Voltage:)	NA

102

Washing Machine	KENMORE 60 Mod. Ser. 21601 (heavy duty)
Dryer	KENMORE Mod. Ser. 61811 (heavy duty plus)
Stove	KENMORE gas Mod. 175.65312, Ser. 881270 (downstairs) HOTPOINT Mod. CTA12C
Refrigerator	SEARS Mod. 106.7627410, Ser. E31119615
Dishwasher	NA
Disposer	SEARS Mod. 175.65312, Ser. 2742031269
Attic Fan	NA
Lawn Mower	BLACK & DECKER elec. 18" mower w deluxe single blade
Additional Tools	(1) lawn mower elec. cord, (2) grass catcher, (3) rake, (4) hoe, (5) 2 snow shovels, (6) hose, (7) 2 garbage cans.

In signing this attachment, the Tenant agrees that the above mentioned appliances and equipment are in the household and are in operable condition when the Tenant moved into the premises.

PLEASE NOTE: The disposer and lawn mower are for the convenience of the tenant(s) and repairs, if any, will be paid by tenant(s).

_____   _____
TENANT   DATE

103

2. PREPARE A HOUSE INFORMATION SHEET

A house information sheet provides the answers to questions that potential tenants are most likely to ask:

- How large is the bedroom? Living room?
- How long will it take to get downtown?
- What bus or subway is close by?
- How much are the utilities per month?

I also put down the neighbors' names, addresses, and telephone numbers for handy reference.

I've included an example of my House Information Sheet. The basic format was copied from the real estate listing form of the Northern Virginia Board of Realtors.

If the house you are buying was listed through a real estate office, the listing card may already have much of the information you need. Otherwise, it's up to you to measure the rooms, and to phone the bus or subway information service to find out about routes and schedules.

Utility payments can only be given to potential tenants as estimates. Utility bills for the previous year can be checked by looking at the receipts of the seller. If the seller doesn't have receipts, the utility companies may supply the information.

The seller's utility bills may not accurately reflect your tenants' bills. Clearly, four tenants may use the utilities more than the couple who previously owned the house. On the other hand, if the sellers had small children who were home all day, the utility bill might be much higher than those your tenants may have if they are out of the house all day at work.

3. LABEL THE MAJOR SHUTOFF SYSTEMS

Locate the main water shutoff, the shutoffs to the outside water spigots, the hot-water shutoff, and the main gas shutoff. Clearly identify each one with a label. In an emergency, you and your tenants will want to know immediately where these shutoffs are located. For example, if a pipe springs a leak and they don't know where the main water shutoff is, you may have a flooded basement before a plumber arrives to fix the leak.

HOUSE INFORMATION SHEET

Address: 123 Main St., Middleton   ZIP 00000   Start Date 3/1/85

	1st Floor	2nd Floor
	L.R. 17'x11'	B.R. 14'x13'
	D.R. 12'x10'	11'x12'
	Kit. 8'5"x8'	
	B.R. 11'x11'	Bath Full
		3rd Level
	Bath Full	B.R.
	Fam. Rm No	Bath
	Other	Other
	Den 11'x10'	

Basement

Size Full
O.S.E. Yes
Cr. Sp. No
R.R. 25'x17'6"
Bath Full
B.R. part of R.R.

Heat Gas
Hot Water Gas
Ut. Rm. 23'x17'8"

Equipment	Yes	No
Stove	x	
Refrig.	x	
Dishwasher		x
Disposer		x
Ex. Fan	x	
Attic Fan		x
A/C units		x
CAC	x	
Washer	x	
Dryer	x	
Storm Wind.	x	
Porch 10'x12'		
Garage None		

HOUSE INFORMATION SHEET (*Continued*)

Rents: B.R. 1 $265   B.R.2 $195   B.R.3 $185   B.R.4 $175

Av. Utility Bills ($125)   Split 4 Ways ($31)

Gas $68   Oil NA   Elec. $40   Water & Sew. $17

Public Transportation: every 12 min.--rush hour

Bus/Subway No.? 24A & 24B   How Often? every 22 min.--other times

Distance? 2 blocks   How Long to Downtown? 25 minutes

Neighbors:

Name(s)	Address(es)	Phone Number(s)
Bill & Sally Smith	121 Main Street	123-4567
Don & Eve Bowman	125 Main Street	891-0112
Eleanor Hunn	124 Main Street	314-1516

Additional Information:

Next, find the circuit breaker or fuse box. Test all the electrical appliances and outlets to find out what circuits they are on. Write down the information on a sheet of paper, and post the information near the electrical box for handy reference.

Actually, you may want to wait until you get tenants for your house, so that they can help you identify which outlets, switches, and appliances belong to which circuit breaker or fuse. You can do this by plugging an appliance into every outlet and then turning on each appliance and light switch. It's much easier to test circuits with other people. If tenants have moved in, station them in different rooms. As you take out a fuse or flip one of the circuit breakers, your tenants can report which light or appliance was affected.

4. MAKE A SCHEDULE FOR WORK THAT HAS TO BE DONE ON THE HOUSE

You may need a plan of action to improve the house. The plan will include:

- what has to be done
- when it should be done
- who you may hire to do the job
- approximately how much the job will cost

You should set priorities. Anything that jeopardizes the health or safety of your tenants must be corrected immediately; smoke detectors, for example, should be installed on each level of the house before the tenants move in. Anything that will increase your rental income should be done next. If in order to rent the basement area you need to install a bathroom, for example, then you should start getting estimates on the bathroom as soon as possible, so work can begin right after settlement.

You can get estimates from contractors before settlement on all work which will have to be done within the first couple of months after settlement. Don't sign a contract with any contractor at this point, though, unless it has an escape clause. The clause should state that the contract is binding on you only if settlement actually takes place.

This is what your schedule might look like:

Task	Scheduled Date	Possible Contractor	Estimate

As each task is completed, you can cross it off your list.

5. CLEAN UP AND DECORATE

Most purchase contracts say that the current owner is supposed to clean the place of debris—usually by the day of settlement. But if you want to rent the house as soon as possible, you can't wait until settlement. The house and the yard should be cleared at once, so that you can start showing the house to potential renters.

If the owners don't look like they intend to get around to picking up for a while, grab your rake and broom. This is no time to stand on principle. Get over to the property and start raking the piles of leaves and picking up any debris. Not only will you begin making the place look presentable to renters, but you'll also start off on the right foot with your neighbors, as they approvingly observe your work to upgrade the property.

Even if it costs a few dollars and some of your time, fix the hinge on the gate, and put a few curtains up. You may even want to bring in area rugs if it will make the place look cozier. In the case of that house we're buying, we may want to place a humongous spider plant in a spot which will effectively screen the electrical substation from sight when a potential tenant comes to view the house.

For this particular house, we may also want to have a landscape plan made, if it doesn't cost too much. Some large nurseries will provide free landscape designs. Then, when potential tenants appear, you can show them the problem area of the house—the backyard— with confidence. You can draw them into your plans, describing where the pine tree will be, how the fence will give them privacy and the bamboo, tranquility. Draw your tenants into your vision of their future home.

6. Meet the Neighbors and Learn About the Neighborhood

Now is the time to meet the neighbors—before settlement. Put yourself in their place. Their main concern is that the people who rent won't get along with the people in the neighborhood, and might even bother them. Their second concern is that the owners and occupants of a rental house won't take proper care of the property; consequently, the value of their own homes will tumble as the rental house runs down.

One of your first tasks, then, is to introduce yourself to the neighbors to help allay their fears. Let them know how carefully you choose your tenants. Let them know your plans to upgrade the house. Show them the landscape drawing, if you have one. Let them know that they are most welcome to phone you at home if there is any problem at all with the house or with the tenants. Give them your phone number at home and at the office, and ask if they would mind giving you their phone numbers as well.

Your house is inextricably a part of its neighborhood. What is good for the property values of your neighborhood is good for your own property value. If the neighbors welcome your tenants, your tenants will be happier than if they were met by indifference or hostility. Your job, even before your first tenant moves in, is to ensure as much as possible that tenants and neighbors will have a cooperative attitude toward one another.

If people realize that you intend to be a good neighbor, they'll supply you with a wealth of assistance:

- They'll lend you and your tenants ladders, wheelbarrows, and lawn mowers when you're working on your rental property.
- They'll tell your tenants which neighborhood kids mow the lawn for a few dollars.
- They'll tell your tenants the best places to shop in the neighborhood.
- They'll keep an extra copy of the house key for you, let in tenants who have locked themselves out, and show in plumbers who need to be let in.

- They'll keep an eye on your house—and, incidentally, on your tenants, too.

The assistance, however, should not be only one-sided. If you have ordered a load of mulch for your garden, make sure the neighbors know that they can help themselves to the extra mulch. If a neighbor phones to say that the tree in your yard is brushing against the electrical wires and may tear the line down in a storm, your response should be immediate. Phone the electric company to prune the limbs, and then phone that neighbor back to explain how you are taking care of the problem.

8. EQUIP THE HOUSE WITH ESSENTIAL ITEMS

Many owners ask if they should furnish their rental houses. My answer is no. Tenants always manage to put together their own collections of furniture. If they don't have furniture themselves, then parents or friends will invariably loan them the essentials, like a sofa and a dining room table.

In fact, it can be more difficult to rent houses when they are furnished. Many tenants already have furniture and are looking for a house where they can use it.

Another advantage to having tenants furnish the house themselves is that they are apt to think twice about moving when they have to lug away sofas and tables and bedroom furniture. A tenant without furniture can easily pack a valise and move out quickly.

There is one other reason for not furnishing the house. Furniture can be a source of friction between owners and tenants if owners feel that the tenants are not treating the furniture properly. My general advice is to avoid situations which can produce friction. Leave all furnishing of the house to your tenants.

I do, however, supply certain items for each house:

- smoke detectors (one for each floor)
- two 32-gallon trash cans
- a rake
- a garden hose with nozzle
- a used lawn mower

- a snow shovel
- a plumber's helper (plunger)

I also provide supplementary heaters, air-conditioning units, and dehumidifiers in rooms that have special heating or cooling problems. I believe that it is your responsibility as the owner to make sure that your tenants are physically comfortable in the house.

You are also going to need seven sets of household keys—one set for each of your four tenants, one for the neighbors, one as a spare, and one for your own use. Ask the present owners how many sets they have, so you'll know how many more you need to make.

Now that you have both your house and the neighbors prepared for your rental, the next step is to find your tenants.

POINTS TO REMEMBER

- A professional house inspection is useful and can save you money.
- There are seven tasks you may want to do to prepare a house and a neighborhood for your tenants:
    1. Take an inventory of all major appliances and fixtures in the household.
    2. Prepare a house information sheet.
    3. Label the major shutoff systems.
    4. Make a schedule for the work that has to be done on the house.
    5. Clean up and decorate.
    6. Meet the neighbors and learn about the neighborhood.
    7. Equip the house with essential items.

FOR FURTHER INFORMATION

I'm sorry, but for this chapter I couldn't find any sources of additional information for you on how to prepare a single-family house for rental. Such books as Leigh Robinson's *Landlording* and Al Lowry's *How to Manage Real Estate Successfully—In Your Spare Time* have chapters which explain how to prepare an apartment for rental, but their procedures are somewhat different than mine.

7

HOW TO FIND GOOD TENANTS

WHO ARE YOUR TENANTS?

The single most important thing you will do to ensure smooth management is to select responsible and considerate tenants—ones who will get along reasonably well with you and with each other.

Who are these singles who will want to share a house with others? Put the concept of the 60s hippie wanting to live in a commune out of your mind. That's not the type of tenant you are probably going to be looking for.

My tenants have had a wide range of professions. Here are just a few of them:

- lab technician
- paralegal
- political fundraiser
- economist
- bank clerk
- assistant manager of a gas station
- marine captain
- graduate student
- coordinator of a health clinic
- lawyer

As you can see, the spectrum is broad. Some of my tenants earned a higher salary than I did. Others earned less than a third of what I made.

A lack of money, then, is not the only reason why people choose to share a house with others (though, of course, the primary reason most people share a house is to save money on rent). Many of these tenants could afford to pay more rent and get an apartment of their own; they choose, however, to spend their money on things other than housing. Some are saving their money to buy a house or a condominium, or to pay for college tuition. Others would prefer to spend their money on flying lessons or trips to Mexico. Still others travel a lot in their jobs; because they aren't going to be home that often, they see no reason to rent an expensive apartment.

Money aside, many singles would rather live in a house than an apartment. They want to be able to go downstairs to use a washer and dryer, instead of going out to use the pay machines in a laundry. Many of these tenants want a private backyard where they can get a suntan or grow their own vegetables.

Although most singles value their privacy, most also like to have people around for a little companionship and additional security. Many potential renters come from families with several siblings. Others have spent some time in college dormitories or have lived in group houses during their college days.

But whatever their other preferences, all tenants want to have some control over who they are going to live with. They want the life-styles of the other tenants to be compatible with their own. Those who are neat don't want to live with others who let the dishes stack up for days. Those who enjoy a quiet lifestyle will quickly leave a household in which a tenant keeps a stereo blaring most of an evening. Nonsmokers may not want to be around smokers.

The first tenant you select is going to be critical to the formation of the household, because he or she is going to set the tone for the rest of the tenants who will follow. Indeed, that first individual is going to be instrumental in helping you select your other tenants.

You, as the owner, are going to have to decide what characteristics you want in your first tenant. You will then have to devise a strategy to get such a person. Obviously you want someone responsible and considerate, someone who will keep the house clean and, ideally, will be able to make simple repairs—in short, someone who is "able to leap tall buildings at a single bound." Unfortunately, the above criteria (other than the last one) are subjective. How do you know if someone is responsible or considerate or handy? When you look for a tenant, you have to stick with objective criteria.

Age and sex are two very objective criteria. They also happen to be important criteria to most tenants who want to share a house with others. Many people who want to rent a shared house have very definite preferences about the age and sex of their housemates. A person of 35 may not want an 18-year-old housemate, and vice versa. Many people also distinctly want to live with someone of the same sex, while others distinctly prefer a co-ed house.

If you run an advertisement that reads "male/female to share a house," three-fourths of your callers will be male. I don't know exactly why. I do know that if you advertise for male/female, you will, in effect, be discriminating against women.

Curiously, you'll get more responses from advertisements which specify the kind of person you want than from vaguely worded ads which imply that you'll take anyone as a tenant. So you must determine in advance what criteria you will place in your advertisement, and what additional criteria you will use for screening, once someone phones.

As mentioned, two of the criteria you may want to put into the ad are age and sex. A third critical criterion is the ability to pay the rent; you should state how much rent you are asking. In addition, you may want to include in your ad such screening devices as "non-smoker preferred" or "no pets, please," but these are not as critical. Once someone phones, you can screen for these traits.

How to find tenants

Once you have decided on the tenant selection criteria to put into your ad, you next have to devise a strategy to find the people you want.

Look carefully at the house and its geographic surroundings. Is it a small house near a university? Then at least some of your tenants may be graduate students. Chances are that young professionals might not want to live in a house that small. Is the house near an army base? Then you may want to advertise at the base.

115

Your rental arrangement is not conducive to the traditional ways of renting a house. A "For Rent" sign would bring many calls from people who did not know they would be expected to share the house. Nor for that matter are real estate offices usually equipped to handle anything other than conventional rentals for a year's lease.

But you have other ways of finding renters, some of which are not available to owners renting out houses in the conventional manner. You can locate tenants through:

- neighbors, friends, and colleagues
- current tenants
- public roommate-referral agencies
- private roommate-referral agencies
- organizational housing offices
- notices on bulletin boards
- newspaper classifieds

Let's go over each of these.

Neighbors, Friends, and Colleagues

If your neighbors, friends, and colleagues know that you have rental houses, they can be helpful in making referrals. The chief advantage to this method is that your friends are likely to have acquaintances of a better caliber than you might find through a newspaper ad, and will in effect have done some of your screening for you. Another advantage to this method is that it's free.

The chief disadvantage is that your friends will probably have a very limited number of acquaintances who want to share a house. Such referrals will also occur sporadically, often at times when all of your houses are full.

Current Tenants

If you already have some tenants, they can be a valuable source of tenant referrals. They often have friends similar to themselves who want to share a house. If your tenants are pleased with your management, they will be happy to let their friends know where they can get good housing at a fair price.

But again, the chief drawbacks are that you won't reach a broad audience through your tenants and that referrals may be made when you don't have a vacancy.

Public Roommate-Referral Agencies

Some communities have publicly funded programs to match house owners with tenants. There is usually little or no charge for utilizing the program. In some areas this service is limited to owners who want to share their own homes with renters, and investors are excluded. Other publicly funded programs work with owners of investment houses.

The target clientele of the publicly funded roommate-referral agencies, however, may be senior citizens, the handicapped, the emotionally disturbed, and lower-income residents. They may or may not fit comfortably into your household as tenants.

If you are interested in this program, phone your local government office. Find out what programs, if any, exist in your locality, and ask whether the office is willing to work with you.

Private Roommate-Referral Agencies

Private roommate-referral agencies usually charge a flat fee, whether or not they find an acceptable tenant for you. The fee may range from $25 to $50 or more. The quality of the service will probably vary from one agency to another. The best agencies do the most prescreening. They will give you a questionnaire and ask you to specify which characteristics you prefer your tenants to have. Personnel from some agencies will even visit your rental house in order to describe it accurately to potential tenants.

You can find the names of private roommate-referral agencies in the yellow pages or in the classified section of your newspaper. Before you engage an agency's services, you may want to check with people who have used the agency to find out if they were satisfied. You may also want to check with your local Better Business Bureau to find out if any complaints have been lodged against the firm you plan to engage.

If your time is extremely limited, you may want to use the services of a private roommate-referral agency. Otherwise, I think it's much more beneficial for you to recruit tenants yourself. For one thing, the agency's clientele is relatively limited, since most prospective tenants prefer to search on their own. For another, an agency is an intermediary—whereas what you ideally want is to have immediate, direct contact with potential tenants. Direct contact promotes personal bonding with your tenants. It also saves an applicant from going through three screening processes—the agency's, yours, and that of the tenants who may already be in the house. The most important thing you must do is to make good tenant selections. As much as possible, direct that procedure yourself.

Organizational Housing Offices

Many organizations and institutions have housing referral offices—or, in the case of universities, off-campus housing offices. It usually takes just one phone call to list your house with that organization. The housing office often has standard questions about your house and about the type of person you are looking for. There is no charge for this service. This use of housing offices is particularly effective if your rental house is near a military base, a university, or a large organization.

Another advantage to using organizational housing offices is that you can target your potential renting audience. For example, you are most likely to wind up with a doctor or a medical student if you advertise at the medical school of a university; you are most likely to get military personnel if you advertise through the housing office of a military base.

Actually, I see no disadvantages to employing this method—only advantages. It's free, quick, and easy. And the applicants who respond will, to some extent, have been preselected by the kind of organizations with which you have chosen to list your house.

Notices on Bulletin Boards

Posting notices on bulletin boards is another free way to find tenants. You may want to post notices in some of the following places, if they are in close geographical proximity to your house:

- libraries
- your place of work
- government office buildings
- churches, synagogues, and mosques
- clubs and associations
- bookstores
- health food stores
- ethnic or vegetarian restaurants
- grocery stores
- apartment complexes—particularly those being converted to condominiums

Again, you can target your audience by posting your notice in places designed to attract a certain kind of person.

The chief drawback to this method is that it is time-consuming to write up the notices and then run all over town to post them. Further, you may have to check your notices every week or two to make sure that they haven't been taken down, or to make sure they still have current information.

Newspaper Classifieds

You will probably get your quickest results by running a weekend ad in the classified section of the largest newspaper in your locality.

Look at the headings of the newspaper's classified section to determine where you should place your ad (under "Roommates," "Rooms, Houses, Apartments to Share," "Furnished Rooms," or "Unfurnished Apartments"?). Each newspaper has its own categories.

You may want to take out two ads—one under "Roommates" for that part of the house in which all facilities will be shared, and another under "Unfurnished Apartments" for that part of the house which has a private suite.

Or, for starters, you may decide to take out only one ad. You don't need a separate ad for each room you intend to rent. Rather, advertise the least expensive area of the house. You can then show prospective tenants the other rooms of the house when they come.

Applicants often decide to take a more spacious room and pay a little more rent once they've seen the house.

Find out if the newspaper has special rates. Some newspapers substantially reduce their rates if you place a 3-line ad for 3 days, or a 2-line ad for a week. Generally, though, the weekend is the best time to run an ad. If you have to choose one day, advertise in the Sunday edition. That way your advertisement will reach the most people.

The chief disadvantage of this method is that it costs money; if you have to run ads for 1 or 2 months, the expense can quickly add up to a significant sum. The other disadvantage is that no matter how carefully you word your ad, you will usually get a motley collection of phone callers—including one or two obscene calls.

Nonetheless, the advantages outweigh the disadvantages. An ad in the classified section reaches far more people than does any other method. You just need the patience to screen the callers. Even if you have to spend a fair amount to advertise, it's worth the money to find good tenants as quickly as possible. If you scrimp on advertising and miss a month or more of rent, your loss of rental income will be far greater than your advertising expense would have been.

My general advice, then, is to try all free methods of advertising— if they are not excessively time-consuming—and to take out an advertisement in the classified section of your largest local newspaper.

How to design an advertisement

Advertisements should be designed to serve two purposes. The first purpose, of course, is to bring you phone calls from people you may want to have as tenants. The second purpose, however, is to screen out calls from people you think would not make good tenants.

It is therefore important for an advertisement or a posted notice to be as specific as possible without being wordy. A well-written ad will save you a lot of time from dealing with people who would not make suitable tenants. There is no need to write a long notice or ad. You just need to give some essential information. You can supply all of the details when people phone.

When you write the advertisement for a housemate, visualize the person you want as your first tenant. Then write the advertisement as though you were that person. You can later explain to callers that you are the owner and that you are looking for the certain kind of tenant described in the advertisement.

So, for example, your notice might read as follows:

HOUSE TO SHARE 3/8
(April 1)

Arlington, North. Female nonsmoker, 25–35, would like to share spacious house with same. House has washer/dryer, fireplace, eat-in kitchen, dishwasher, and yard. Two blocks to bus. Near shopping.

Rent is $195/month plus utilities (about $40/mo.). Please phone Lois on weekends or after 7:00 P.M. at 123-4567.

House to Share 123-4567	House to Share 123-4567	House to Share 123-4567	House to Share 123-4567	House to Share 123-4567	House to Share 123-4567	House to Share 123-4567	House to Share 123-4567	House to Share 123-4567

Type or neatly print your notices on brightly colored cards to get the attention of passersby, and post them on the bulletin boards of the locations you have selected.

Put a date on the notice, and mention when the vacancy will become available; otherwise, people may not know whether or not the notice is out of date.

The same advertisement, condensed to fit into a 3-line ad in the classifieds, might read as follows:

Arlington, N. F. nonsmoker, 25–35 to shr hse w same.
Washer/dryer, fpl. 2 blks to bus.
$195+. 123-4567

Look carefully at the notice and at the advertisement. What makes them clearly worded? Three factors do. Clearly worded advertisements give the reader information about (1) the house itself, (2) the characteristics of the tenants in the household, and (3) the rental terms.

1. The House Itself

It's essential to give the geographical location of the house. Other positive features should be mentioned as well; these include proximity to public transportation and such amenities as a washer/dryer, skylights, wall-to-wall carpeting, and a fireplace.

2. The Characteristics of the Tenants

Potential renters always want to know if they would fit into the lifestyle of the household. As mentioned previously, the age range and sex of current tenants are important to most people, as are such characteristics as smoking habits.*

3. The Rental Terms

Always include the amount of rent in your advertisement, and indicate whether or not utilities are included. There is no sense in wasting the time of people who can only pay $125 a month if your rental is for $195.

Helpful Abbreviations

I've included a list of helpful abbreviations for your ads. Don't overdo them, though. People reading the classifieds may get confused if you use too many abbreviations.

cac	central air-conditioning
wwc	wall-to-wall carpets
w/d	washer/dryer
apt	apartment
bsmt	basement
br	bedroom
ba	bathroom
fpl	fireplace
yd	yard
shr	share
w	with
nr	near

* Advertisements to secure a tenant for an accessory dwelling unit have to be phrased differently if placed under "Apartments" than if placed under "Houses to Share." Newspapers are not permitted to print apartment ads which indicate sex or age preferences. We'll discuss this later.

Now that you have carefully set your lures to attract your first tenant, it's time to sit back and wait to see who phones.

TELEPHONES AND TELEPHONE ANSWERING MACHINES

If you own several houses, you may want to install a separate telephone line in your house to be used strictly for business purposes. That way you won't disturb the rest of your household with your business calls. It's also tax deductible as a business expense.

Install the business line in a quiet, secluded area of the house—perhaps in your study or in a finished basement. Place the phone on a desk, within easy reach of the files you maintain for your properties.

I would also strongly recommend that you buy an answering machine. If you don't, you'll have to spend weekends and evenings glued to your telephone while awaiting the calls. You'll also have many a meal interrupted by telephone calls. With an answering machine, you can:

- schedule a time to return calls at your convenience,
- record essential information, including the caller's name, home phone number, and office phone number, and
- reduce the number of obscene calls you receive.

I have the least expensive kind of answering machine—one that plays my message and allows people 30 seconds to leave their message. More expensive machines have an unlimited message time, can tell you how many phone calls you have received, will stop the tape when people hang up rather than record the long tone sound that follows, and allow you to phone your answering machine from another telephone to find out what messages you may have received.

The feature I don't have, which would be most useful to me, is that which allows you to phone your answering machine from another telephone to get messages. That way you could check your calls during lunch break while you are at your regular 9 to 5 job. In addition, on several occasions I have been at a rental house for an hour or more waiting for someone to show up who never did. When I've returned home, I've found the recorded message explaining that the person wouldn't be able to keep the appointment.

Whatever machine you decide to buy, keep your recorded message short and friendly, and avoid trying to be cute or apologetic about using an answering machine.

My message goes like this: "Hello, and thanks for calling. This is Doreen. Please don't hang up. If you phoned about the ad for a house to share, it's still available. I can't come to the phone right now, but I would like to talk with you. At the sound of the tone, please leave your name and number both at home and at work, and I'll get back to you just as soon as I can. Wait for the beep and leave your message. Thank you."

The Obscene Phone Caller

Be prepared to get one or two obscene phone calls if you don't have an answering machine. Actually, you might get a rare obscene phone call even with an answering machine, though I'd imagine a person would have to be in pretty bad shape (I was going to say "pretty hard up") to talk obscenely to a machine; nonetheless, it can happen.

If you are new at this business, obscene phone calls may first scare you, but after awhile you'll simply become exasperated or bored with them. Here's a surefire way to handle obscene phone calls: As soon as you realize the nature of the call, don't say a word. Simply put the phone down off the receiver and walk away. When it finally sinks in that nobody is listening, the caller will hang up.*

Don't act scared or hang up in a panic, and don't talk to him. If you react to him in any way, he will continue to harass you. Do not blow a whistle in his ear. If you do, he may phone you at three o'clock in the morning and blow a whistle back at you.

---

* One of my housemates had a most effective way of handling one obscene caller who graphically described certain services he would have liked her to perform on him. She listened carefully to this fellow's proposal, and when he finished, she coolly responded, "No, I don't believe I would care to, but I'm sure that your mother would." The caller, aghast, quickly hung up and never phoned back.

Keep a List of Callers

By all means, keep track of the people who phone. List them in a single notebook, not on scraps of paper or on the margins of your blotter. Your notebook could have pages with the following columns:

- date
- person's name
- home telephone number
- office telephone number
- comments
- appointment

You will get information for the first four columns from the recorded message left on your answering machine. You'll be able to fill in the comments column when you speak with the caller and find out more information about the person. Jot down in the appointment column the time and day you set for the scheduled visit.

Your list will provide a clear record. You'll know when you have scheduled each caller to look at the house, and you will know a little about each person when they show up. The accompanying example shows the format I use.

The list of callers can be useful to you in other ways, too. You will know how to get in touch with a prospective tenant for follow-up if the caller misses an appointment or if you need to change or confirm an appointment. You'll also have a ready list when the time comes to let all the applicants know whether they have been accepted as tenants. Further, if a tenant in one of your houses unexpectedly moves out within a month or so, you may check the list for a person you liked but did not choose as a tenant. Even if that person has already taken other accommodations, she may know of others who are looking for places to rent.

WHAT TO SAY TO POTENTIAL TENANTS ON THE PHONE

You should be able to do much of your screening on the telephone. I've gotten reasonably good at this. I can often tell within a few

LIST OF CALLERS

Date	Person's Name	Home Tel.	Office Tel.	Comments	Appointment
3/17	Winnie O'Donnell	345-6789	101-1121	25; intern for Agency for Intn'l Dev.; just moved from OH; in last apt. 2 yrs	Sat. 1:00
	Maureen Land	314-1516	171-8920	32; USDA economist for 3 yrs	Sun. 2:00
	Shirley Smith	212-2232	425-2627	27; hairdresser; unable to pay deposit	No appt.
3/18	Marie-Jo Vernat	282-9303	132-3334	30; French; journalist from Morocco; attached to Embassy	Sat. 1:30
	Lois Lewis	353-6373	839-4041	26; membership coordinator for nonprofit assoc. for 2 yrs	Sat. 2:00
	Anne Raffini	424-3444	546-4748	26; paralegal; has a dog	No appt.
	Renee Noto	495-0515	253-5455	28; coordinator of GW health clinic; 1 yr in previous residence	Sun: 1:30
	Susan Molde	565-7585	960-6162	29; lawyer with Justice Dept.; travels a lot; 10 months in previous residence	Sun. 1:00

minutes if the caller might work out as a tenant or not. The more thorough your screening is on the telephone, the more time you will save by showing the house only to reasonably good prospects. Remember, you are not in the used car business, nor do you own an apartment complex with numerous vacancies. You do not want a lot of people to come look at your house; you want only a few well-screened prospects who have a pretty good possibility of becoming tenants.

What do you say to your callers that will sound friendly, yet will effectively screen them, and not sound excessively prying? Well, first put yourself in their shoes. Address their concerns first, before asking them questions about themselves.

When potential tenants phone, they will want to know more about the house; they will want to know if they will feel comfortable with others in the household; and they will want to know more about the rental terms.

Have your House Information Sheet handy, and immediately ask the callers whether they have specific questions or would prefer to hear your "running monologue." Most will want your monologue.

I tell the callers that I will let them know everything good and everything bad about the house, plus a few neutral things. Then I tell them that one of the neutral things is that I don't live in the house—that I'm the owner and do the initial screening. I then explain the characteristics of tenants in the household I'd like to put together. For me this means relatively quiet people who like to be in a house that's clean and reasonably picked up, and who are considerate of others. I explain that whoever moves in first will be instrumental in choosing the kind of housemates they would like to see make up the rest of the household.

Then I describe the most and least attractive features of the house. For example, I mention the white brick fireplace, the beamed ceiling in the living room, the washer and dryer, and the fact that public transportation and shopping are within walking distance. Following this, I let the caller know that the available bedroom is not large, that the closets are small, and that the house is on a busy street.

If you are honest about the drawbacks, you will achieve three positive results:

1. The callers will identify you as a trustworthy person.
2. When the callers come to look at the house, they will be

prepared for the worst, and so they will often wind up reassuring you that the problem isn't really that bad.

3. If a caller absolutely needs a large bedroom because she has a king-size bed, two bureaus, and a gigantic desk, there is no sense in wasting your time and hers by setting an appointment if the bedroom is 11 by 12 feet.

Conclude your running monologue by describing the most important terms of the rental agreement. I explain that although there is only a month-to-month written agreement, each tenant makes a verbal commitment to stay a minimum of 6 months, and hopefully much longer. I explain that I require the first and last month's rent in addition to a security deposit, and then I explain why I require this sum of money. I also explain my rental system to callers, assuring them that they will only be required to pay their own share of the rent, even if we can't find other renters right away. At most, they will pay only one-third of the utilities. In the winter, particularly if your house is in a cold region of the country, your first tenant may otherwise be concerned that she alone would have to pay an enormous heating bill by herself.

In the last part of your monologue, let the caller know that the vacancy will not be filled on a first come, first served basis and that you will meet all prospective tenants before making a decision. There are several reasons for saying this:

•   Callers should not feel that they have to make an appointment with you immediately, thereby cramming your schedule.

•   You will be able to meet all prospective tenants and pick the ones you want most.

•   As you will see later in this chapter, you are going to need some breathing space before making a decision.

Although you have billed your remarks as a monologue, the caller will interrupt you many times with questions and comments and, hopefully, with little chuckles at the small witticisms you throw in.

You will find that your request for a security deposit will screen out some callers right away. Others may feel that your household sounds too uptight for them. Still others will decide that the location may be too noisy. Callers who would not make suitable tenants often screen themselves out. This self-screening is to your mutual benefit.

You may even pause to inquire whether you've knocked them out yet. If they say, "No, not yet," then ask if they have any questions that you haven't answered. If so, answer all questions as honestly as possible.

That done, it's your turn. You will say, "Now, may I ask you some questions about yourself?"

SCREENING CRITERIA

You may want to ask questions related to the caller's:

- age
- type of work
- hours of work
- length of time employed
- length of time in the area
- length of time in current residence
- reason for wanting to leave current residence
- smoking or nonsmoking habits
- ownership or nonownership of pets
- ability to pay the rent and the initial deposit
- expected length of residence as your tenant
- ownership or nonownership of a waterbed

There are three key elements that you should look for:

1. Has this individual been steadily employed and, if so, for how long?
2. Why is she leaving her current residence, how long did she live there, and how did she get along in the last place?
3. Is this person willing and able to pay the sum that you have requested for the first month's rent, the last month's rent, and the security deposit?

On occasion, you may decide to be flexible with one of these three key elements. You may allow someone who is unemployed to move in, providing you know that the person has a substantial bank account. You may allow someone to pay the initial deposit a little at a time over a 2-month period. You may decide that the person who is having a miserable time in her current residence because her roommates are into acid rock would really work out quite well with you. Nonetheless, if you completely ignore any of these three elements, you may be in for some unpleasant surprises after the tenant has moved into your house.

Essentially what you are looking for in the callers is stability—personal stability in their places of employment and in their places of residence.

Red flags: proceed with caution

1. The Person Who Wants to Move In Immediately

Beware of the caller who wants to move into your house immediately. Usually, the only exception you would make is for someone who has just come into town and is staying in a hotel.

Most people have to give 30 days notice before leaving their current residence. If they are prepared to move at a moment's notice, this could mean that they are:

- being evicted
- having serious problems with one or more people in their current residence
- impulsive by nature, perhaps likely to move out of your house on the spur of the moment, too

2. The Person Who Demands to Know the Address of the Property and Wants to Come Over Immediately

Although many people may ask for a more specific location of the house, don't give callers an address until you have completed your screening and you are sure you want to show them the house. Rather, when asked for an exact address, I usually give the names of two nearby cross streets and explain that I'll give them an exact address afterwards, if the party is still interested.

Beware of callers who state that they want to come over immediately and ask for an address before they have asked you any questions about the house. There is an air of desperation in such a request. Good potential tenants will want to ask you questions about the house and the rental terms before deciding if they want to look at the house.

3. THE PERSON WHO HAS MOVED FREQUENTLY AND/OR CHANGED JOBS FREQUENTLY

Be careful of the person who has had more than two jobs or more than two places of residence within the past year. Often, such a person has some personal or economic problem which has caused this instability. However, don't be afraid to use your own judgment. If the reasons for the job/residence changes seem understandable, you may want to, at least, show the house to the caller.

4. THE PERSON WHO ARGUES ABOUT YOUR DEPOSIT REQUIREMENTS

If you explain the reasons why you need to get the first month's rent, the last month's rent, and a security deposit, and the caller responds that she sees no reason for the deposit because she is a trustworthy person, I immediately conclude that the caller is not a trustworthy person. I simply explain that I understand that I'm asking for a lot of money, but that it's a requirement for all of my tenants. I thank the person for calling, tell her I'm sorry it won't work out, and say goodbye.

The person who argues about the deposit will be the first person to damage the house and move out without notice. Good tenants will understand why you need the security deposit. They will have enough commitment to staying with you and being a good tenant that they won't object to the deposit. As you will see later, in my management system the deposit is not only a protection for me, but also for each of my tenants. Good applicants appreciate the protection that my requirement for a security deposit affords them.

131

5. The Person Who is Currently Living with Friends or Family

When callers let you know that they are now living with friends or family, find out how long they have been in that situation and why. Sometimes, people who have just been evicted or have just cc ne out of a mental health or correctional facility have no other place to go but family or friends. Their backgrounds may or may not exclude them from being your tenant, but you should be aware of any potential problems.

6. The Person Who Works at Home or is Between Jobs

On rare occasions, I have taken in a tenant who was unemployed. Usually, though, it behooves you to look for a full-time worker or a full-time student. Your tenants should work outside of the house. They should not be permitted to conduct business from your house, for not only would such an arrangement usually violate zoning codes, but the rest of the tenants in that household would usually feel uncomfortable about having their residence turned into a place of business.

7. The Person Who Objects to the Personal Questions You Ask

I quickly terminate the conversation with the person who objects to my personal questions by saying, "I have a feeling that this isn't going to work out."

There must be honesty and open communication between owner and tenant from the start. It is imperative to get a housing and employment history, and sometimes to get more personal information if, from the conversation, you sense that the person doesn't expect to share household chores, or perhaps plans to have her boyfriend move in.

The person who is offended by your questions will not make a good tenant.

8. The Person Who Owns a Junky Car

Watch out for the applicants who drive up in junky cars. I don't mean old cars. I mean cars with smashed headlights, badly dented doors, torn seats, and an accumulation of trash scattered on the floor.

It is almost guaranteed that a tenant with a junky car will keep your house the same way the car is kept.

Scheduling the voice on the phone

After you have screened a prospect over the telephone and have determined that the caller might be a suitable tenant, make an appointment for that person to see the house and to meet you. Schedule several appointments in one afternoon and give each person a specified time— possibly half an hour apart. That way you won't have to keep going back and forth to show the house to one person in the morning, another in the afternoon, and another in the evening.

Some real estate books suggest that you schedule several people at once, making applicants feel the pressure of competition. I most wholeheartedly disagree! If you schedule everyone at once, you will have no time to spend with each individual. You want to know that person. Hopefully, you will have a business relationship with that individual for some time—perhaps 2 or 3 years. You want your tenants to feel comfortable with you and to like the house. You don't want them to feel pushed in any way.

How to reduce the number of no-shows

Inevitably, some of the people you have scheduled to look at the house won't show up for the appointment. This can be frustrating, because you may waste half an hour or more just pacing around the house for nothing.

You can reduce the number of no-shows by saying the following when you schedule someone: "May I ask a favor? If, for some reason, you decide that you won't be able to make the appointment, would you mind phoning to let me know?" Once they have verbally promised to let you know if they aren't coming, they will usually (but not always) do as they promised.

Meeting the voice on the phone

Bring a list of those you have scheduled, and greet every potential renter by name at the door. Show the caller the whole house, and point out convenient features and amenities. If you have plans to upgrade the house, or to make certain repairs, let the person know what you intend to do and when you intend to do it.

SAYING YES

If you like the person and think that she would make a responsible tenant, let her know that you like her, and ask what she thinks of the house.

As a general rule, I suggest that you neither make a decision yourself nor force the prospective tenant to make a decision on the spot. Both of you should have time to think it over. Further, you have previously told callers that it's not first come, first served. You should stick by your word.

If I like someone very much, I might say something like this: "I like you, and think you would work out fine as a tenant. I don't know if this place is something you might be interested in."

If she responds that she is quite interested in the place, ask her if she would mind if you phoned her back tomorrow evening at 6:00 P.M. to get a final decision.

SAYING NO

Fortunately, human nature is such that if you do not feel comfortable with a potential renter she won't usually feel comfortable with you either. Your caller may let you know that she has other places to see.

How do you say no to an individual who wants to rent from you? Explain that you have promised to show the house to others, and that no decision will be made until you have seen everyone. Let her know when you will phone her with a decision. Then make sure to phone at the promised time.

When you phone, let her know that you appreciated having her look at the house, but that someone else was selected. Now if you have just bought a house and you have four vacancies, that rejected individual may want to have one of the other places in the house. Try to think of an honest reason why you think things wouldn't work out—hopefully without hurting the individual. Here are some examples.

- Given the nature of the person's job, you weren't sure that she would stay for a while.
- Her work hours might bother other tenants in the house.
- You weren't sure that other tenants would be amenable to having a baby grand piano in the living room.

Or if you can't think of anything else, just say that you're sorry, and you're not sure you can explain why, but you feel somehow that things wouldn't work out. Or say that because you would like to interview more applicants, you plan to run the ad for a few more weekends. As a kindness to the person, though, you may want to let her know as nicely as you can that she is out of the running. Honesty which is not tinged with emotion, and is not judgmental is usually appreciated.

Let me tell you my most harrowing tale of turning down an applicant: I was in the process of screening applicants for the basement area of one of my rental houses. The three women upstairs said they preferred to leave the selection process to me. I was still a bit of a greenhorn, though, about screening over the phone. One of the appointments turned out to be a fellow who had long, greasy hair and glazed eyes. He was wearing Levi tops with the sleeves ripped out. He took one quick look around the rooms and said, "Like man, I'll take it!" He then reached into his pocket and took out a wad of money.

I said, "Now, just a minute. Remember that I said that this was not first come, first served."

He glared at me, and I felt the tension rising. He said, "What's the matter, dontcha like me?" He said, and I quote, "I won't deal dope. I won't crack the ladies upstairs. What's the matter? Dontcha like me?"

Needless to say, I was terrified. But I took a deep breath, looked him straight in the eye, and quietly said, "Frankly, you scare the hell out of me."

My remark stopped him cold. The tension disappeared. He sat

down on the floor. So I sat down on the floor, too. Then he looked at me and asked, "Why?" So I replied that he looked as though he had gone through some difficult times that he wasn't completely finished with yet.

He said that he had been through some rough times, but he was okay now, and he wanted to rent the place.

I responded, "Look, remember that I told you that I wouldn't rent the place on a first come, first served basis?"

He nodded.

"Well," I continued, "I told everyone the same thing, and I have other appointments scheduled. Now you wouldn't want me to go back on my word, would you?"

He shook his head, no.

I kept talking. "I'll call you tomorrow night at six to let you know my decision. Okay?"

He asked me if I would really call him back, and I told him that I would. Exactly at six the next evening, I phoned him back to let him know he *didn't* have the place. He accepted my decision and told me how grateful he was that I had kept my word to phone him back.

How do fair housing laws affect TENANT SELECTION?

So far I've talked about tenant selection as if you had the absolute right to accept and reject people on any basis whatsoever—but you don't have that absolute right. On the other side of the coin, many people believe that federal fair housing laws require owners to rent to any person who can pay the rent—and this is not true at all.

You have the right to decide that you want only nonsmokers, say, or vegetarians, or people with good credit references. In many states, you can decide that you don't want to rent to certain types of jobholders, such as lawyers or people who work the night shift. You can even decide to rent only to someone who has a clean car.

The point is that fair housing laws prohibit only certain types of discrimination. There are two major pieces of federal legislation which bar discrimination in housing. One is the Civil Rights Act of

1866, which prohibits discrimination on racial grounds. The other is the Fair Housing Act of 1968, which bars discrimination based on race, color, religion, sex, or national origin in connection with the sale or rental of most housing; note that the federal Fair Housing Act does not prohibit tenant selection based on age. In addition to federal laws, most states have fair housing laws, as do countless numbers of local jurisdictions. These state and local laws may provide tenants with additional protections which bar discrimination based on marital status, physical disability, blindness, age, mental disability, and a whole host of other criteria.

The Federal Fair Housing Act and many of the state and local fair housing laws exempt some owners who only make a few rental transactions from some provisions. No owner, however, is permitted to advertise in a discriminatory manner. For example, public newspapers would not accept an ad which specified "Christian household" or "whites only." If this were printed the publishers would be brought into court for discriminatory advertising on the basis of religion and race.

Despite state and federal laws, if you look at the classified section of newspapers under "Houses to Share" or "Roommates," invariably publishers allow advertisements to specify age and sex preferences, even if state and local laws technically forbid this. On the other hand, you will not be allowed to specify age or sex in classified advertisements if you have listed your accessory dwelling unit under "Apartment for Rent." Indeed, tenants in the rest of the house may not care as much about the sex or age of the person in the accessory unit as long as that person won't be sharing the same bathroom and kitchen.

Screening Based on Race, Color, Religion, or National Origin

My strong advice to you is not to discriminate on the basis of race, color, religion, or national origin. Not only is such discrimination illegal, but it is simply not your place to do such screening. No matter what you think your tenants want, and no matter what you think the neighbors want, don't do it. Even if you think that you are capable of conning the callers into thinking that they are being turned down for other reasons—when the real reason is race, color, religion, or national origin—don't do it.

An Instance When Discrimination Almost Occurred

Let me give you a personal example of how I almost discriminated on racial grounds.

When I bought my third house, I made the rounds, introducing myself to all of the neighbors surrounding the property. None of the neighbors were enthusiastic about having a group house nearby, but after speaking with me, they were prepared to adopt a wait-and-see attitude. One neighbor, though, sighed and said, "A group house, huh? Well, I hope you're not going to have any blacks there."

I was taken aback. Now part of my management philosophy is to be on good terms with the neighbors. I didn't know what to say. I blurted out the truth—that I didn't discriminate on the basis of race, but that in any event she probably didn't have anything to worry about. Blacks rarely responded to my ads for houses to share in Arlington, Virginia.

Who was the first caller for my ad? A young, black, West Indian woman. She was attending graduate school full-time and holding down a job, as well. She reminded me of myself when I was working my way through college.

I showed her the house. Nonetheless, mindful of my neighbor's comments, I had her fill out a rental application and told her that other applicants would be looking at the house, too. Her application would be just one of many I would be considering.

The thought went through my head that maybe I could stall her and select other tenants. I was afraid. If she moved in first, would I have difficulty finding other tenants to move in with her? And what would the neighbors say?

I went home with her application, sat down, and thought about the situation for a while. The more thinking I did, the more ashamed I became of myself. I still remember how, at the age of 5, I was chased through the streets of a Montreal neighborhood by older kids yelling "dirty Jew" at me. Fifteen years ago in some areas of the country I would not have been allowed to get credit to buy a house because of my sex. It is a very terrible thing to feel that people may not see you as an individual human being, but as an entity to be automatically despised or disregarded. And I know I am not alone. Twenty years ago, many people would have stigmatized you if you were divorced. And how many of you had ancestors who came to this country with strange accents and minority religions? How, then, can you turn around and discriminate against someone else? I couldn't.

The next day, after checking her references, I phoned Elris to let her know that I'd be delighted to have her as a tenant if she still wanted to move in. She moved in. The two of us selected the rest of the household.

What happened? The rest of the tenants, who by the way were white, were selected in record time. And there was never a complaint or even a racial comment from the neighbor who originally objected to black tenants. The only comment made by that neighbor was about how pleased she was with my tenant selection.

So, there you have at least one example that worked out very well. Don't discriminate. At the same time, never feel pressured to accept someone as a tenant just because the person is handicapped, or foreign, or from a racial or religious minority. You are not running a social service agency. References have to check out. It is absolutely imperative that both you and the people in the household feel comfortable with individual tenants. Personalities and lifestyles must fit in with the rest of the household. A shared household is not an apartment complex. You can't go strictly by some formula for a rental application. The chemistry among the people in the household must work.

If I were ever asked advice from my tenants, I would tell them, "For the purposes of tenant selection, put stereotypes aside and look at each applicant as an individual. If you like the person, fine. If not, don't select that person."

I am happy to report that in the 8 years that I've had renters, no tenant of mine has ever made a racial or ethnic slur, nor have any tenants ever told me that the reason they didn't want someone was because of race, religion, color, or national origin.

POINTS TO REMEMBER

- The most important thing you will do to ensure smoothe management is to select good tenants.
- You can find tenants through:
    - neighbors, friends, and colleagues
    - current tenants

- public roommate-referral agencies
- private roommate-referral agencies
- organizational housing offices
- notices on bulletin boards
- newspaper classifieds

- Advertisements or notices should include information on:

  - the house itself
  - the characteristics of the tenants in the household
  - the rental terms

- Look for tenants who:

  - are steadily employed
  - have a history as a good and stable tenant
  - are willing to pay your security deposit

- You must have selection criteria, but don't discriminate on the basis of race, religion, color, or national origin.

FOR FURTHER INFORMATION

There are two classic works on residential property management for owners with small- to medium-sized apartment buildings. Both books include excellent sections on tenant selection:

Lowry, Albert J.: *How to Manage Real Estate Successfully—In Your Spare Time*, Simon and Schuster, New York, 1977.

Robinson, Leigh: *Landlording*, 3d ed., Express, P.O. Box 1373, Richmond, California 94802, 1980.

In addition, *The Monopoly Game* by Dave Glubetich devotes a section to tenant selection. It is well worth reading.

Lectures given around the country by Donald Berman of Reno, Nevada, are also instructive. He supplied some of the material in this chapter under "Red Flags: Proceed with Caution."

8

THE MANAGEMENT SYSTEM

The ancient Greek philosopher Heraclitus once said, "You can't step into the same river twice," to which a student of his added, "You can't step into the same river once." By this they meant that everything is in a state of flux.

There is no such thing as one management system to meet everyone's needs for all time. If you own one investment house, your system will be different than if you own twenty houses. The system I'm going to explain is designed for people who own a relatively small number of rental houses.

Although my management system has evolved over the past 8 years and will undoubtedly continue to evolve, the underlying principle on which it is based has remained constant: *Satisfied tenants are the foundation on which your whole investment sits.* With satisfied tenants, you can succeed even with a mediocre management system. Without satisfied tenants, the most sophisticated management system in the world won't produce a profitable return from your rental.

That said, it's still important to set up the best management system you can. Having a systematic approach to management will not only increase your profits, it will also make your relationship with your tenants more pleasant. Most problems that arise between owners and tenants occur because of a lack of communication, which leads to a misunderstanding about what is expected and what is fair. If your tenants understand your management system and perceive that it is sensible and fair to all parties, you will avoid most management problems.

141

Your management system: Lao-tzu and Han Fei Tzu

There are two schools of thought on management I'd like to discuss. I'll call these the schools of Lao-Tzu and of Han Fei Tzu.

Lao-tzu and Han Fei Tzu were Chinese philosophers. Lao-tzu believed that there is a natural order—a Way—which is both a gentle and a powerful force in the universe. Countries and people, he said, are the happiest and most productive when guided by the Way and governed least by rulers. He maintained that rules and regulations are oppressive, complicating people's lives and making productivity and creativity more difficult.

Han Fei Tzu, on the other hand, believed that clearly defined laws and rules are essential to a well-run society. People must be guided by precise laws, so they will know their obligations and responsibilities, and there will be no question about what constitutes correct behavior.

Which view is correct? I am reminded of the story about two men who came to a rabbi to settle a dispute. One man presented his side of the story, and the rabbi, having listened carefully, said, "You are right." Then the other man presented his diametrically opposite view, and the rabbi, scratching his head, said, "You are right, too." "But we both can't be right," clamored the first man. The rabbi thought for a moment and replied, "That, too, is right."

Which view is correct? Both, perhaps, when it comes to devising a management system. Tenants are the happiest when managed least. And tenants are also the happiest when there is a clear management system.

What I'll do in this and coming chapters is to show you how to set up such a management system for singles. Step by step, I'll show you what to do from the time a person applies to become your tenant until the time a tenant leaves your house.

Turning an applicant into a tenant

Your management system starts when you turn an applicant into your first tenant. After showing the house to a number of people, you will find one who likes the house and with whom you feel comfortable. You will phone that individual back at the time you said you would call, and tell her that if she is still interested in moving in, you would like to have her as a tenant. At this point, you may want to tell her that you can't formally accept her as a tenant, however, until you have checked her references.

The Rental Application

You will need some essential information in order to check references. The accompanying is an example of my tenant application form. Refer to the Appendix for an example of a more detailed application for lease form used by the Northern Virginia Board of Realtors.

TENANT APPLICATION FORM

1. Name of prospective tenant _SARAH SHANE_
2. Home phone _123-4567_ Office phone _891-0111_
3. Present occupation _PROGRAM ANALYST_
4. Name and address of firm _CPI, INC._

   100 RIVER ROAD

   MIDDLETOWN
5. Name of supervisor _JOE YUCKENFLUSTER_
   Telephone number of Supervisor _213-1415_
6. Previous occupation (if employed less than 6 months at present job) _NA_
7. Name of previous supervisor _NA_
   Previous Supervisor's telephone number _NA_
8. Address(es) of applicant for last 2 years

Address	Dates	Landlord	Phone
999 Rose St. #5 MIDDLETOWN	1983-85	HARRY SHMEGEGI	161-1718

9. Name, address, and phone number of nearest relative
   BILL SHANE (FATHER) 765 E. 42nd ST., N.Y. (212) 111-1212

10. Name and phone number of two friends locally
MARY WINTERS   235-6017   BILL FERRO   123-9768
Comments:

Supervisor says Sarah Shane is a good worker;
She's been with the firm for 3 years.

Shmegegi says rent was always paid on time, and
she kept the apartment neat & clean; however, she
had numerous small complaints -- for example, the
time she asked management to come immediately to
fix the drip in her faucet at 9 p.m.

As you can see, my tenant application form is pretty basic. I don't believe in asking for information unless I know what I'll do with it.

Most rental applications are much more detailed, as perhaps they should be when one is leasing a whole house at a relatively high rent for a year or more. Many applications have a lot of personal questions, such as "What is your salary?" "Have you ever declared bankruptcy?" "What kind of car do you drive?" and "How much do you spend each month for car payments? —credit card charges? —child support?"

Frankly, I don't care about the answers to these questions. People can make $50,000 a year and never pay their rent on time. Others can earn $10,000 and be painstakingly conscientious about meeting financial obligations. I only care about three things:

1. That the applicant is steadily employed or is a full-time student.
2. That the applicant has a history of being a stable and responsible tenant.
3. That the applicant is able and willing to pay both a security deposit and the first and last month's rent before moving in, or at least to pay the entire sum within a short time after moving in.

Now let me tell you a secret. I don't always check references. After speaking with them by phone for a few minutes, I usually have a fairly good instinct about whether people will be suitable tenants. After meeting them in person, even without having checked their references, I'm pretty sure if they would make good tenants.

Nonetheless, I still get information on each prospective tenant. It is useful to have the office telephone numbers of your tenants in case you need to phone them at work. It is important to have the name of a nearest relative in case of some future emergency.

Those of you who are more cautious, though, may want to design a rental application with more of those questions from typical applications used by real estate offices. When you phone supervisors or former landlords, ask some open-ended questions and some specific questions. For example:

- How long have you known the applicant?
- In what capacity?
- Generally, how would you describe her as a worker (tenant)?
- How does she get along with the rest of the people in the household (at work)?

For Landlords
- How did she keep the place?
- Did she have any difficulty paying the rent on time?
- Do you know why she is leaving (or left)?
- If you could, would you rent to her again?

Cautious owners should be sure to check with a previous landlord, not with a current one. Current landlords are sometimes so eager to get rid of problem tenants that they will give an unjustifiably good reference to a bad tenant. Previous landlords, on the other hand, have nothing to lose by giving an accurate description of their former tenants.

Some unsavory applicants will ask a friend to pretend to be a previous landlord. The friend will then give a glowing recommendation when you phone to check references. However, if you ask specific questions—like "How much rent is the person paying?" and "Why did the applicant leave his or her previous residence?"—make-believe landlords will begin to stammer. They won't know what the friend told you. You'll easily be able to discover the deception.

If you really want to make sure that the person giving a reference is being honest with you, here's a slightly devious way. Ask the applicant how much rent she paid at her previous residences. When you phone previous landlords, add $100 to the amount of rent she listed, and ask if the applicant paid this imaginary rent. An honest reference will say, "No." I've never used this trick, but two people checking references on former tenants of mine have used it on me.

Professional property managers often require an applicant to pay an extra $20 or more for a formal credit check performed by a credit bureau. It is rare for anyone other than professional property managers to require applicants for house sharing to submit to a formal credit check. Most applicants would balk at the idea and, in my opinion, there is no need for you to complicate your rental procedure by requiring one. Unless you are very unsure of yourself, you should be able to get the information you need by doing your own checking from the information the applicant has provided on the rental application.

Last Steps to Take Before the Applicant Becomes Your Tenant

It's time to meet with the applicant in person again, once you have checked out the references to your satisfaction. I usually ask the person to come to my house to complete the rental procedure over a cup of tea. At that time:

- I explain my management system to her.
- She signs two copies of the rental agreement—one for her and one for me.
- She hands over a check for the sum of the first month's rent, the last month's rent, and the security deposit.
- I hand her a key to the house.
- I give her a welcome letter.

The rental agreement and the Welcome Letter form the basis of my management system, and I'll discuss both of them shortly.

146

HOW TO GET THE SECOND, THIRD, AND FOURTH TENANTS

An enormous feeling of relief comes over me once I have my first tenant. In a way, I feel like I am no longer alone in this venture. I have a partner.

The next step, after the rental agreement is signed, is to discuss with your new tenant how the rest of the household will be assembled. Explain your screening criteria, and ask what she thinks of them. Sometimes your new tenant will suggest a different age range. Sometimes she'll tell you she definitely does not want to live with a smoker. Change your screening criteria, if you have to, to meet the preferences of your new tenant.

Then, ask her what times would be convenient for her to meet with prospective tenants who might want to share the house with her. You will advertise for tenants and screen them by phone, but it will be up to her to meet the applicants and show them the house. She will make the final decision about the people she wants as tenants. In fact, I tell my tenants that I would prefer to have a vacancy and miss out on some rent than to have someone with whom they don't feel comfortable.

I phone my first tenant before the applicants show up. I let her know who is coming, at what time, and what my initial impression of each individual was from the telephone interview. I then ask her to phone me back after the last applicant has looked at the place. We discuss her reaction to each applicant: Whom did she like? Who seemed interested? Which ones would she like as housemates?

Some new tenants try to be too accommodating. They may say that a prospective tenant is okay, either because they don't want to hurt me financially or because they are tired of showing the place to so many people. You have to probe any "okays." You may have to explain to your tenant again that the two of you need to hold out for people who really would be compatible, rather than to select someone who is just okay. Tenants don't have to become best friends, but they do have to feel comfortable with each other.

Once your second tenant is selected, you have two partners. Your two tenants may decide to interview for the third and fourth tenants together, or they may decide to take turns. It's up to them.

Only after my tenants have selected them do the applicants come to my home, individually, to meet with me for the first time. I go through the same rental procedure with each new tenant, explaining my management system in general and the rental agreement in particular.

THE RENTAL AGREEMENT: THE WRITTEN RULES OF THE GAME

Tenants usually have very little knowledge about the rules of the rental game. As a result, many don't understand why an owner will charge them for some repairs and not for others, or why an owner will choose to make certain improvements requested by the tenant but refuse to make others. Likewise, a sudden rent increase may be inexplicable to tenants and cause resentment, even if they have gone for years without a rent increase.

Tenants should be made aware from the beginning that they will control their own household to a great degree—but that they will also have clear rules to follow. And they should understand that you, too, will be as strongly committed to carrying out your own responsibilities as you will be committed to seeing that your tenants carry out their responsibilities. It is definitely a two-way street.

The framework of your management system is the written agreement. Long, tedious leases and rental agreements filled with legalese may make an owner feel protected against any contingency. But in truth, nothing will protect you from every contingency. You are dependent to a large extent on the good faith and trust of your tenants, no matter what you think your legal rights might be.

I have therefore opted to make my agreements short and easy to understand, so that my tenants know clearly what their rights and responsibilities are. You don't have to cover every possible problem that may occur in the course of a year. Particularly in month-to-month agreements, as mine are, you should be able to speak with your tenants periodically, resolving any problems that may arise but are not addressed in the rental agreement.

Here is the agreement I use. I've inserted circled numbers by those items which I'll discuss in the following pages. Other items in the agreement will be discussed in the "Welcome Letter" section at the end of this chapter.

148

RENTAL AGREEMENT

THIS AGREEMENT HAS BEEN MADE between those parties named below, hereinafter referred to as Tenant(s) and _DOREEN BIERBRIER_ , hereinafter referred to as Owner.

The term "Tenant" refers to the individual signators of this Rental Agreement. The term "Tenants" denotes all tenants in the household. "Tenant(s)" means either "Tenant" or "Tenants" or both, as determined by the Owner. Responsibilities of a Tenant pertain only to that individual. Contractual obligations of Tenants are binding on each Tenant and denote both individual and joint responsibility of all Tenants.

In consideration of a monthly rent stated below, Tenant(s) are entitled to share the residence at _123 MAIN ST., ARLINGTON_ on a month-to-month basis.

The following points are agreeable to the Tenant(s) and the Owner, and are mutually binding:

1. Rent will be due the first day of every month.
2. Tenant, before occupancy will pay the first month's rent and an equal amount toward the last month's rent.
3. Tenant will pay a security deposit of _$150._ before occupying the premises. Within 30 days after departure, if all obligations have been paid, and if the premises have been maintained in satisfactory condition as determined by the Owner, the deposit will be returned to the Tenant. Any deductions will be itemized in writing and sent to the Tenant.
4. Tenant(s) will assume full responsibility for all gas, electricity, water, sewer, waste removal, and telephone bills until the last day of legal tenancy.
5. In the event there are fewer than 3 tenants in the household, an individual Tenant will pay no more than one-third of the bills for gas and electricity, and the Owner agrees to pay the remaining share. If a Tenant has not paid his or her share of the utilities after terminating the agreement, Owner reserves the right to use part of the Tenant's security deposit to meet the Tenant's obligation to the household, if sufficient funds are available after other obligations have been paid. However, Owner does not assume any liability if a Tenant fails to pay his or her share of any utility bill.
6. Owner will assume expenses for the major maintenance, cleaning, and repair of the furnace, roof, water heater, central air-conditioning, gutters, and outside plumbing, and repairs to equipment and appliances (except for the lawn mower and disposer) when required if they have been used in a proper manner. See attached "Inventory of Owner's Appliances and Equipment."
7. Owner will pay to exterminate carpenter ants, termites and other wood-boring insects, and waterbugs. The expense to eradicate all other insects, including cockroaches, will be borne by all Tenants.

149

RENTAL AGREEMENT *cont'd.*

8. Tenants will assume responsibility for minor maintenance such as re-placement of fuses, filters, light bulbs, washers in faucets, and batteries in smoke alarms. In addition, Tenant(s) are responsible for changing screens and storm windows and for repairing screens and cracked window panes and door panes unless they can demonstrate that the damage was beyond their control. Tenant(s) are responsible for repairing any damage to the premises or the appliances which was caused by Tenant(s) misuse or negligence.

9. Tenant(s) will keep the premises, including all plumbing fixtures, as clean and safe as conditions permit and will unstop and keep clear all waste pipes and outdoor drains. Unless the cause is beyond their control, Tenant(s) are responsible for loss or damage from freezing of water pipes or plumbing fixtures or from the stopping of water closets and drains, which will be repaired at the expense of the Tenant(s).

10. Tenants, at their own expense, will keep up and preserve in good condition the lawn and garden and will remove ice and snow as necessary to keep walkways clear. Tenants at their own expense will keep the premises neat and free from rubbish and/or hazards, and maintain wood-piles, if any, at a distance from any structure. The Tenant occupying the lowest level of the house is responsible for clearing leaves and debris from the outdoor drain(s).

11. It is expressly understood and agreed by and between the parties of this agreement that unless liable under law, Owner will not be liable for any damage or injury to any person or persons which may occur on the premises for the duration of this agreement; nor will the Owner be liable for any personal property which is stolen or damaged due to flooding, leaks, fire, malfunction of equipment, structural problems, or for any reason whatever. All persons and personal property in or on the premises will be at the sole risk and responsibility of the Tenant(s).

12. The premises will be used as a single-family household for no more than 4 unrelated persons and for no other purpose or additional number of people whatever except for temporary guests. A temporary guest is herein defined as someone occupying the premises for no more than 10 days in the course of a year. Further, all Tenants are entitled to share all living areas, to have access to all outside doors, and to utilize a common cooking facility.

13. Tenant(s) cannot sublet the premises without the express consent of the Owner.

14. No pets are permitted on the premises without the express consent of the Owner.

15. No alterations, additions, or improvements may be made on the premises without the express consent of the Owner. Any alterations, additions, or improvements will become the property of the Owner when the Tenant(s) depart, unless the room can be restored to its original condition.

RENTAL AGREEMENT *cont'd.*

⑨16. Tenant(s) agree to allow the Owner at any reasonable hour, by appointment, to enter the premises to inspect the same, to make repairs, or to show the premises to any parties.

17. Tenant(s) and Owner will, by mutual consent screen and select new Tenants to fill vacancies.

⑩18. This agreement and the tenancy hereby granted to a Tenant may be terminated at any time by either party by giving the other party not less than 30 days prior notice in writing. Terminations initiated by the Tenant must end on the last day of a month.

All the undersigned parties have read this agreement, agree to abide by its terms, and each has a copy of this agreement.

Date	Monthly Rent	Amt. of Sec. Dep.	Date Occupancy Will Begin	Amount Attached	Date Termin.	Comments
3/13/84	$205	$150	4/1/84	$355		Last month's rent of $205 will be paid by 3/20/84

Mari J. Kaplan
TENANT

Doreen Bierlien
OWNER

Date	Monthly Rent	Amt. of Sec. Dep.	Date Occupancy Will Begin	Amount Attached	Date Termin.	Comments
3/15/84	$195	$150	4/1/84	$540		

Eric Adams
TENANT

Doreen Bierlien
OWNER

Date	Monthly Rent	Amt. of Sec. Dep.	Date Occupancy Will Begin	Amount Attached	Date Termin.	Comments
3/22/84	$325	$150	4/15/84	$637.50		1st month's rent prorated @ $162.50

Diana Harris
TENANT

Doreen Bierlien
OWNER

151

Date	Monthly Rent	Amt. of Sec. Dep.	Date Occupancy Will Begin	Amount Attached	Date Termin.	Comments
4/5/84	$195	$150	5/1/84	$195		Last month's rent of $195 to be paid by 4/30; security deposit of $150 to be paid by 5/15.

Jane Gardner
TENANT

Doreen Bierlein
OWNER

Date	Monthly Rent	Amt. of Sec. Dep.	Date Occupancy Will Begin	Amount Attached	Date Termin.	Comments

TENANT   OWNER

1. Rental Agreement

A signed rental agreement forms the legal basis of the business relationship between you and your tenants. The agreement may be made for a set period of time, such as a year. An agreement for a predetermined length of time is called a *lease*. A rental agreement may also be open-ended, with no fixed termination date, and be on a month-to-month basis, as mine is.

I recommend that you have month-to-month agreements with all of your tenants. Why a month-to-month agreement and not a year's lease? For several reasons:

- If the tenancy is not satisfactory, you or your tenants should be in a position to terminate the agreement within a short period of time.
- Many singles do not know their plans for a full year. They will agree to rent a place much more readily if they are not bound by a year's lease.
- Even with a legally binding 1-year lease, there is no assurance that a tenant will not be obliged to move because of a job change, a military transfer, or marriage.

- If you do need to raise the rent, you may do so without waiting until the term of the lease is up.

- Month-to-month rental agreements encourage tenants and owners to be more courteous to each other, because both parties know that the tenant can leave (or be asked to leave) with a month's notice.

The major drawback to a month-to-month rental agreement is the lack of a commitment, in writing, that the tenant will stay for any length of time longer than a month. It can be a very tiresome process for an owner to have to rent and rerent to tenant after tenant month after month. It is therefore important to obtain a verbal commitment from a prospective tenant that, if she signs the rental agreement, she signs with the understanding that she will stay at least 6 months. The verbal commitment may not be legally binding, but the vast majority of tenants will honor their pledge. In fact, most stay a year or two before leaving.

Rental agreements should be tailored to fit your particular circumstances. At a minimum, however, all agreements should contain:

- the names and signatures of the parties
- the location of the house which the tenant is renting
- the date occupancy will begin
- the amount of the rent
- the date when the rent will be paid

The terms of the rental agreement you design for yourself should be in accordance with the laws of your state and locality. Such laws may determine the answers to the following questions:

- How much is the owner permitted to ask for a security deposit?
- Should the security deposit be placed in an escrow account?
- Is a tenant entitled to interest on a security deposit, and, if so, how much?
- Does the owner have to return the security deposit within a certain amount of time?
- How much notice must an owner give when requiring a tenant to leave?

A phone call to the appropriate office of your local city or county government should provide you with the answers to these questions. The switchboard operator may connect you with a tenant-landlord commission, a rental accommodations office, a zoning section, a housing section, a consumer affairs office, or whatever other public agency handles tenant-landlord relations in your locality.

In addition to my rental agreement, you may want to study the phrasing of other agreements. You can pick up sample leases and rental agreements from:

- stationery stores
- real estate offices
- public tenant-landlord offices
- private apartment owners' associations

2. Rent

As gasoline runs a car, rent runs your business operations. You must receive rent regularly to pay the expenses associated with the house, and hopefully to give you a positive cash flow.

Tenants should be absolutely certain that you expect them to pay the full amount of rent on time each month. On this point you are not flexible. Well, at times you may be a little bit flexible . . . if an unusual circumstance occurs, and if they give you advance notice, and if they tell you exactly when they will pay you. But don't let them know in advance that you may occasionally be flexible.

Rent should be due on the same day of the month—usually the first—for everyone; otherwise, you will only confuse yourself trying to remember which tenant was supposed to pay on what day.

If someone moves in during the middle of the month, prorate the rent for that one month, and make the rent due on the first day of the month starting from the following month.

3. First and Last Month's Rent

Collect the first and last month's rent before a tenant moves in. The reason for collecting the last month's rent in advance is to make sure that you get at least 30 days notice before someone leaves. If you don't get the last month's rent in advance, it is possible for a tenant to mention casually on the last day of the month that she is

154

leaving the next day. Then you would have to scramble to find a tenant fast, and it would be virtually impossible to avoid a vacancy.

Check your state laws first, though. Some states prohibit prepayment of the last month's rent.

4. SECURITY DEPOSIT

A security deposit is a refundable payment made to owners by tenants as an assurance that the tenants will carry out their responsibilities according to the terms of the rental agreement.

The maximum amount of money that you are permitted to collect as a security deposit may be governed by state law. Some states limit the amount to 1 or 2 months of rent. When I started renting to tenants 8 years ago, I arbitrarily thought that $50 would be sufficient. The amount I now require for a deposit is $150 per tenant. The size of the deposit is not based on how much rent a tenant pays. Each of my tenants now pays $150, regardless of the fact that their rents vary. That figure will undoubtedly go up as inflation continues.

Most states don't require an owner to hold a security deposit in a separate escrow account. In other words, the money may be put directly into the owner's personal account. Some states do, however, require that an owner pay interest on the tenant's security deposit. Usually the interest you are required to pay is a relatively low passbook rate. If you pay interest on a security deposit, you will have to report the amount to the tenant and to the IRS at the end of the year on Form 1099.

State laws may also regulate how quickly an owner must return a security deposit to a tenant—often within 15 or 30 days. Any deductions should be itemized in writing. I usually itemize all deductions, make a photocopy of any bills paid from the deposit, and enclose these in the envelope when I mail the tenant the remainder of the deposit.

As a protection to the other tenants in the household, I will use a departing tenant's security deposit to pay that tenant's share of any unpaid utility bills (see the Rental Agreement, item 5).

5. UTILITIES

Have your tenants pay for all utility, water, and sewage bills. That way, your tenants will be more conscious about energy conservation.

When the utility bills are high, they will only be upset with the utility companies or with themselves.

It is human nature not to be very energy conscious when someone else is paying the bills. You can imagine your frustration if you were paying for the heating bill and you walked into your rental house in the middle of winter and saw the thermostat set at 78°F and a window wide open.

As much as possible, don't place yourself in a position in which you and your tenants are pitted against each other. If you paid for the utilities, you would have to charge a higher initial rent to cover the cost of the utilities, and you would have to raise the rent each time the utility companies raised their rates. Hefty rent increases would cause your tenants to become upset with you. It is much better if tenants are allowed to vent their frustration directly at the utility companies.

You may want to provide your tenants with the telephone numbers of all the utility companies they will need to contact. But let the tenants figure out who in the household will pay what bills. Stay out of it. Let them organize themselves.

Be aware that in some localities a lien can be placed against an owner's property if water and sewage bills are not paid. Some owners of rental houses have been surprised to learn that there is a long-standing lien against their property for hundreds of dollars because of the unpaid bills. It's therefore a good idea to check with the appropriate office every 6 months to make sure that the water and sewage bills have been paid.

6. MAINTENANCE AND REPAIRS

Most of the items numbered 6 through 10 in the rental agreement are self-explanatory. You will soon see (in the "Welcome Letter" section) how I describe these points to my tenants.

Generally, I believe that owners should assume responsibility for the maintenance and repair of the structural part of the house and for the repair or replacement of major appliances. The major exception to this is the unclogging of waste drains, which (with rare exceptions) I've made a tenant responsibility.

Some owners of rental houses make the tenants responsible for the payment of any repair less than a certain amount—say $50. The rationale behind this approach is that tenants won't be bothering the owner about every minor problem that the household may have; in addition, of course, owners hope to save money on such repairs.

But I don't think it's advisable to give tenants the responsibility for paying for all minor repairs. I'd prefer to be "bothered" by the tenants if something is not working in the house. Sometimes tenants will not make those small repairs when they know that they will have to pay for them. By the time the owner discovers the problem, the minor repair has likely become a major repair. The leaky sink trap, which might have cost a few dollars to fix, may end up costing you a few hundred dollars when you have to replace an entire water-damaged floor.

In addition, if tenants are responsible for all minor repairs, they may decide to do the work themselves. Some jerry-built repairs may mean, at best, that the repair will only last for a short while before the problem recurs. At worst, the do-it-yourself repair may be hazardous to the household.

7. LIABILITY AND INSURANCE

No matter what your agreement says, you may be responsible for damage to a tenant's property or for injury to persons on your property. You may be liable if it can be proved that you were negligent in the care of your property, or that you knowingly failed to disclose certain defects (e.g., basements that flood) to your tenants.

You should protect yourself with several kinds of insurance coverage. Essentially, your insurance should protect you from three kinds of loss:

1. direct damage to the property (e.g., if the house burns down)
2. liability for damage or injury to others while they are on your property
3. loss resulting as a consequence of damage to the property (e.g., loss of rent because rooms are uninhabitable after a fire)

Laws vary from state to state, and insurance coverage varies from company to company. The best way to make sure that you have all of the coverage you need is to find a good insurance agent to analyze your situation and advise you.

I suggest that you find an insurance agent who is not associated with one insurance company, but can deal with all companies. That way, the agent is free to choose from among several companies to find you an insurance policy which best meets your needs.

The types of coverage that you should consider when you own an investment house are these:

Fire Insurance and Extended Coverage   The basic coverage you need is protection against loss from fire and other hazards. Most mortgage companies require owners to have a fire insurance policy to protect, if nothing else, the lender's financial interest in the property.

What is called "extended coverage" will insure your property not only against fire, but against such other calamities as explosions, smoke, wind, and lightning. The specific types of protection that you need depend on where your properties are located. You may, for example, want earthquake coverage if your properties are located near the San Andreas fault, or flood insurance if your houses are close to some parts of the Mississippi delta.

For insurance purposes, you should estimate the worth of the house based on how much it would actually cost to rebuild it, and not on its assessed value or its market value.

Now most disasters which occur do not destroy an entire house, foundation and all. Nor, of course, will a fire or most other natural catastrophes destroy the land on which the house is built. Most insurers therefore require owners to carry a policy covering 80 percent or more of the value of the dwelling that could be destroyed. If the property has 80% coverage, the insurance company will compensate in full for any damage caused up to the stated amount.

If the property were underinsured, though, the insurer would only compensate an owner in part, by means of the following formula:

$$\frac{\text{Insurance Carried}}{\text{Insurance Required}} \times \frac{\text{Amount of}}{\text{Loss}} = \text{Recovery}$$

For example, let's say that you have a property worth $100,000 which should be insured for $80,000. Instead, you carried coverage for only $40,000. A fire destroys $20,000 worth of the property. How much compensation would you receive?

$$\frac{\$40,000}{\$80,000} \times \$20,000 = \$10,000$$

To make sure that your property is properly insured, you may want to carry an *inflation guard* endorsement. This automatically increases the amount of your insurance coverage, adjusting it upward as inflation increases your property's value.

An inflation guard endorsement is just one of several coverages an owner may want to have. Other endorsements, also called "attachments" or "riders," include the following:

Vandalism and Malicious Mischief covers your costs for repairing damage caused by the malicious mischief of people who destroy your property.

Personal liability covers your financial responsibility for damage to persons or property as a result of your omission or commission of acts to safeguard your property.

Contents covers your belongings—such as dishwasher, refrigerator, or lawnmower—if they are damaged or destroyed by a named peril. *Please note that this coverage only covers your property and does not protect the personal property owned by your tenants.*

Fair rental value covers the loss of rent you may incur while having damaged property put back into habitable condition for rental.

Workers compensation is not an endorsement, but a separate policy. It covers expenses incurred when someone you hire is injured while performing work for you. You would only need this coverage if you employed people who did not carry their own workers compensation insurance. Be careful, though, if you pay a tenant to make some repairs, or offer reduced rent in exchange for making some repairs. You may be liable for medical expenses if your tenant is injured while performing the task. You may even be liable if you hire some neighborhood kid to cut the grass and he is injured on the job. You are less likely to be liable if you include within your rental agreement certain responsibilities of tenants—such as mowing the lawn and changing storm windows or screens—for which you provide no compensation.

State laws regarding workers compensation differ, so you may want to ask your insurance agent what liability you have in your state.

Homeowner's Insurance Policies   If you own two or three rental houses, you may be able to put the liability coverage for the rental properties on your own homeowner's policy for a reduced rate. If you own more than a couple of rental houses, you may need to have an "Owners, Landlords, Tenants Policy."

Most homeowner's policies consist of a package of several of the coverages thought to be most useful. The coverage provided in the packages is less expensive than if you bought each coverage separately.

There are at least six kinds of insurance packages, but Form HO–2 and HO–3 are the most common packages for homeowners. The insurance packages have two sections: Section 1 covers damage to the house due to named perils; Section 2 includes liability insurance to pay for injuries to others caused while they are on your property. Section 2 also pays for damage caused to the property of others, such as when a tree on your property falls on your neighbor's car, and you are judged to be liable.

In order for a homeowner's policy to cover additional rental properties, Section 2 has to have an endorsement to the basic policy. You will, however, have to purchase a separate policy for each investment house to provide the same protection for them as you have under Section 1 of your homeowner's policy for your personal residence.

8. ZONING CLAUSE

Item 12 in my rental agreement is in conformity with the zoning requirements of Arlington County, Virginia—the local jurisdiction in which all of my properties are located. In my county, zoning ordinances permit four unrelated singles to share a single-family dwelling, provided that they have access to all common living areas, can enter the premises through any door, and use a common cooking facility. I included item 12 in my agreement to help prove, if I were ever questioned, that my rental arrangement is in conformance with local zoning ordinances.

Look at your local zoning ordinances under the definition for a single-family dwelling, and use language from that definition to create your own zoning clause.

9. INSPECTIONS

Some owners like to make frequent surprise visits to their rental houses to see how their tenants are keeping the house. I have neither the time nor the inclination to make frequent surprise visits. In any event most rental agreements implicitly give tenants the right to "quiet enjoyment of property." I always phone my tenants ahead of time when I have to make a repair, show the place to prospective tenants, or inspect the household.

If you rent a house to a family or a group in the conventional way, with a year's lease, you should have a different system for inspections than I have. You would conduct an inspection of the house with the tenants before they move in, noting any existing damage. You would again inspect the house with the tenants either before they moved out, or a couple of months before you decided if you wanted to renew your lease agreement with them. Having inspected the house, you would charge the tenants for any items that were damaged (beyond normal wear and tear) during the course of their tenancy.

Check-in and check-out inspections are impractical when you own several rental houses, each occupied by four tenants who rent on a month-to-month basis. You would spend too much of your time just making inspections.

Nonetheless, inspections are essential. Some inspections you will want to do yourself, as you will see in the next chapter. Tenants, though, will be able to make many inspections themselves. Actually, if you think about it, new tenants make ideal inspectors. They notice every nail hole in the wall, every cracked window pane, and every dirty window sill. You will see how the tenant inspection system is set up when you read the Welcome Letter.

10. TERMINATION OF TENANCY

Terminations initiated by tenants should end on the last day of the month because it's usually easier to find new tenants who need to move in on the first of the month. In some states, owners are also required to set the last day of the month as the termination date when they ask tenants to leave.

Notice by either party should be made in writing. If a tenant gives you verbal notice, ask her to send you a written note explaining when she will move out. If you don't receive the note, send the tenant a written letter verifying that her rental agreement will terminate on a certain date. With notice in writing, you are less likely to run into legal difficulties in case you agree to rent the place to someone else and, at the last moment, your old tenant decides she really wants to stay.

Okay. So much for the points in the rental agreement which are of particular interest to owners. Let's now discuss the items of interest both to you and to your tenants. I've incorporated the most important topics in the following Welcome Letter.

The Welcome Letter

Dear Tenant,

I am very pleased that you are going to be moving into one of the houses I own.

I always sit down and have a chat with new tenants about the house, about payment of the rent, and about the respective responsibilities of owners and tenants. Sometimes, though, I have forgotten to mention one point or another. So, I decided to write this letter to make sure that your concerns are covered as completely as possible, and that all important topics are discussed.

A rental agreement is a contract that spells out the responsibilities of owners and tenants toward each other, and toward the upkeep of the house. It is the responsibility of owners in most residential agreements to maintain and repair the structural parts of the house, such as the roof, the furnace, the water heater, and the central air-conditioning. Beyond that, though, each state and local jurisdiction has different laws and customs pertaining to rentals. Even within a locality, leases and rental agreements vary widely in terms of what the tenant is responsible for and what the owner is responsible for.

What I've tried to do is devise a management system which, if I were a tenant, I would think is fair. If, after reviewing the rental agreement, you have questions let me know.

Here are some of the key points.

Rent

According to my rental system, you are only responsible for your own rent. If someone else in the household leaves or does not pay rent when it's due, it's not your responsibility to pay that person's share of the rent.

All rent is due on the first of the month. It's late after the first. And I absolutely have to have the full amount of the rent. There are no acceptable reasons for nonpayment. I must make mortgage payments, and I'm dependent on your timely payment of the rent to do so.

You can mail the rent to me or drop it off at my house.

Most rental agreements have late charges—penalties if the rent is late. My agreement does not. I trust you to make timely rental payments. However, if your rent doesn't arrive by the fourth or fifth of the month, you can expect to get an anxious call from me asking when the rent will arrive.

Rent Increases

Don't worry. Even though our agreement is on a month-to-month basis, I normally raise the rent only once a year, and then by a relatively modest amount. Unless the economy gets totally out of hand, I don't see this policy changing.

Security Deposits

Your security deposit is a protection for me as well as for other members of the household. If, after you leave, some damage is discovered—a broken towel bar, cracked windows, etc.—I'll fix the problem, deduct the charge from your deposit, and send you a copy of the paid repair bill along with the remainder of your security deposit.

In some group houses, a tenant may leave without paying his or her share of the last utility bills. I've tried to protect the household by holding deposits until the last bill is paid. I will pay a tenant's share of utility bills to the household if there is money left over from the security deposit after any damage is paid. I'll then send xeroxed copies of the bills to the tenant who has departed, along with a cover letter itemizing the deductions.

Interest on security deposits: Some states require owners to pay interest on the security deposits they are holding from their tenants. In this state, owners are not required to pay interest on security deposits if they own ten or fewer units or houses, as I do.

Preventive Maintenance

I am firmly committed to providing you with a safe, well-maintained house. Although tenants in this area are usually expected to clean the gutters and oil the furnace, I'll perform these services for you—

just to make sure that your furnace is in top operating condition. That way your utility bills will be lower, and I'll make sure that the furnace lasts longer.

On the other hand, I must depend on you for certain preventive maintenance tasks. One of the most important is changing the filter on any forced air furnace or central air-conditioning system every month when in use. Not only will the system last longer, but installing clean filters is one of the easiest ways to reduce household utility bills.

Lawn, Yard, and Walkways

In some areas of the country, owners are responsible for seeing that the grounds are maintained. Here, though, tenants are completely responsible for mowing the grass, weeding, pruning, and maintaining the yard. Tenants are also responsible for shoveling the snow off the sidewalks around the house, and for clearing the walkways of ice and snow. Tenants occupying the lowest level of the house are also responsible for seeing that the outdoor drain remains clear of leaves and debris.

For your convenience, I've provided the houshold with some garden tools and a snow shovel.

Vegetable Gardens

In every household I've ever owned, one or more tenants have passionately wanted to have a vegetable garden. Tenants have dug up the lawn for a garden plot and, the first year, proudly showed me their zucchinis. By the second or third year, this enthusiasm dampened, and the former vegetable garden was likely to be overgrown with weeds.

Nonetheless, I don't mind if you make a garden, as long as your plot is relatively small and is in an unobtrusive spot.

Firewood

For some reason, tenants feel compelled to buy a cord of wood if the house has a fireplace. But most households don't even use one-fourth of a cord of wood during the winter season. As a result, as the years pass your woodpile becomes one huge mass of rotting wood, which makes a terrific home for carpenter ants, termites, and various and sundry other little beasts. I strongly recommend that you buy a few artificial logs at the grocery store. If you absolutely must follow your compulsion to buy a massive amount of firewood, please stack it at least 5 feet away from any other existing structure—and, ideally, put the logs on a platform raised above the ground.

Creepy Crawly Things

Carpenter ants, termites, and waterbugs sometimes invade houses through no fault of the tenants. Elimination of these pests is definitely my problem, unless I discover that the reason for the infestation is tenant-related—the tenants say, left rotting wood by the side of the house.

On the other hand, tenants may bring cockroaches into detached houses quite inadvertently. For example, sometimes, when furniture has been stored in an apartment complex which has cockroaches, unbeknownst to the tenant cockroaches infest that furniture. When the new tenant moves the furniture into a house, the little critters also move in.

Surprisingly, cockroaches can be found just as easily in clean houses as in dirty houses, so it's no reflection on your housekeeping habits if cockroaches are found. Nonetheless, extermination of cockroaches is a tenant responsibility.

Other bugs and ants (other than carpenter ants) may infest a house if opened food is left lying around. Or sometimes in summer, bugs just enter from the outside. Tenants can usually eliminate these pests by keeping the place clean and by buying a relatively inexpensive insecticide to spray.

Plumbing Problems

Some plumbing problems are completely my responsibility, while others are the responsibility of the household or of an individual tenant.

Here's what I'll take care of:

- cleaning roots from an outside sewer pipe
- repairing leaks in corroded plumbing
- replacing plumbing fixtures which aren't working properly because the parts are worn out

You are responsible for clearing any drain which backs up. Now, if the plumbing backs up in older houses, tenants are inclined to say to owners, "Look, the pipes are old, and there have been many residents of this place before I moved in. The pipes might be clogged from the accumulation of debris from previous tenants. Why should I have to pay if the toilet gets clogged or a drain doesn't work?"

Owners invariably reply that there are several tenants in the house. How does the owner know if one of the tenants didn't flush some object down the drain, or put something in the garbage disposer which shouldn't have been put down?

Arbitrarily, then, the custom in this area is to have the tenants pay for all clogged plumbing in houses, unless the cause of the problem is clearly beyond the control of the tenants.

Electrical Fixtures

Practically all problems connected with electrical fixtures are mine, unless you are responsible for overloading circuits with appliances.

Major Structures and Appliances

As I mentioned, nowadays landlords are usually responsible for correcting structural problems and problems related to the:

- roof
- central air-conditioning
- furnace, boiler, or heat pump
- water heater

In addition, unless the problem is related to tenant negligence, I'll pay for problems related to the:

- window air-conditioning units (if any)
- washer
- dryer
- refrigerator
- stove

166

- dehumidifier (if any)
- dishwasher (if any)
- portable electric heater (if any)

However, you are on your own for maintaining and repairing the lawnmower and the garbage disposer (if any). The last two items are there for the convenience of the tenants. If you want to use these items, it is up to you to see that they are maintained and repaired.

Improvements

Usually, the house and the room that you see when you decide to rent the place are the house and the room that you get. The theory is that the rent you agree to pay is based, in part, on the condition of the place as it is.

When you move in, you are most welcome to itemize any damage or malfunction that you find. For your convenience, I will give you an inspection sheet, which you can return to me (the inspection sheet is at the end of this letter). We may be able to correct some of the problems you encounter or take money from the security deposit of your room's departing tenant to pay you to correct other problems.

Please feel free to suggest ways in which you think I can improve the house. I'll consider what you have to say, particularly if your suggestions will increase the value of the house, or if you volunteer your services to help make the improvement. Whether or not the improvement is made will also depend partly on how strongly I feel that the improvement has to be made, and partly on how much money I have available at the time of your request.

Outside painting is my responsibility. For inside touch-up painting, I'll supply the paint and loan you the painting implements if you are willing to supply the labor.

Supplies

Tenants are responsible for paying for supplies. What are supplies? They are those items which are likely to be used up in maintaining a household over the course of a year or two. These include:

- spark plugs for the lawnmower
- plastic window covers for the winter
- fuses
- filters
- weather stripping

Insurance

Many renters know that practically all owners carry insurance. Many renters don't realize, however, that our insurance just protects us owners and our possessions. We can't get an insurance policy to cover possessions that don't belong to us.

If renters want to protect their own belongings, they have to get a renter's insurance policy. In addition to protecting your possessions against theft or damage, the policy would cover you if you inadvertently caused some accident, such as a grease fire in the kitchen.

Choosing New Tenants

I'll assume the responsibilities of paying for newspaper advertising and of making an initial screening of all tenants. I completely depend on you, though, to meet the applicants to see if you feel comfortable with them.

Don't worry. I'll never force a household to accept a tenant just so I won't miss the rent. I'd rather miss rent than have someone with whom you don't feel comfortable.

Repairmen

If you have previously lived in an apartment, you may be used to having the apartment manager arrange all repairs, as well as let in the workmen. Houses are different than apartments. They are geographically dispersed. An owner would go nuts trying to run around opening doors for the repairmen in the different houses.

If repairs are needed, I'll schedule the job to be done at a convenient time for you. Or you can often leave a key in a secret place outside. Or if you have made friends with the neighbors, they may occasionally let a repairman in if you ask them nicely.

However you do it, letting the workers in is a household responsibility.

168

Dangers to Health and Safety

Please report any condition to me at once which you think may be hazardous. While you are one of my tenants, your health and safety is one of my primary concerns. If at any time you are in the house in a situation which you feel might be dangerous, don't worry about the property—get out of the house at once and report the problem to the proper authorities—the fire department, the police, the gas company, me.

One thing I ask of you. I've supplied your house with smoke alarms. Smoke alarms don't go off if the batteries are dead. Replacing batteries is a household responsibility. Test your alarm periodically. Make sure it works. Replace any weak batteries immediately.

Please note: For your own safety, and to protect the house, all tenants should know where the water shutoffs, and the circuit breaker or fuse box are located. If you don't know, ask another tenant.

Tenant-Landlord Disputes

I have yet to encounter a tenant with whom I couldn't work to solve problems together. However, if some question arises and we can't agree on its resolution, I suggest that we ask for guidance from Arlington County's Tenant-Landlord Commission. The staff members can supply information on state and county laws, and tell us what is customary for the area regarding tenant and landlord responsibilities. The telephone number is 558-2355. If you have a question, phone them.

Let me once again welcome you. I'm delighted you decided to move in. If you have any questions, please let me know. My telephone number is 527-1780.

Sincerely,

Doreen

Doreen Bierbrier

Attachments:

Move-In/Move-Out Procedure
Tenant Checklist
Inventory of Owner's Appliances and Equipment

MOVE-IN PROCEDURE

Go through your room and the rest of the house, Tenant Checklist in hand. After you have made your inspection, check all the appliances in the inventory sheet attached to your rental agreement to make sure that everything is there and works.

If you encounter some problems, show them to one of the current tenants in the household. Report any problems to me, if you expect to get reimbursed for remedying the problems.

Please make one copy each of your completed Tenant Checklist and inventory to keep for your own records. Return the original to me within 1 week after moving in. If you don't return the forms within 10 days, I'll assume that everything is okay, and may charge you for any damage or problem found when you leave.

When you move out, the next tenant will complete the same form.

MOVE-OUT PROCEDURE

If you are moving out, you should complete the following steps:

1. Provide me with written notice at least 30 days before you leave.
2. Check the condition of your room and of the house against the Tenant Checklist and the inventory you completed when you moved in.
3. Report any problems to me before you move out. I may be able to explain how to remedy the problem inexpensively.
4. Leave your room or rooms the way you would want if you were the new tenant moving in.
5. Either give your key(s) to me or to someone in the household.
6. Leave me your forwarding address, so that I will know where to return your security deposit.

_____   _____
Tenant's name   Address of house

TENANT CHECKLIST

In your own room(s) are the following clean?	Yes	No	Approx. charge if not clean
Windows (inside) and window sills	__	__	$1/window or sill
Carpets and floors	__	__	$5/room
Walls	__	__	$5/wall
Baseboards	__	__	$2/baseboard
Bathroom (if for your sole use)			
Toilet	__	__	$5
Tiles, caulking, tub, and shower stall	__	__	$10
Washbasin	__	__	$2
Refrigerator (if for your sole use)	__	__	$15
Stove (if for your sole use)	__	__	$25
Kitchen countertop (if for your sole use)	__	__	$2
Shelves and cabinets (if for your sole use)	__	__	$2/cabinet (inside) $2/cabinet (outside)

In your own room(s):

	Yes	No	
Are there any stains on the floors or carpets?	__	__	$2–$50
Is all trash removed?	__	__	$2–$20
Are all walls free of nails, nail holes, and damage?	__	__	$2/nail hole $5/larger hole
Do any walls need to be touched up with paint?	__	__	$2 or more
Are any windows cracked or broken?	__	__	$25/window

TENANT CHECKLIST *cont'd.*

Is any light fixture broken?	___	___	$35/fixture
Do any light fixtures need light bulbs?	___	___	$1/bulb
Are leaves and debris swept from the back entrance if you regularly use this entrance?	___	___	$2

In the common areas of the household:

Household may be liable

Are any light fixtures broken or damaged?	___	___	$35
Does the smoke detector have a functional battery?	___	___	$3
Are there cockroaches or any other insects in the house?	___	___	?
Is there a clean filter in the central heating and cooling system?	___	___	$2
Are there any broken or cracked windows?	___	___	$25 each
Is there any damage to the following?			
Floor and carpets	___	___	?
Bathroom fixtures	___	___	?
Kitchen countertops	___	___	?
Kitchen cabinets	___	___	?
Porch (if any)	___	___	?
Garage (if any)	___	___	?
Are all items in the inventory sheet now present and in operable condition?	___	___	?

If you are moving in:

Do you know where the spare key to your house is located if you lock yourself out?	___	___

172

TENANT CHECKLIST *cont'd.*

Do you know where the following are
  and how to turn them off?
    Main water shutoff   __ __
    Hot water shutoff?   __ __
    Outside water shutoffs?   __ __
    Circuit breaker or fuse box?   __ __

If you are leaving:

Have you returned your key to Doreen
  or to someone in the household?   __ __ $5
Forwarding address: _____

                 _____

Comments: _____

_____

_____

_____	_____	_____	_____
Date	Signature of tenant moving in	Date	Signature of tenant moving out

THANK YOU VERY MUCH. BEST WISHES TO YOU.

Return to: Doreen Bierbrier
5002 N. 14th St.
Arlington, VA 22205

INVENTORY OF OWNER'S APPLIANCES AND EQUIPMENT

Address _____

DESCRIPTION

APPLIANCE/ EQUIPMENT	DESCRIPTION
Hot Water Heater (Capacity,)	
Heating/Cooling System	
Humidifier (Capacity:)	
Dehumidifier (Capacity:)	
A/C Unit(s) (BTU's:) (Voltage:)	
(BTU's:) (Voltage:)	
(BTU's:) (Voltage:)	

174

Washing Machine _____

Dryer _____

Stove _____

Refrigerator _____

Dishwasher _____

Disposer _____

Attic Fan _____

Lawn Mower _____

Additional
Tools _____

In signing this attachment, the Tenant agrees that the above mentioned appliances and equipment are in the household and are in operable condition when the Tenant moved into the premises.

PLEASE NOTE: disposer and lawn mower (if any) are for the convenience of the tenant(s) and repairs, if any, will be paid by tenant(s).

_____   _____
TENANT   DATE

POINTS TO REMEMBER

- Satisfied tenants are the foundation on which your whole investment rests.
- Use a rental application to get essential information from applicants and to help you screen potential tenants.
- Written rental agreements should be clear; they should protect the rights and define the responsibilities of both owner and tenants and be fair to both parties.
- Tenants should be instrumental in selecting other tenants who will live in the same household.

FOR FURTHER INFORMATION

The following books, previously mentioned, will be valuable to you as you devise your own management system:

Glubetich, Dave: *The Monopoly Game,* Impact Publishing, San Ramon, California, 1977.

Lowry, Albert J.: *How to Manage Real Estate Successfully—In Your Spare Time,* Simon and Schuster, New York, 1977.

Robinson, Leigh: *Landlording,* 3d ed., Express, P.O. Box 1373, Richmond, California 94802, 1980.

I highly recommend these additional resources:

Blumberg, Richard E., and James R. Grow: *The Rights of Tenants,* Avon, New York, 1978.
An excellent national survey of the legal rules of the rental game, although *The Rights of Tenants* is definitely written from the tenant's viewpoint.

Harwood, Bruce: *Real Estate Principles,* 3d ed., Reston Publishing, Reston, Virginia, 1983.
In a readable fashion, it summarizes key real estate concepts, some of which are important to owners of rental houses: e.g., insurance, essentials of a valid contract, and rental marketing strategies.

Lao-tzu: *Tao Te Ching*
The *Tao Te Ching* gives reader's an insight into the universal Way, with useful concepts for living your life—and oh yes, for managing rental houses, too.

THE MANAGEMENT SYSTEM

There are many translations of Lao tzu's work. The first one I read was *The Way of Life*, translated by Raymond B. Blakney and published by The New American Library, New York, 1955. It has great explanatory notes.

A more recent translation, which has beautiful photographs of nature interspersed with text, is *Tao Te Ching*, translated by Gia-fu and Jane English and published by Vintage Books, New York, 1972.

Peters, Thomas J and Robert H. Waterman, Jr.: *In Search of Excellence*, Warner, New York, 1982.

When I read this best-seller, I realized that the same concepts that make little management systems work well apply to huge corporations as well.

Townsend, Robert: *Further Up the Organization: How to Stop Management from Stifling People and Strangling Productivity*, Knopf, New York, 1984.

This is an excellent guide to letting people participate in management, so that everyone can help everyone else to succeed and have a good time doing it.

In addition to the above-mentioned publications, John Schaub gives outstanding lectures around the country on how to buy and manage single-family homes. One of his lectures is on tape and can be obtained from

Impact Publishing Company
2110 Omega Rd., Suite A
San Ramon, CA 94583

9

COMMON PROBLEMS

When I was in Hawaii training to become a Peace Corps volunteer for the Philippines, I was asked by the camp psychologist how I thought I would adjust to life there. I replied, "Okay, I think." The psychologist then said, "So you don't think you'll have any problems?" I looked at him quizzically, and responded, "Of course I'll have problems. Why should living in the Philippines be different than the rest of my life?"

Having problems and frustrations is just part of life. You solve or mitigate some problems and others will occur. This is to be expected. Don't be upset when they come. Do, though, try to avoid problems as much as possible. If some problems are unavoidable, try to understand the causes of each problem in order to solve it. Then attempt to arrange things in such a way that the problem will not arise again in the future.

In this chapter we'll go over some of the most common situations that owners face, and suggest possible ways to handle them.

FIVE MAJOR WAYS TO AVOID PROBLEMS

The best way to handle problems is to avoid them. To avoid major management hassles:

1. Choose a structurally sound house.
2. Choose responsible tenants.

3. Set up a clear management system which both you and your tenants accept as fair.

4. Be responsive to tenant complaints and suggestions. (Remember, though, that being responsive does not always mean saying "Yes.")

5. Understand that there is practically no way that you can over-communicate with your tenants.

Even if you have done all five things reasonably well, some problems will inevitably occur in your house. On the other hand, you are not likely to have the kinds of problems common to owners who rent houses in a conventional way to families or groups.

For example, it is highly unlikely that you wouldn't know that a tenant has unexpectedly moved out on you. The other tenants in the house would report the disappearance at once. It is also highly unlikely that you would ever be locked out of your rental house. Some troublesome tenants in conventional rental arrangements change the locks on the doors, barring entrance to the owner. Singles wouldn't dare try such a maneuver, because they would be locking out their fellow tenants. If the housekeeping became too slovenly, you could rest assured that at least one or two members of the household would alert you to what is going on—whereas managers whose tenants have conventional leases are often shocked to see the condition of their rental houses when they make their annual inspections.

Here are some problems that you might encounter when you rent to singles.

TEN COMMON PROBLEMS

Late Payment of Rent

My rental agreement doesn't contain a penalty if a tenant pays the rent late. I rely on "moral suasion," which to date has proved highly effective. If I haven't received a rent check by the fourth day of the month, I phone the late-paying tenant to ask why.

Other owners, however, have a clause in their agreement which says something similar to this:

If payment of rent is received by Owner after the (fifth) day of the month, Tenant covenants and agrees to pay the sum of ($25) as a late charge.

Some late-charge clauses also say that the tenant shall in addition pay a certain sum (e.g., $2) per day for each day that the rent is not received after the fifth day. Please be aware, however, that some courts have ruled that an owner cannot collect a late-payment penalty in excess of the costs incurred. A $15 or $25 administrative charge may be acceptable—considering the time, letters, and telephone calls a landlord made to collect the late rent—but a $75 charge might be questioned if the tenant disputed the amount in court.

Another method to encourage tenants to pay rent on time is to set the rent between $15 and $25 higher than you originally planned to. You then offer the tenants a $15 to $25 rent reduction if they pay the rent on or before the first of the month.

I've used this rent reduction method with an otherwise good tenant who habitually forgot to pay rent until reminded. At the end of the year, when it was time to raise the rent, I sent the tenant the following addendum:

Addendum to the Rental Agreement

This is an addendum to the rental agreement originally signed on February 3, 1982, between _____(Tenant) and Doreen Bierbrier (Owner) for the property located at _____ .

It is mutually agreed that the rent will increase to $315 per month as of March 1, 1983. However, if the rent for any month is received by the Owner on or before the first of that month, the rent due for that month will be only $295.

Tenant	date	Owner	date

By using the rent reduction method, you will make your tenants much happier than if you had penalized them with a late charge. The one tenant with whom I had to have this agreement now often gleefully comes over with the rent on or before the first of the month so she can triumphantly pay her special "lower" rent. Occasionally, she still forgets to pay the rent on time, but then I eagerly call her to collect my extra $20 under the guise of collecting the "full" rent this month.

Please note: The example I have given is for tenants who have every intention of paying the full rent on time each month. I have never had a tenant who consciously attempted to make late rent payments regularly. If you have tenants who make up heart-breaking stories on more than one or two occasions, you need to explain to them that you need the full amount of rent on time each month. If the rent continues to come in haphazardly, you may want to proceed to the section on "Owner-Initiated Terminations."

Nonpayment of Rent

I don't believe in nonpayment of rent for any reason whatsoever. Interestingly, although I've never verbally laid down the law on this issue, no tenant had ever tried to test me by withholding the rent. The closest one tenant came was when he told me that his waterbed business was going into bankruptcy and that he wasn't sure he could pay next month's rent.

I said, "You've been an excellent tenant for over a year. If you need a place to stay when you leave, you can sleep on my sofa in the living room for a couple of weeks. You've already paid the last month's rent, so you don't have to worry about that. Just give me a written note saying that you're leaving, so I can start showing your place to potential renters as soon as possible."

The tenant paid his rent on time the following month, and I never heard another word from him about not being able to pay the rent.

Renting is a business. Your tenants have parents, brothers, sisters, and friends if they must borrow money to pay the rent. It is not your responsibility to subsidize a tenant to the tune of $200 or $300 per month. When a tenant doesn't pay rent, that money will come out of your own pocket to pay for the mortgage. Further, the other tenants in the house will be given a bad example to follow, should they ever run into financial difficulty.

The sooner you get the nonpaying tenant out, the better. If you now have such a tenant, proceed to the section on "Owner-Initiated Terminations."

Poor Yard Maintenance

Poor yard maintenance is another problem which owners of rental houses may encounter. The grass may not be mowed as often as you would like to see it mowed; hedges may not get cut back; roses may not get pruned; leaves may not get raked. And a poorly maintained yard can be a major expense to remedy, as well as an irritant in the neighborhood.

What can you do?

Well, in part, you can create conditions which encourage your tenants to maintain the yard. Make sure that they have a lawn mower and a rake. Don't say anything if the lawn is a little shaggy, but if it really starts getting out of hand, mention the problem to the household. If the lawn still doesn't get mowed, your next step could be to suggest that they hire someone to mow the lawn. If action still isn't taken, you may explain to the household that you will hire someone to mow the lawn and will present the household with the bill.

Actually, the lawns at all of my houses have been mowed on a more or less regular basis, and I've never had to say a word to my tenants . . . well, come to think of it, I did have to mention the shaggy lawn to a household on one occasion. Weeding and pruning are more problematic. I've resigned myself to weeds and crabgrass. As long as the lawn is green and is mowed, I don't care about the weeds.

If some plants or bushes (such as roses or hedges) require heavy pruning, consider pulling them out. For one house with an exceptionally tall and heavy hedge, I arranged with a neighbor to split the cost of having it pruned.

Some houses have yards with steep slopes, and it's difficult for tenants to mow the lawn on a slope. Consider planting ivy or some other ground cover on the slope. That way it won't need mowing.

Cars Parked Off the Driveway

If your tenants can physically do it, they will park their cars by the side of the driveway when another tenant's car is already in the driveway. The tires will make deeper and deeper ruts in the yard. Eventually, the ruts will be deep enough to hold rain water and form a muddy pond.

Even if you ask your tenants not to park off the driveway, the temptation is usually too great for them. What can you do? Plant shrubs and flower beds alongside the driveway. Or make a rock garden—with jagged rocks alongside the driveway.

Sloppy Housekeeping

If I enter a house and see newspapers lying around and beds unmade, what do I say? Nothing. How your tenants choose to live is their own business.

On the other hand, if dirty dishes are stacked up, the garbage has not been put outside, and open food is lying around, I would definitely say something. This is a health and sanitation hazard. Explain your concern to them. If the situation is very bad, I would let the household know that you plan to make a surprise visit within the next few weeks to make sure the condition has improved. Or you can rely on other tenants in the household to make periodic reports to you on the condition of the house. Usually, at least one or two tenants in the household should be on your side. If the sanitation hazard persists, let the chief offender(s) know that you fear for the safety of the household, and that you will regretfully have to ask the offender(s) to leave. See "Owner-Initiated Terminations."

Bounced Checks

On 3 occasions in 8 years, tenants' checks have been returned to me for insufficient funds. One was a bank error.

If a check is returned to you, first phone the tenant to let her know that it bounced. Ask why. Then regardless of the explanation (especially if you have a relatively new tenant who has no track record with you), let her know that you believe her but need the rent. Ask the tenant to come over within 24 hours to pay the rent either with cash, a cashier's check, or a certified check.

If you know the tenant well, and trust her—and if she explains that the check was returned because of a bank error, or that she now has sufficient funds in the account to cover the check—then believe her. Nonetheless, go immediately to the bank and cash that check. Phone the tenant again if the bank still refuses to honor the check. Explain that you trust her and are willing to wait another day, but that you must have the rent in hand. Ask her what you should do; let her know that it's her option whether she wants you to try the bank again or wants to come on over to your home with a payment which will be immediately negotiable. If the tenant does not cover the check, proceed to the section on "Owner-Initiated Terminations."

Most rental agreements have a clause which states:

> Tenant agrees to pay Owner an administrative charge of ($25) for each check returned for insufficient funds or for any other reason.

I don't bother with the clause, because I am sure that when an occasional check bounces it's an oversight on the tenant's part and that he or she will make the check good immediately on notice. It's punishment enough for the culprit to have to scurry to the bank for cash or for a negotiable check and then to run over to my house to give it to me in person.

If you receive more than one bounced check from a tenant in the course of a year, it's time to have a chat with that tenant. Three bounced checks within a year and the tenant should be out, as far as I'm concerned.

Tenants who bounce checks should be made to realize that a bounced check sets off a whole chain reaction. Your check to the mortgage company could be returned for insufficient funds if you were counting on all of the rent checks to be good. You would then have to pay a penalty fee yourself. At the very least, you would have to make an extra run to the bank with the new check.

Unreported Repair Problems

The usual cause of tenant failure to report repair problems is twofold:

1. Tenants feel that the owner won't be responsive.
2. Tenants are afraid that they will have to pay for the repair themselves.

The best way to encourage your tenants to report problems is to fix problems as soon as possible after they are reported. If it is impossible to fix something right away, at least let your tenants know that you are trying.

As a rule, tenants will immediately report problems which affect their comfort—like clogged plumbing. But whatever the problem, they will be quicker to report a tenant-caused problem when they know that the owner won't get mad at them, and will give them useful information about how to fix the problem as quickly and as cheaply as possible.

Repeated Appliance Breakdown

Sometimes owners are informed in short succession that the water heater needs to be replaced, that the washer and dryer need major repairs, and that the refrigerator isn't freezing.

Many owners jump to the conclusion that the tenants are mistreating the appliances, which may or may not be true.

You should of course check with the tenants in the household to make sure that they are using the appliances correctly. But you should also be aware of the possibility that your appliances have all reached the end of their useful lives at about the same time. It stands to reason that new appliances may have been installed in the house at the time it was built. The 15-year-old washer may give out at about the same time as the 15-year-old dryer, which may require replacement at about the same time as the 15-year-old water heater.

For your interest, I'm including in the Appendix a chart showing the expected useful lives of major appliances.

Guests Staying Too Long

If the guest of one of your tenants is staying for a limited time and there are no complaints from the other tenants in the household, I keep my eyes shut to the situation.

If a girlfriend or a boyfriend actually moved in with the intention of staying, or if there were any complaints from another tenant, I would feel forced to ask the tenant to ask his or her friend to leave. If the tenant did not meet my request, I would ask the tenant to leave. See "Owner-Initiated Terminations."

Wear and Tear

Most leases specifically exempt a tenant from having to pay for what is termed "reasonable wear and tear." Yet this term is often subject to different interpretations by tenants and owners. Quite frankly, there aren't always clear guidelines for distinguishing between what is damage and what is wear and tear.

Obviously, holes in the wall, where the tenant used it as a dartboard, or cigarette burns in the wall-to-wall carpeting are clearly damage. But what about the nail hole where the tenant put up a picture? And what about a dent in the refrigerator? There are no clear answers to these questions.

Owners need to realize that nothing lasts forever. Carpets wear out, paint chips and peels, and doors and windows warp. The costs of routine maintenance and of replacing worn appliances and carpeting should be borne by the owner. These costs, after all, are covered in part by the rent and in part by IRS depreciation allowances.

TENANT-INITIATED TERMINATIONS

Almost all terminations will be amicably initiated by your tenants. Common reasons tenants leave are because they are getting married, they are moving to another state, or they have gotten a promotion and have decided to take more expensive accommodations.

Be positive toward the outgoing tenant, no matter how disappointed you might be. Let the outgoing tenant know you are really sorry to see her go. You are sad for yourself, but happy for her. There's no point in terminating your business relationship on an unhappy note.

Once a tenant has given notice, discuss the upcoming vacancy with the remaining tenants. Ask them what type of replacement they would like to have and when they would be available to meet prospective tenants. The process for finding a replacement tenant is the same as the procedure for tenant selection described in Chapter 7.

Your last official communication with departing tenants will be the letter you send them along with the remainder of their security deposit. A sample letter follows:

October 4, 1985

Barbara Bates
2163 Lee Highway, #10
Arlington, VA 22201

Dear Barbara,

At last—your security deposit. Anne gave me copies of the last utility bills yesterday, and we prorated your share. I paid her for the following:

C & P Telephone	$13.91
Water & Sewage	13.25
Gas	3.73
Electricity	17.19
Total	$48.07

I believe I owe you $101.93 from your original deposit of $150. Please feel free to check the math and the bills. If you have any questions, you are welcome to phone Anne or me.

Barbara, I very much appreciated having you as a tenant these last 2 years, and I wish you and Don the best.

Sincerely,

Doreen

Doreen Bierbrier

Enclosures:
  Check for $101.93
  Copies of bills

OWNER-INITIATED TERMINATIONS

For more than half of the sections on common problems, I have asked you to look under this section. Owner-initiated terminations is a solution of last resort and should be used very rarely, for it will invariably wind up hurting both you and your tenant. It should only be used with extreme reluctance.

The best way to terminate a tenancy is by convincing a tenant to give you notice. People always feel better when they are the rejecter rather than the rejectee. To get them to reject you, you have to explain the nature of the problem and let them know that the situation can't go on this way. They can then tell you either that they will change their ways or that your position is unreasonable and they're going to look for other accommodations—so there! In the latter event, you can look dejected and say, "Well, if you think it's for the best."

If the problem tenant does not give you notice within 1 or 2 months, or if you don't have time to dilly dally, you will have to take the termination process into your own hands.

Now I'm not suggesting that you act like the queen in *Alice in Wonderland* whose solution to most problems was to shriek, "Off with their heads!" although nobody actually got executed. Quite the contrary. Once your decision is made, you should behave like the executioner in the following story:

In olden days in China, criminals convicted of a capital offense were beheaded.

One particular executioner took great pride in his work. He honed his blade so sharply that prisoners felt no pain in being executed. To spare prisoners the terror of kneeling at the chopping block, this executioner would quickly dispatch them as they climbed the scaffolding to the block.

The executioner's reputation spread. Prisoners specifically asked for him when they were given the death sentence.

The executioner kept perfecting his technique. And then one day, much to everyone's amazement, a prisoner reached the top of the scaffolding with his head still on his shoulders. The prisoner looked at the executioner, and demanded to know why he hadn't been executed yet.

The executioner smiled and replied, "Please nod."

If you make a decision to terminate a tenancy, carry it out. Try to ensure that the procedure is carried out as efficiently and as painlessly as possible—so that your tenant feels minimal pain, preserves maximum self-respect, and is at the same time out of your house.

First, purge yourself of any traces of vindictiveness or bitterness. There is no place for that. We are talking about business.

Second, identify the problem, and separate the problem from the tenant. In other words, the problem is not that *Mary isn't paying her rent;* the problem is that *you are not receiving rent which you must have to pay the mortgage.* The problem is not that *Joe is an inconsiderate slob;* the problem is that *you are worried that the garbage thrown on the floor is a health hazard and is disturbing the rest of the household.* Your tenant should be encouraged to see the problem through your eyes. Do not get angry with your tenant, either verbally or in writing. Never threaten. The main emotion which you should seek to convey, and which you should indeed feel, is one of regret that things have not worked out.

Once you have made the decision that a tenant will be leaving, speak with the other tenants in the household. Keep them fully informed as to what you are about to do and why. They will be on your side, particularly if the person being asked to leave has caused problems in the household.

Then get in touch with the problem tenant. Say something complimentary, identify the problem, and set a target date for the tenant to leave. Next, put all of this in writing and send it to the tenant by certified mail. A letter sent by certified mail carries with it the aura that the request is official, and that it is the first step, if need be, in an inexorable legal process.

Ideally, this should be done just after the tenant has paid rent. You will thus be giving the tenant closer to 60 days of notice instead of 30.

Here is an example of a termination letter:

June 10, 1985

Sheila Weber
1114 Stewart St.
Arlington, VA 22205

Dear Sheila,

As you know, you moved into the house on Stewart Street about 6 months ago.

In many ways I have considered myself fortunate to have had

you as a tenant. You always paid the rent on time and pitched in with the household chores.

I have been aware for some time that your friend, Steve, has moved into the household. Now, personally, I like Steve. However, Arlington County only permits 4 unrelated people to live in a single-family dwelling. In addition, your rental agreement does not permit long-term guests. But you know this; we've talked about this matter before.

The only way I know to resolve the problem at this point is to ask both of you to find other accommodations. Only a 30-day notice is required, according to the terms of our rental agreement, but you are welcome to stay until August 1 if you need the extra time. Let me know if you decide to move out earlier; if another tenant moves in before August 1, I'll prorate the rent and return that portion to you.

As things now stand, I'll be advertising and showing your room starting in July, and will try to coordinate schedules with you in order to inconvenience you as little as possible. I'm sorry things didn't work out.

Sincerely,

Doreen

Doreen Bierbrier

Evictions

Most books on real estate management devote a chapter, or at least several pages, to the eviction process. But I don't plan to discuss the legal process of eviction. If you follow the advice in this book, hopefully you will never have to go through a formal eviction—and it's just as well that you don't consider it an option.

Although the eviction process will eventually get the tenant out, you will often have a very disgruntled tenant on your hands in the meantime. Disgruntled tenants are liable to commit vandalism, to be obnoxious toward prospective tenants when they come to look at the place, and to try to linger on, despite court orders. They can make life generally unpleasant for you and for the other tenants in the household. Further, going through an eviction process will cost you money on top of the money you may already have lost from unpaid rent or vandalism. And even if the court requires the tenant to reimburse you, good luck trying to collect the money.

It is far better to cooperate with the tenant you've asked to leave. If possible, give close to 2 months of notice right after the tenant has made a rent payment. If the tenant needs to stay a few extra days, try to work it out. Help the tenant to leave in the least uncomfortable way possible.

If you still feel that you must learn how to carry out a formal eviction, you can get this information by phoning your local government offices. Ask to speak with the court clerk or with a member of the tenant-landlord commission.

SUMMING UP HOW TO HANDLE TENANT-RELATED PROBLEMS

Before we go on, I'd like to sum up one of the principles of my management style: *Vulnerability can be beneficial; weakness is a disaster.*

Your tenants should know that you are dependent on them. After all, if they really wanted to, they could cripple you financially. They could destroy the house. They could all leave at once. They could never be available to meet new tenants. You are vulnerable. Curiously, if your tenants sense that they could hurt you if they chose to, they won't. On the contrary, they will usually try to protect you.

On the other hand, if you are weak—if you compromise your principles—you will be destroyed. If a tenant says, "Don't raise the rent, or I'll leave," tell the tenant "I hope you decide to stay, but the rent is going up." Even if it will mean a vacancy, do not be intimidated. Whatever your vulnerability to financial loss, don't show weakness.

If tenants know that you will stick to your principles even if it hurts you financially, they won't try either to threaten you or to get away with something that isn't fair.

I am reminded of the story of two masters of the martial arts who met one day. The younger master challenged the other to a fight to see who would be champion. The older master did not want to fight, and said, "If two tigers fight, one will be severely injured, and the other will surely die." But the young challenger kept prodding and prodding. Reluctantly, the older master agreed to the fight, and they met at the appointed time the next day. There was a moment of stillness as each sized up the other. Just before the attack was to begin, each assumed the martial stance. After a moment, the challenger relaxed and said in concession to the other, "You have won."

People sense the strength, weakness, and fear of others. If your tenants know intuitively that you will keep your word and that you will quickly enforce the rules, which they know to be fair, both for yourself and for the household, they will rarely try to oppose you.

So far we have talked about tenant-instigated problems. The rest of this chapter deals with other situations with which owners must grapple.

RENT INCREASES

Tenants will be surprised to learn that one of the most distasteful problems an owner faces is how to raise the rent. Specifically, owners want to know when to raise the rent, how much to raise the rent, and how to present the rent increase to tenants in a palatable way, so that they won't get upset and leave.

When to Raise the Rent

The best time to raise the rent is before a new tenant moves in. The new tenant, never having paid your rent at the old rate, won't likely be upset with your new rate. As far as the new tenant is concerned, the rental rate at your house is merely a *fait accompli.*

It is more difficult to raise the rent for tenants who have been with you awhile. To many owners, the timing of rent increases is a total mystery. "I hadn't raised the rent in years," one will say, "and when I finally raised it just slightly, my tenants left; some even moved to more expensive accommodations. What have I done wrong?"

Most often, the source of the problem is the owner's unpredictability. Tenants don't like to be taken by surprise. An unexpected increase in rent may offend their sensibilities. Tenants usually will not balk at a rent increase as long as they know from the outset that they can expect it on a regular basis—generally once a year.

193

How Much to Raise the Rent

It is difficult to know how much to raise the rent, because there are no clear guidelines or formulas.

You may want to check the classifieds to find out what rates are currently being asked for similar rentals. You may want to phone a few large apartment buildings in your locality to find out the percentage rents have increased in the past year for efficiencies and one-bedroom apartments. Ultimately, though, you have to pull a figure for the rent increase out of the air.

How to Present the Rent Increase

About 60 days before your scheduled increase, just after you have received a rent payment, send a letter to the tenant who is due for a rent increase. Psychologically the 60-day period will give the tenant time to get used to the idea of the increase; the impact won't be immediate.

The letter should state how much the new rent will be and when it will be due. Remind the tenant to pay an additional amount that first month to cover the increase in the last month's rent.

How do you explain the increase to your tenants? Many owners and management firms have marvelously inventive rent increase letters. Usually the letters say something to the effect that although management has tried everything it knows to keep costs down, costs have risen—maintenance costs, repair costs, taxes. Therefore, management is being forced by circumstances beyond its control to raise the rent. If the rent isn't raised, management will go bankrupt, be forced to sell the building, and become destitute. By the time you have finished reading the letter, you are almost ready to give management more rent than they've asked for, just to help them out.

Now, such rent increase letters are not completely concocted out of thin air. Expenses have indeed continued to rise. Nonetheless, when push comes to shove, rents are primarily set by the marketplace. If the managers of an apartment complex increase the rent exorbitantly because the boiler had to be replaced and the roof repaired that year, they will find their tenants departing for comparable apartments where the rent is much lower. Conversely, I have yet to see an owner reduce the rent because no major repairs were needed that year and none would be needed in the foreseeable future.

Many owners find it indelicate to tell their tenants the truth— that renting is a business. Like any other business, you are trying to make a healthy profit while keeping your customers satisfied by providing excellent service at competitive prices. You set your rent by doing a market analysis (however crude) and then by doing your best to set competitive rates.

Here's an example of the kind of rent increase letter I write. However you write yours, try to personalize it for each tenant you address.

January 3, 1985

Dan Klein
123 Main Street
Arlington, VA 22207

Hi, Dan,

It's hard to believe that as of March 1 you will have been with me for 3 years. That makes you the "old-timer" of the household.

As of March 1, your rent will go from $295 to $315. The rent payment in March will be $335—which is the $315 plus $20 to be applied to the last month's rent.

Generally, rent increases in this area seem to be about 10 percent this year. Your rent increase of $20 is only a 7 percent rise. I'm trying to keep my rent increases below market rate for my tenants.

Dan, I've really appreciated having you as a tenant these last few years. If you have any questions, don't hesitate to call me.

Sincerely,

Doreen

Doreen Bierbrier

THE MAINTENANCE SCHEDULE

Your tenants have the major role in taking care of the house on a day-to-day basis. They are the ones who will vacuum the wall-to-wall carpets, clean out the lint collector in the dryer, and mar or not mar the walls. There is no way you can monitor the daily behavior of the tenants in your house. You have no choice but to choose your tenants carefully, and then to trust them.

You do, however, have a role in house maintenance. It's helpful if you set up a maintenance schedule to ensure that essential maintenance tasks get done on a regular, rather than a hit-and-miss, basis. Most of the tasks will be routine preventive maintenance. Other tasks, like replacing a worn-out carpet or painting the outside of a house, should only be done when needed.

At the beginning of every year, I make out a separate maintenance schedule for each of my houses. The accompanying sheet illustrates what a completed maintenance schedule might look like. Let's go over each of the tasks on the sheet.

Annual Inspection

Owners should visit their houses at least once a year to inspect the premises for damage or disrepair.

Phone the household a week before you'd like to visit, and schedule a mutually agreeable time with your tenants. Not all of them have to be there, but at least one tenant should be with you when you make the inspection.

When you phone, ask the tenant to find out from the others about any problems the household may be experiencing—leaky faucets, the lack of some caulking in the bathroom, loose wallpaper—whatever. Also ask what improvements, if any, they would like to see in the house. This information should be given to you before you make the visit.

When you come over, you may want to bring tools and supplies to fix some minor problems while you are there. You'll also have done your homework and gotten rough estimates of how much the suggested improvements will cost.

To make a check of the premises, take the inspection sheet you used when you were buying the place. Make sure that all of the

196

MAINTENANCE SCHEDULE

Address: 123 Main Street

Year: 1984

Task	Scheduled	Performed	Person/Firm
1. Annual inspection	April	4/17	me
2. Gutters cleaned	November	11/21	Patrick Hayes
3. Heating/cooling system serviced	November	11/13	J. R. Stephens
4. Water and sewage payment checked	April	4/17	me
	June	6/15	me
	December	12/10	me
5. Termite inspection	NA		
6. Christmas gift for tenants	December	12/11	me
7. Other			
Clean carpets	October	10/5	Mr. Steam Clean
Paint garage	May	5/30	2 tenants and me

197

inventory listed on your Inventory Sheet is still in the house. Check to see if there is additional damage beyond normal wear and tear.

After the inspection is over, report what you have found to your tenants. At the same time, discuss any concerns they may have. If you have the money, and if you think that an improvement suggested by the tenants would increase the value of the property, let them know when you plan to schedule the work. If they have suggested several improvements and you don't have enough money for all of them, ask them to select the one improvement they want most. Then get it for them.

Gutters Cleaned

Most gutters should be cleaned at least once a year. One of the most common reasons for water damage in a house is that exterior water is not draining away from the house properly.

If you clean the gutters yourself, you will quickly learn how much debris can accumulate in gutters. Houses surrounded by trees may need to have their gutters cleaned several times a year.—Other houses may have gutters with barely a leaf in them.

When you clean the gutters, check to make sure that they are firmly attached to the house. Also be sure that the downspouts drain water off at a distance from the house.

Heating/Cooling System Serviced

Different kinds of heating/cooling systems require different maintenance schedules. If they are not serviced, they become inefficient, increasing the utility bills. This is bad for the tenants. Unmaintained heating/cooling systems also don't last as long. This is bad for you.

Oil burners need to be cleaned twice a year. Many owners have a service contract with a firm to provide automatic routine maintenance.

Some gas furnaces and boilers require oiling twice a year—when the cold season starts and when the season is over. Other furnaces, boilers, and heat pumps just need servicing once every several years. Find out what the maintenance requirements are for the heating/cooling system in each of your houses and provide maintenance accordingly.

While you are lubricating your furnace, or while you are making a house inspection, look at the flame in gas furnaces. It should be blue. If the flame is burning yellow, it means that the furnace needs to be adjusted or cleaned.

Water and Sewage Payment Checked

Your tenants will be responsible for paying water and sewage charges if you follow my rental agreement. If these bills are not paid, a lien can be placed against your property and you will be forced to pay the bills long after your tenants have left.

Twice a year, check with the public department which handles billing for water and sewage in your locality, and make sure that the payments are up to date on each of your houses.

Termite Inspection

Termites are common in my area of the country. I don't schedule a termite inspection every year, but having that task on the schedule reminds me that I may want to consider having a professional inspection that year.

Christmas Gift for Tenants

I usually buy a holiday gift for my households as a way of saying "thank you" for being considerate tenants. The gifts in the past have been a dried fruit platter, a box of expensive chocolates, and a fruit cake—something the tenants can split four ways.

Do not buy a gift for your tenants unless you sincerely like them and want to show your appreciation. A gift given in a perfunctory manner without genuine affection will mean nothing to you and nothing to your tenants.

Other

Depending on the idiosyncrasies of the house, you may want to put such special tasks as these under "Other":

- kudzu sprayed
- chimney cleaned

- lawn dethatched
- carpets cleaned

REPAIRS AND MAINTENANCE

You may want to put some repairs and other maintenance jobs on your House Maintenance Schedule under "Other" if you know about them in advance. For example, you may want to put down:

- Paint the garage.
- Fix the loose banister.
- Replace the living room light fixture.

Other repair jobs will just crop up unexpectedly and will have to be remedied on the spur of the moment.

You will save yourself a fair amount of money if you learn to:

- change switches and outlets
- unclog plumbing
- fix leaky faucets
- replace electrical fixtures
- remove and replace sink traps
- replace the mechanisms inside toilet tanks
- spackle walls
- caulk
- paint

For those of you who are relatively inexperienced with household repairs, don't worry. The best way to learn is simply to jump in and do them. There are many excellent books available on household repairs and maintenance. I primarily rely on the Reader's Digest *Complete Do-It-Yourself Manual*. It's excellent. For $1 you can get a small corollary book by the Reader's Digest called *Women's Guide to Household Emergencies* (I suspect you'll find it useful even if you're a man). Many a time I've gone to a property, Reader's Digest guide in hand, to read the "recipe" for the cure of a problem while I'm doing the job.

Of course, the best way to learn how to do something is to watch people who know what they are doing. A neighbor may help you, but usually you will hire a professional carpenter, electrician, or plumber for a task you don't know how to do. Watch them work and ask a lot of questions. The good ones enjoy explaining their work to an eager student. You'll soon learn that some jobs are quite simple; for example, you may never again need to pay an electrician $30 to change a light switch, because you may learn to do it yourself in a few minutes for a couple of dollars. On the other hand, you'll learn that some jobs require specialized tools and are beyond your capabilities.

If you are a good customer, professionals will often give you free guidance, explaining over the phone how you can fix something yourself. The personnel of plumbing supply stores, hardware outlets, and electrical supply stores will give you excellent advice as well.

A SIMPLE SOLUTION TO MANY REPAIR PROBLEMS

Rather than try to explain how to fix common problems, let me suggest a simple general solution to all problems: *If something goes wrong, make sure your tenants try the easiest solution first.*

When your tenants phone you about problems, here's some expert advice you can give:

- If the garbage disposer isn't working, make sure your tenants press the reset button.
- If an air-conditioning unit isn't working, ask whether it's plugged in, and whether the circuit breaker switch is in the ON position.
- If the toilet is clogged, ask if they have tried using the plunger.

You will be amazed at how many problems you can remedy by telephone.

I recommend that all owners know how to make minor repairs. Even if, eventually, you decide to hire someone else to do the work, you'll still find it valuable to understand the costs involved and the explanations of the workers you have hired. You'll also be more likely to have a relationship based on mutual respect with the people you're doing business with.

At some point, however, owners will begin to ask themselves if it wouldn't be worth it to hire someone to do many of the repair and maintenance tasks that have to be done. For one thing, the expenses incurred are tax deductible. So, if you are in the 50 percent tax bracket, your $40 repair bill would only cost you $20 after factoring in your tax savings. Hiring someone would also save you from the hassle factor. While it might take you 3 frustrating hours to replace the mechanism in a toilet tank, a plumber might do it in 1 hour, and do a better job at that.

If owners doggedly do all the work on several rental houses, they could burn themselves out and come to hate their investments. There's no sense to that. If you have an investment, you may as well enjoy it.

No matter how adept you are, I suspect you'll come to agree with me that good, honest, reliable plumbers, electricians, and carpenters are worth their weight in gold.

How to find good, honest, reliable Tradespeople

If you own several rental houses, you should come to know professional tradespeople better than you know your lawyer (hopefully, you'll be utilizing your tradespeople more than your lawyer). You need to find one or two people you can trust in each of the following fields:

- roofing
- painting
- heating and air-conditioning
- plumbing
- electrical
- carpentry

In addition, a handyperson who can repair a loose banister, put in a ceiling, fix leaky faucets, and clean the gutters all on the same visit is indeed a treasure.

I am very fortunate to have found and worked with some excellent people. I'd like to take the opportunity to thank my favorite landscape architect, Don Bowman; my plumber, J. R. Stephens, his sidekick, "Dusty," and his wife, Dottie; Block's Plumbing Supply; Patrick Hayes; Quality Electric; Mark Sather and his wife, Denise; Pond Roofing; Robert Morrison of Morrison Waterproofing; Fred Mosser of Southern Exterminating; and Allen Gerstel of Office Furniture Outlet.

How do you find good tradespeople? Many consumer guides will give you the following advice:

- Ask neighbors and friends for the names of people who have done good work for them.
- Check the yellow pages, and phone the firms in your area; compare prices for the same work.
- Check the Better Business Bureau to see if any complaints have been lodged against the firm you are thinking of hiring.
- Make sure that the person doing the work has adequate insurance, so that you won't be liable if a worker has an accident on the job.

I have also found that the staffs of plumbing supply stores and of other outlets in which contractors do business will be happy to recommend good tradespeople. Many tradespeople in one field also know tradespeople in others and would be glad to give you the names of some.

In addition, the staff of county inspection units know good work when they see it. They also know the reputations of many of the tradespeople in the county. Find out when the county inspector is coming to check on the furnace or bathroom you had installed. Then, accompanying the inspector through your house, ask him what he looks for when he makes an inspection, and ask which tradespeople the inspector thinks do good work. Inspectors will often tell you which ones they think are good and which to stay away from.

Danger Signals

If you are looking for reliable tradespeople, watch for these danger signals. Avoid people who:

- dress too well
- drive flashy cars
- criticize many aspects of the house
- say the job will cost a lot, and can't think of any way to save you money when you ask if you can do something less expensive (e.g., the waterproofer who insists that you need an expensive French drain, and ignores your suggestions that you merely regrade around the house)
- talk incessantly about something other than their profession (e.g., the painter—or for that matter your doctor—who talks about investments in the stock market while purportedly examining your problem)

"Stand By Your Man"

Once you find people who provide prompt, competent service at fair prices, stick with them.

Get estimates on large jobs from two or three other tradespeople. Then compare their prices with that being asked by your steady tradesperson. If there is a large discrepancy in price, ask why the discrepancy exists. If the explanation is not satisfactory, you may want to consider hiring the new firm for that job. However, the cost of the job is only one factor. The cheapest price is not inexpensive if the work is shoddy and the service undependable. I'm almost always inclined to stick with people who have proved to be reliable, even if, at times, their bills may be somewhat higher than their competitors's estimates.

I vastly prefer to do business with people I know and trust. That way, although major jobs must be put in writing, most business can be conducted as my grandparents did business in the old country, where people's words were their bonds. These relationships don't get built overnight. They take years to develop. But believe me, they are worth it.

MISCELLANEOUS MANAGEMENT TIPS

- When you go on a trip, give your tenants the names and phone numbers of your tradespeople. If an emergency comes up while you are away, your tenants can check the list for the appropriate person, phone, and explain the nature of the problem. Let your tradespeople know that if, in their opinion, some work has to be done immediately while you are away, do it. You will cover the bill.

- When your tenants request some small improvement (such as putting locks on windows or painting their bedrooms), encourage them to buy the supplies themselves, to deduct the amount of the supplies from their rent, and to send you the receipt along with their rent check. If the task is simple, tenants can do the work themselves and save you time.

- When your tenants call you about a needed repair, ask them if anything else needs to be repaired, maintained, or painted. That way you or your handy person can perform several tasks on the same visit.

- If you plan to do some repairs or maintenance work yourself, try to plan it at a time when at least one tenant is home. Tenants appreciate seeing an owner do something other than collect the rent every month.

- Know which hardware stores are closest to each of the houses you own. Jot down their store hours on the list of phone numbers you keep, and check the list before leaving for a job. That way you will avoid the frustration of finding the hardware store closed when you try to pick up a part you need for the repair work you are in the middle of. Some people keep a notebook of hardware stores, lumber yards, and plumbing supply stores in their cars for easy access.

- Find out which neighbors near each rental house have ladders, wheelbarrows, and other equipment you may ask to borrow.

- If you ask them, many of the tradespeople who make repairs of one type in your house will report back to you on conditions of other types which they consider to be hazardous or caused by negligence in the household.

- People who specialize in one field, such as gutter cleaning, may offer you a discount if you mention that you own several houses that need the same service. Even if you don't own several houses, you can ask the neighbors near the rental house

205

if they need the same service; by grouping together, you all may be able to get a discount. The tradesperson will of course benefit too, having increased his earnings by working on several houses in one location.

- You may be able to save some money on major repairs and improvements by telling the tradesperson that you would be willing to pick up the supplies or do some of the simpler tasks yourself.

- Be cautious about buying used appliances from individuals. A used air-conditioning unit sold at a fantastically low price is not so great when you later discover that it doesn't cool properly. On the other hand, some private individuals have businesses on the side. They may specialize in repairing lawn mowers and have several on hand for sale. Others pick up refrigerators from apartment buildings being rehabilitated and sell them at a fraction of the original price. You can get some excellent buys from such individuals.

- Look for those outlets which sell major appliances that are new but have minor, cosmetic damage. It won't matter to you or your tenants if there is a small dent or scratch, and you may be able to save $50 to $100.

POINTS TO REMEMBER

- Here are five major ways to avoid management problems:

    - Choose a structurally sound house.
    - Choose responsible tenants.
    - Set up a clear management system.
    - Be responsive to tenant complaints and suggestions.
    - Communicate, communicate, communicate with tenants.

- You can solve most tenant-related problems by clearly explaining the nature of the problem to the tenant and by relying on moral suasion to get them to solve the problem.

- If possible, tenants should initiate their own terminations. If you must terminate a tenancy yourself, do the following:

- Get the support of the others in the household.
- Send a certified letter to the tenant who will be leaving; in this letter, explain the nature of the problem and set the last day of tenancy.
- Try to accommodate departing tenants, doing your best to make the termination as comfortable as possible.

- Let your tenants understand from the outset that modest rent increases will be made on a regular and predictable basis.

- Learn to do basic repair and maintenance work yourself.

- If something goes wrong, make sure that your tenants try the easiest solution first.

- Be loyal to those tradespeople who have given you prompt and competent service at a fair price.

FOR FURTHER INFORMATION

Complete Do-It-Yourself Manual, Reader's Digest, Pleasantville, New York, 1973.

Lowry, Albert J.: *How to Manage Real Estate Successfully—In Your Spare Time,* Simon and Schuster, New York, 1977.

Robinson, Leigh: *Landlording,* 3d ed., Express, Richmond, California, 1980.

U.S. Department of Agriculture, Extension Service: *Simple Home Repairs . . . Inside,* GPO 0–290–711, April 1973.

U.S. Department of Housing and Urban Development: *Protecting Your Housing Investment,* HUD–346–PA(7), 1980.

Many localities have state- or county-run agricultural extension services, which will provide you with valuable, free assistance. They can identify insects you bring to them and suggest ways of exterminating the pests. Among their many other services, they will test your soil and make recommendations to improve it.

For literature on how to work with a contractor, check with your local government offices.

10

RECORD KEEPING

Record keeping is often considered one of the least interesting topics for discussion. I don't know how to spice up this chapter, other than to tell you that if you read this section carefully, you may get a few ideas about how to increase your profits and lower your tax liability. Now that I have your attention, let's proceed.

WHAT RECORDS DO YOU NEED?

I don't believe in collecting information, unless I know what the information can be used for. As a result, I try to keep my record-keeping system as simple as possible. I have a small notebook in my car to record mileage related to my rental properties. At home, I have a large, month-to-month desk calendar and three record-keeping systems.

One of these three systems is a master *management schedule* for all of my houses. In addition, for each house I have a separate binder in which I keep the records and correspondence related to that individual property; these *house information binders*, as I refer to them, do not include month-to-month financial transactions. Instead, all of the financial transactions which occur in the course of a year are recorded in separate *financial records*, one for each house.

There is nothing fancy about these record-keeping systems. You can create your own management schedule and financial records by buying 3-ring, looseleaf notebooks. You may want to buy notebooks with different-colored covers, so that you can easily identify which notebook belongs to which property. In addition, you'll need to get some lined, 3-holed paper, a ruler, and a pen.

My house information binders are a little fancier. Each of the binders has six dividers inside, with two prongs at the top of each divider. I staple an accordian folder to the back for the warranties and other materials pertaining to the appliances in each household. You can get these specialized binders for a few dollars each at some stationery stores. You'll also have to buy a 2-holed paper punch to use on the documents you are collecting.

Let's go over each of the three record-keeping systems.

A Management Schedule

A management schedule is a master file for the scheduled chores which need to be performed at all of your houses.

There are twelve pages in the management schedule, one for each month. At the beginning of the year, write down on the appropriate page when each tenant is scheduled to be notified about his or her yearly rent increase. Make another entry under the month that the higher rent is supposed to be paid, to remind yourself to check whether the tenants are paying the new, higher rent when they are supposed to.

After all notifications of rent increases have been duly recorded, check the house maintenance schedule for each house. Transfer all tasks on the schedule sheets to your master management schedule, listing each task under the appropriate month. Jot down when the water and sewage bills have to be checked, when routine maintenance has to be performed, and when the scheduled repairs are to be made.

Look at the notebook at the beginning of each month to check what activities need to be performed or scheduled that month. At the end of the month, check the management schedule again to make sure that the tasks have been completed.

The accompanying example illustrates the format of a management schedule, along with typical tasks for October, November, and December, although ordinarily each month would have its own separate page.

MANAGEMENT SCHEDULE

October

Task	Scheduled	Done	Comments
Notify Jane Doe of 12/1 rent increase		x	Letter sent 10/3
Check water/sewage bills to make sure they've been paid			
• House 1		x	OK
• House 2		x	$72.05 due from last bill
• House 3		x	OK
Oil furnace motors			
• House 1	10/15	x	Scheduled with J. R. Stephens Co.
• House 2	NA		
• House 3	10/18	x	Me

November

Task	Scheduled	Done	Comments
Clean gutters	11/10		Scheduled with Patrick Hayes
• House 1		x	
• House 2		x	
• House 3		x	
Notify Mike Smith of 1/1 rent increase	NA		Moved

December

Task	Scheduled	Done	Comments
Check to see if Jane Doe paid higher rent	12/4	x	She forgot to pay toward last month's rent; has been called
Christmas gifts • House 1 • House 2 • House 3		 x x x	

A House Information Binder

It will prove helpful to you to prepare a separate house information binder for each of your properties. Each binder should contain most of the essential information and documentation pertaining to a particular rental house. But it should not contain your monthly financial transactions, which should be kept separately.

Each house information binder could contain the following sections:

1. Agreements and Rental Documents
   (a) tenant applications
   (b) rental agreements
   (c) management agreements
2. Incoming Correspondence
   (a) insurance policies
   (b) tax assessments
   (c) letters from tenants, lenders, utility companies, local government offices, etc.
3. Outgoing Correspondence
   (a) your letters to tenants, lenders, utility companies, local government offices, etc.
4. Additional Information
   (a) house information sheet
   (b) house maintenance schedule

    (c)   landscape plan
    (d)   contracts with firms making improvements to the house
    (e)   documentation of capital improvements

5. Settlement Documents
    (a)   deed of sale
    (b)   deed of trust
    (c)   settlement sheet
    (d)   purchase contract
    (e)   plat survey
    (f)   inspection report
    (g)   appraisal
    (h)   covenants or bylaws
    (i)   insurance documents

6. Warranties and Guarantees
    (a)   for major appliances
    (b)   from contractors

Periodically, the house information binders have to be purged of outdated documents. There's no point in keeping a copy of most old insurance policies or of most older correspondence.

From time to time, though, you'll need to look up information on a rental application, an insurance policy or warranty. For tax purposes, you'll also need the documentation for some of your settlement charges the year you bought your house; you'll need that information again when you sell your investment.

It's helpful to have all of the documentation for a single property in one place.

Financial Records

Keeping records of financial transactions is mandatory. The IRS requires it. Bookkeeping performed on a regular basis each month will also make your management system more efficient, for you will see at a glance which tenants are delinquent with the rent.

To some extent, the annual summation of your financial record will show you whether you are making or losing money. If you own and manage houses for the long haul, though, and don't expect to sell them in a year or two, the figures for an individual year won't mean as much. In some years you may have to replace a roof or a furnace, and you will see your profits eaten up. On paper, either you may not be making much in a particular year or you may feel as though you were rolling in profit.

As you read the rest of this chapter, please keep in mind that tax laws and interpretations change. Further, different laws may apply in specific situations. I strongly recommend that you find a tax advisor who is familiar with tax laws as they apply to real estate. At a minimum, you should have clear, well-organized records for your tax advisor. Ideally, you should know as much as you can about the tax laws— so that at least you can ask intelligent questions and make thoughtful suggestions about how you can decrease your tax liability.

To keep track of all financial transactions, take the different-colored 3-ring notebooks you have for each rental house you own and, in black ink, mark the address and the telephone number of the household on the cover. Divide the notebooks into three sections: "Income," "Expenses," and "Capital Expenditure." Let's go over each section.

Income

You need to record all revenue generated by each rental house under "Income."

When checks come in, immediately write "For Deposit Only" on the back of each check. If the rent is paid in cash, count the money in the presence of the tenant who paid it, give the tenant a receipt, and make a copy of the receipt for yourself. You can deposit the money immediately, if you choose, but place the copy of the receipt with your other checks which haven't been deposited yet, so you can record all the payments at the same time.

One day every month—let's say the fourth day of every month— record in the notebook for each house the payments its tenants have made that month. Note on a separate sheet of paper the names of any tenants from whom you haven't received rent. You will want to phone tenants delinquent as of that fourth day to find out why they haven't paid.

This is the format I use to record income:

INCOME

Date	Source of income	Item	Amount paid	Security deposit	Balance due

INCOME *cont'd.*

Let's go over the columns.

Date refers to the date you receive or record payment from your tenants.

Source of income will usually be your tenant.

Item will almost invariably be a rent payment or a security deposit. Save yourself time by simply using an "X" to indicate the routine payment of rent. But write in a brief description here if the income is for something else—such as for a late charge or for money collected from a tenant who damaged the floor.

Amount paid is the rent or any other monies collected (except for security deposits, which are recorded in the next column).

Security deposits are recorded separately, because they don't count as income when, at the end of the year, you total your rental income for the IRS. Security deposits don't count as anything until you actually charge a tenant for some expense and take the money from the tenant's

216

security deposit; the money you have deducted is then classified as income to you and is reported as such to the IRS. If you return a tenant's deposit in full, however, the IRS doesn't want to know anything about either the collection or the return of a security deposit. You will usually use the security deposit column only twice for each tenant—once when the tenant pays the deposit, and once when you return it. Use brackets around a sum of money to indicate a subtraction from your account.

Balance due should rarely be used. You record in this column the amount of money a tenant owes you. Sometimes, before a tenant moves in, I'll allow that tenant to make a partial payment toward the first and last month's rent and the security deposit. I then record the amount still owed in two places—in the "Balance due" column and on my desk calendar (on the date the tenant has promised to pay the outstanding balance). When the outstanding balance is paid, I record the income under "Amount paid" or "Security deposit" and then put a line through the amount that had been recorded under "Balance due."

In other situations, you may have an outstanding balance that remains on your books until the tenant leaves. Let's say that you have a charge for late payment of rent; a tenant pays the rent late one month, but refuses to pay the late charge. Record the unpaid late charge under "Balance due." When the tenant moves out, check to see if any outstanding balance remains on the books. If so, deduct that amount from the departing tenant's security deposit.

Expenses

There are more categories for expenses than for sources of income. To find out what headings to use, I suggest that you look under the "Rental and Royalty Expenses" section in IRS Schedule E, *Supplemental Income Schedule*. Using IRS headings for bookkeeping will save you the time of translating your own categories into IRS categories at tax time.

When you pay your bills, keep receipts of all your expenses. Either paperclip them to the back of each page where you have recorded the expense, or put them in a manila envelope. Hang on to your cancelled checks to prove that you paid your bills.

For your own records, you don't have to use all of the headings in Schedule E; you may never use such IRS categories as "Commissions" or "Utilities" or "Wages and Salary." At the beginning of each year, head a few sheets of paper with the major categories you are most likely to use, and place then under "Expenses" in your financial records for each house. My major headings are these:

- advertising
- cleaning and maintenance
- repairs
- supplies
- other expenses

The following are other major expenses, which I call end-of-the-year expenses:

- auto and travel
- insurance
- interest
- taxes

I usually wait for my end-of-the year statements from lenders to find out how much interest, taxes, and insurance I have paid for each property. Therefore, I don't keep track of the above expenses on a month-to-month basis in my financial records.

The auto and travel expenses include, in my case, only the expense incurred for mileage. I keep track of my mileage for each property in a notebook, kept in the glove compartment of my car. At the end of the year I tally up the mileage for each property. I then multiply my total mileage by the cost-per-mile allowance (which is given in the printed tax instructions); the result is my "auto and travel" expense.

You can also use actual auto expenses if you think this method will give you a greater deduction than the standard allowance. This method used to be particularly advantageous if you had an expensive car, because it allowed you to deduct a certain amount of depreciation for your car.

The Tax Reform Act of 1984, however, appears to eliminate the possibility of depreciation for vehicles placed in service after June 18, 1984 for most investors. You should ask your tax adviser about the changes.

To calculate actual expenses, figure out how many total miles you have driven in the course of a year, and the number of miles you have driven for business purposes. The formula to calculate actual auto expense is:

$$\frac{\text{Business Miles}}{\text{Total Miles}} \times \frac{\text{Total Expense}}{\text{(including depreciation)}} = \text{Business Expense}$$

Total expense would include the costs you have incurred for gas, oil, repairs, insurance, tags, tune-ups—anything related to the car. Just make sure to collect receipts and evidence that you have paid the amounts you said you have paid.

If you own a distant rental property, remember to keep an itemized list of all travel expenses, including the cost of your plane or train ticket; these are deductible, if you made the trip for reasons connected with your rental property.

If you follow the suggestions in this book for buying rental houses, though, your houses should be close to your own residence—so most of your travel expense should be for mileage. Every time you make a trip to your rental houses or a trip on their behalf, take your notebook from the glove compartment and write down the last few digits from your car's odometer before you start your trip. When you return home, check the odometer again and complete your entry. This is what a page of your mileage notebook might look like:

Date	Property	Purpose	Start	End	Total
1/3	House 1	Repair leak	417	424	7
1/20	House 2	Meet with tenants	511	515	4
3/28	House 1	Buy paint supplies (ABC store)	901	909	8
4/19	House 1	Paint garage	222	229	7
4/20	House 1	Paint garage	229	236	7
7/5	House 3	Meet with contractor (123 Fairfax Dr.)	999	013	14

Your other record keeping will be done at home. There, you will enter the month-to-month expenses for each rental house directly into its financial record, which will have a page for each category of expense. Here is an example of how to set up a format for a category—repairs, let's say:

REPAIRS

Date	Item	Paid to	Amount
2/18	Patch roof	Pond Roofing	$ 75
4/12	Fix basement leak	Morrison Waterproofing	$125
8/3	Unclog outside drain	Root-M-Out	$110

You can set up a similar format for each of your other major categories. Here are some examples of expenses you can claim:

- Advertising

  - newspaper advertisements
  - posting of rental notices   (if there is a fee)
  - tenant-referral services   (if there is a fee)

- Cleaning and maintenance

  - cleaning of carpets
  - floor waxing
  - window cleaning
  - cleaning of gutters and downspouts
  - maintenance of furnace, boiler, and air-conditioning unit(s)
  - interior and exterior house painting

- Repairs

  - repairing a plumbing leak
  - roof patching
  - fixing a loose bannister
  - repairing a washer, dryer, furnace, refrigerator, and other fixtures and appliances

- Supplies

    - carpet shampoo
    - floor wax
    - paint and painting supplies

- Utilities (if you pay for these expenses)

    - gas
    - heating oil
    - electricity
    - water and sewage

- Insurance

    - hazard insurance
    - liability insurance
    - all types except title insurance

- Interest

    - interest on mortgages and deeds of trust
    - interest on liens
    - points at settlement amortized over the life of the loan (if they represent prepaid interest or were paid for the forbearance of money)
    - interest on home improvement loans
    - *Note:* You can't deduct amounts you paid for penalties, although you can deduct the interest on a penalty payment as an expense.

- Legal and other professional fees

    - attorney's fees to draw up a rental agreement or (God forbid) initiate an eviction
    - accountant's fee to set up your bookkeeping system

- Taxes

    - property tax
    - local benefit taxes for the purpose of maintenance or repairs

- Wages and salaries

- the salary (not a fee or a charge for services which would go under "Repairs") you pay the handyperson you employ to repair your houses

- Other
    - a business phone in your personal residence
    - your work clothes, if used solely when you provide maintenance and repair services to your rental houses
    - postage and stationery used for your correspondence and payment of bills in behalf of your rental houses
    - Christmas gifts to your tenants
    - *Note:* If you have an area of your personal residence used exclusively and regularly for managing your rental houses, you may also be able to deduct certain additional expenses and to claim depreciation on that part of your personal residence classified as a home office. See IRS Publication 587, *Business Use of Your Home.*

Capital Expenditure

The last section of your financial record is "Capital Expenditure." It will probably be the section in which, on a year-to-year basis, you have the fewest entries. It is also one which requires you to grasp the more complicated concept of depreciation. Yet grasp it you should, because the IRS allowance for depreciation may save you the most tax dollars.

So let's now see what kinds of capital expenditure you may have and how you can use depreciation to reduce your taxes.

How you can profit from DEPRECIATION

Basically, the IRS assumes that major items called *capital improvements* will wear out over time and have to be replaced. If these items are used in the production of income, the IRS allows you to deduct that amount of loss, or *depreciation,* which you have incurred that year for the item that is wearing out.

Here are some examples of capital improvements:

- the house itself (minus the land)
- furnace, air conditioner, heat pump, boiler
- water heater
- refrigerator, stove
- washer/dryer
- installing a patio or fence
- converting an unfinished basement into an accessory dwelling unit
- replacing a roof
- installing a new kitchen floor

In fact, the IRS is correct—items do wear out over time. In terms of prices, however, houses usually go up in value rather than decline. So the "loss" you show the IRS each year due to depreciation is usually a "paper loss." During the first few years of ownership, investors can usually show a loss even if they have a positive cash flow from rent. This "loss" may offset other income received by investors, enabling them to reduce their tax liability.

For faster write-offs, it's best to have as many items as possible fall under the "Expenses" heading, rather than under "Capital Expenditure," because you can deduct the full amount of the expense in the year you made the purchase. If you have a capital expenditure, you will have to depreciate it a little at a time over several years. Unfortunately, the IRS does not give you wide latitude to select the category of your choice. You generally must depreciate any items over a given amount.

How to Determine the *Basis* of Your Rental House

To figure out how to calculate depreciation, you must first determine what the *basis* of your property is. It is relatively easy to calculate the basis of most capital improvements; the basis is merely the purchase price of the items, if you bought them for use in your rental property.

It is harder to calculate the basis of your house. But figuring the basis of your house is important, because this calculation is usually the most important factor in determining whether you will save or lose thousands of dollars in taxes.

If you have just bought a house with the intention of renting it out immediately, then the basis of your house equals the *purchase price* plus the *acquisition costs* minus the *cost of the land*. You have to subtract the price of the land because the land on which a house is built does not wear out, and thus cannot be depreciated.

Add the Acquisition Costs   The following are items which may be charged to the buyer at settlement, or close of escrow; you add these items to the purchase price of the house in order to determine its basis:

- attorney's fees
- abstract fees
- appraisal fee*
- charges for installing utility service
- option costs
- points or origination fees which were charged to process the loan*
- transfer taxes (these may be expensed at your option)
- title insurance
- amounts which the seller owed but which the buyer has agreed to pay, such as:
  - back taxes or interest
  - recording or mortgage fees
  - charges for improvements or repairs
  - selling commission

Subtract the Land's Value   After determining the basis of your property, you must then subtract the value of the land, which is nondepreciable. For larger write-offs, it's to your advantage to assign as much value as possible to the house, and as little as possible to

---

* Technically loan costs including appraisal fees which lenders require should be amortized over the life of the loan. For simplicity's sake, however, they are often included in the property's basis and depreciated.

the land. The IRS, though, may ask you to explain the objective criteria you used for making this allocation.

There are several ways to determine the land-to-house ratio. Three of them are presented here:

1. PROPERTY TAX ASSESSMENT

One way to calculate the land-to-house ratio is to look at the property tax assessment of the rental house for the year in which the purchase was made. See what percent of the assessment was for the land, and what percent was for the house.

Example: You buy a rental property for $92,500. The assessed value of the house is $95,500, of which $42,700 is allocated to the land and $52,800 to the house. By dividing $42,700 by $95,500, you see that the land's value is about 45 percent of the entire property value. You would thus allocate 45 percent of your $92,500 purchase price to the land and the remaining 55 percent to the house, which would make the land worth $41,625 and the house worth $50,875.

2. COST OF LAND PER SQUARE FOOT

Another way to calculate how much of your purchase price goes to the land and how much to the house is to calculate the square footage of your lot, and then to find out how much it costs per square foot to buy land in that area.

Example: You buy a rental property for $92,500. The house sits on a lot of 5,000 square feet. You learn from developers in the area that a nearby vacant lot sold for $7.65 per square foot. You then determine that the land on your property is worth $38,250, or $7.65 × 5,000 square feet; the house is worth the remaining $54,250. The allocation between house and land would thus be about 41 percent for the land and 59 percent for the house.

3. INSURANCE REPLACEMENT VALUE

A third way to determine how much of the purchase price went to the house, exclusive of the land, is to look on the insurance policy for the figure showing how much it will cost to replace the house. Compare the replacement cost with the purchase price of the house to find out how much of the total purchase price went to the house and how much to the land.

Example: You buy a rental property for $92,500. Your insurance company insures the house for $65,000. Therefore, you would allocate about 70 percent of the purchase price to the house ($65,000 divided by $92,500) and 30 percent to the land.*

How to Figure the Basis if Your Rental House Was Previously Your Personal Residence Let's say that you are converting a house in which you have previously lived into rental property. To determine the basis of the house, you have to take the cost basis of your house when you acquired it, and add the cost of any capital improvements which you have made since you bought the house. Then subtract from it any depreciation that you took in previous years, any casualty losses, and (of course) the cost of the land.

Look at the figure you get, and compare it with the market value of the house (minus the cost of the land) at the time you converted it to a rental. You have to use *whichever figure is less* when determining the basis of your house.

Different Methods of Depreciation

Before 1981, the IRS permitted investors to take depreciation in several different ways, including:

- *straight-line method* in which the taxpayer deducted an equal part of the cost or basis of the property every year for the estimated useful life of the property
- *declining-balance method* in which the taxpayer had larger initial tax write-offs for depreciation by subtracting depreciation from the cost of the property before computing the next year's depreciation
- *sum-of-the-year-digits method* in which the taxpayer multiplied the cost of the property by a different fraction every year

If these seem complicated to you, they must have seemed complicated to others, too. A simplified Economic Recovery Tax Act of 1981 was passed. This tax act contained the Accelerated Cost Recovery System (ACRS), which not only simplified the calculation of deprecia-

* Note: All three examples assume that the $92,500 price includes acquisition costs.

tion but also gave investors additional tax savings by allowing a faster write-off for most capital improvements placed in service between January 1, 1980 and March 15, 1984.

Originally, I had a long and detailed section in my manuscript about how to calculate depreciation based on the Economic Recovery Tax Act of 1981. Congress, however, passed the Tax Reform Act of 1984 while I was writing this. The Tax Reform Act, among other changes, lengthened the depreciation period for rental houses from 15 years to 18 years. The law applies to rental property purchased after March 15, 1984 (unless you had a binding contract to purchase prior to that date). The new depreciation schedules are not available as of this writing.

Not knowing what other changes are in store for us, I decided to fudge the issue by suggesting that you consult your tax advisor and the latest IRS publications to determine how to take depreciation on your property.

Instead, I'll just show you how I might have kept a financial record on a house purchased in 1983.

Preparing a Financial Record: A Case Example

FINANCIAL RECORD: 123 MAIN STREET

INCOME

Date	Source of income	Item	Amount paid	Security deposit	Balance due
4/15	Sue Gordon	1st mo. last mo.	$ 97.50 195	$150	
4/15	Leah Sparrow	1st mo. last mo.	97.50 195	150	
4/17	Winnie Doe	1st mo. last mo.	123.67 265		$150 paid 5/3
5/1	Dan Scott	1st mo. last mo.	315 315	150	
5/1	Leah Sparrow	x	195		

FINANCIAL RECORD *cont'd.*

5/3	Winnie Doe	x	265	150	
5/3	Sue Gordon	x	195		
6/2	Dan Scott	x	315		
6/2	Sue Gordon	x	195		
6/3	Leah Sparrow	x	195		
6/4	Winnie Doe	x	265		
7/3	Dan Scott	x	315		
7/4	Sue Gordon	x	195		
7/4	Winnie Doe	x	265		
7/5	Leah Sparrow	x	195		
8/1	Sue Gordon	x	195		
8/1	Winnie Doe	x	265		
8/3	Dan Scott	x	315		
9/2	Dan Scott	x	315		
9/2	Sue Gordon	x	195		

FINANCIAL RECORD *cont'd.*

9/3	Winnie Doe	x	265		
9/20	Ann Hammond	1st mo. last mo.	195 195	150	
10/1	Sue Gordon	x	195		
10/1	Winnie Doe	x	265		
10/2	Dan Scott	x	315		
11/2	Ann Hammond	x	195		
11/3	Sue Gordon	x	195		
11/3	Winnie Doe	x	265		
11/4	Dan Scott	x	315		
11/15	Leah Sparrow	Return deposit		<150>	
12/1	Dan Scott	x	315		
12/1	Winnie Doe	x	265		
12/2	Sue Gordon	x	195		
12/2	Ann Hammond	x	195		
	Yearly total:		$8,853.67		

EXPENSES

Advertising

Date	Item	Paid to	Amount
3/15	Ad	Washington Post	$18
3/22	Ad	Washington Post	18
8/3	Ad	Washington Post	18
		Yearly total	$54

Cleaning and Maintenance

Date	Item	Paid to	Amount
12/1	Clean gutters	Patrick Hayes	$ 30
12/7	Clean carpets	Robinson's	75
		Yearly total	$105

Repairs

Date	Item	Paid to	Amount
4/21	Fix toilet	J. R. Stephens	$40
9/21	Patch roof	Pond Roofing	35
		Yearly total	$75

Supplies

Date	Item	Paid to	Amount
5/16	Trap for sink	Block's Plumbing	$ 6.53
8/11	Paint	Sears	28.45
8/22	Caulk	Hechingers	3.49
		Yearly total	$38.47

Other

Date	Item	Paid to	Amount
5/1	Checks (for rental and own use)	$20.84 @ ⅓ for rental First American Bank	$ 6.95
12/10	Christmas Gift	Hecht Company	$10.47
		Yearly total	$17.42

CAPITAL EXPENDITURE

Date	Improvement	Cost	Recovery period
4/15	House (less land)	$65,665	15 yrs
5/10	Washer	329	5 yrs
8/2	Fence	750	10 years
12/20	Furnace	1,250	15 yrs

END-OF-THE-YEAR EXPENSES

Auto and travel (106 miles @ 20.5 cents/mile)	$ 22
Insurance	$ 259
Interest	$5,625
Taxes	$ 665

POINTS TO REMEMBER

- In addition to a mileage notebook placed in your car, you may want to have three record-keeping systems:
  - *a management schedule* to remind you what tasks have to be performed for all of your houses
  - *house information binders* containing essential documents and correspondence for each house
  - *financial records* in which you record all month-to-month financial transactions, including all income generated from each house and all expenditures

- Financial records are essential for tax purposes, because the IRS requires you to report all:
  - income
  - expenses
  - capital expenditure

- Consult your tax advisor to make sure that you take every tax deduction to which you are legally entitled.

FOR FURTHER INFORMATION

The best source of practical, up-to-date real estate tax information I've come across is the syndicated newspaper column by Robert Bruss. He also wrote a book called *The Smart Investor's Guide to Real Estate* (Crown, New York, 1983). The book includes answers to the most common tax-related questions people ask about real estate.

In addition, *J. K. Lasser's Your Income Tax*, published each year by Simon and Schuster (NY), has some of the clearest explanations available on how to prepare your taxes. My CPA highly recommends it.

The IRS also has many free publications which attempt to explain to the average citizen how to compute taxes. The most important for our purposes is Publication 527, *Rental Property*. Other publications are the following:

Publication 17	*Your Federal Income Tax*
Publication 463	*Travel, Entertainment, and Gift Expenses*
Publication 523	*Tax Information on Selling Your Home*
Publication 529	*Miscellaneous Deductions*
Publication 550	*Investment Income and Expenses*
Publication 552	*Recordkeeping for Individuals and a List of Tax Publications*
Publication 587	*Business Use of Your Home*

11

ACHIEVING SUCCESS

Who is wise? He who learns from every person.
Who is strong? He who has conquered himself.
Who is rich? He who is content with his lot.
Who is honored? He who honors others.

"Ethics of the Fathers"

What is success? What brings happiness? These seem to be eternal questions.

If you look at people who write and talk about how to make a lot of money, typically most of them show you how successful they are by telling you stories of how, having started out poor, they now own two Ferraris, a pink Cadillac, and a luxury vacation home in Vail, Colorado. They tell you that they are their own bosses; they don't have to report to a 9 to 5 job like most other suckers; if they wanted to, they could take a trip to Tahiti tomorrow.

"So," you may ask yourself, "is this success? Is this it? Is this what I should be striving for?"

Money, indeed, is supposed to be an objective indicator of success in our democratic society. Unlike some societies in which people are trapped by birth in certain social classes, in our society the myth is that whether you are born a Rockefeller or have come from the slums, everyone has an opportunity to get rich and thereby—which is probably more important to most people—to gain social status.

Surprisingly, the American myth has a large amount of truth to it. People who come from poverty-stricken backgrounds do "make it" here with perseverance. But there are other dimensions to "making it" than money.

Those rich movie stars who take drugs and smack their cars up against trees—are they successful? Bored wives of wealthy executives who speak endlessly about problems with their servants, their clothes, their parties—are they successful?

Perhaps more important than having money is how you make money. The real challenge is to make a comfortable living from work you enjoy—from work which is ethical—from work which enriches you and the people with whom you come into contact. Because just as surely as you shape your work, the work you choose to do ultimately shapes you.

Now I imagine there is a lot of excitement in running around the country cutting deals, buying and selling properties before dashing off to Tahiti. But there is also pleasure in walking along the streets of your community and being greeted with a warm smile from a former tenant, or with a hug from a neighbor who lives next to one of your rental houses.

Being free to do anything you want—to follow rules only if you see fit to do so—to set your own working hours at your personal whim—is not necessarily a pleasurable experience, nor is this type of freedom necessarily liberating.

One of the most gratifying experiences of my life was as director of a family planning program in Tulare County, California—particularly that first year when we actually set up the program. The office hours were 8 A.M. to 5 P.M. Most mornings started for me at 7 A.M. when Dr. McGrew, a pathologist, Dr. Gates, an ob-gyn, and I got together for a cup of coffee before our respective offices opened. Two or three nights a week, our entire family planning staff held evening clinics for low-income residents. The clinics opened at 6:30 P.M. and lasted until 11 P.M. or midnight. Wages were based on a 40-hour work week, and were low anyway. There were no funds for overtime; there was no compensatory time. If you considered that we regularly put in 50 or 60 hours of work a week that first year, most of our salaries may have been only a little above the minimum wage.

Were we "free"? No. We had rigid clinic schedules. Were we

"rich"? Not in terms of money. Yet staff morale was exceedingly high.

Now what will happen when you manage rental houses? Will you be free? No. You will have to make sure that the rent is collected and will have to keep records. You will have to respond to the needs of your tenants, maintain the property, and obey the rules laid down by your state, your local jurisdiction, and your own sense of fairness.

If you look at your rental house as a commodity and at your tenants as incidental and necessary evils for you to get a tax shelter and a profitable return on your investment, you will find that you are not at all free. You will resent every tenant request as an interruption of your time, and you will resent the cost of every repair. What money you do manage to make will be hard-won.

If, on the other hand, your first concerns are to implement a fair management system and to work with your well-chosen tenants, then management will become relatively easy. Tenants will help you. Neighbors will help you. Tradespeople will help you.

What is a little surprising is that if you follow the precepts in this book, not only will you enjoy managing rental houses, but you will probably make even more money from your investment than you thought possible. Curiously, you will rarely stop to think if you are free or successful or rich. You will do what you do, just for the sake of doing it well. The extraordinary profit just follows.

I think Lao-tzu would smile, don't you?

APPENDIX

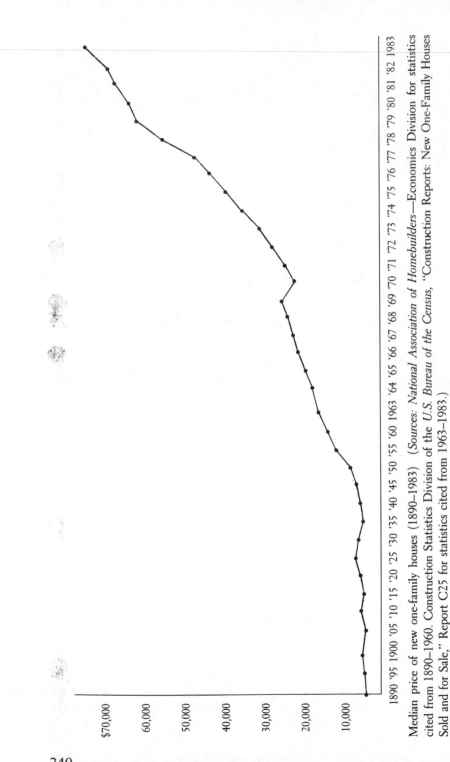

Median price of new one-family houses (1890–1983) (Sources: *National Association of Homebuilders*—Economics Division for statistics cited from 1890–1960. Construction Statistics Division of the *U.S. Bureau of the Census*, "Construction Reports: New One-Family Houses Sold and for Sale," Report C25 for statistics cited from 1963–1983.)

MEDIAN PRICE OF NEW ONE-FAMILY HOUSES (1890–1983)

Year	Median sales price	Year	Median sales price
1890	$ 4,422	1966	21,400
1895	4,500	1967	22,700
1900	4,881	1968	24,700
1905	4,311	1969	25,600
1910	5,377	1970	23,400
1915	5,159	1971	25,200
1920	6,296	1972	27,600
1925	7,889	1973	32,500
1930	7,146	1974	35,900
1935	6,296	1975	39,300
1940	6,558	1976	44,200
1945	7,476	1977	48,800
1950	9,446	1978	55,700
1955	13,386	1979	62,900
1960	16,652	1980	64,600
1963	18,000	1981	68,900
1964	18,900	1982	69,300
1965	20,000	1983	75,300

WHAT TO LOOK FOR WHEN INSPECTING A HOUSE

- Is all the wood in the house above the level of the soil?
- Does water drain away from the house?
- Does the crawl space have adequate clearance and ventilation?
- Are there signs of dampness in the basement?
- Have earth-filled porches or other structures separated from the house?
- Is the roof overhang sufficient (18 to 30 inches)?
- Has the caulking around doors, windows, and joints been maintained?
- Are the gutters and downspouts intact?
- Is the attic ventilated?
- Is the roof decking completely covered, especially at the roof edge?
- Does the roof sag, indicating possible rafter decay?
- Is the paint peeling or blistering?
- Are the decorative and other items attached to the house likely to admit or trap moisture?
- Is the plumbing, including drains, free of leaks?

- Do any doors or windows stick? Are any frames decayed?
- Is the caulking around tubs, sinks, and showers intact?
- Are the floors level? Do any areas feel spongy when walked on?
- Do the ceilings have water damage?
- If the house is in a zone of high termite hazard, is there a structural pest control contract on it? Does the contract include a guarantee?
- Was the soil under the house treated with insecticide during construction? Afterward?
- Has the soil under the additions been treated?
- Are any termite shelter tubes visible on the foundations? On the pipes?
- Does the crawl space contain stumps or wood debris?
- Are there any small holes in unfinished wood (in the crawl spaces or elsewhere) with powder under them?
- Will an expert inspect the house for termites or other structural pests before the sale?

242

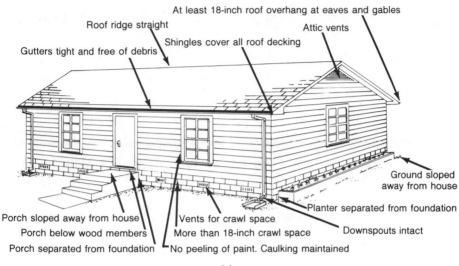

Roof ridge straight

At least 18-inch roof overhang at eaves and gables

Attic vents

Shingles cover all roof decking

Gutters tight and free of debris

Ground sloped away from house

Planter separated from foundation

Porch sloped away from house

Vents for crawl space

Downspouts intact

Porch below wood members

More than 18-inch crawl space

Porch separated from foundation

No peeling of paint. Caulking maintained

(a)

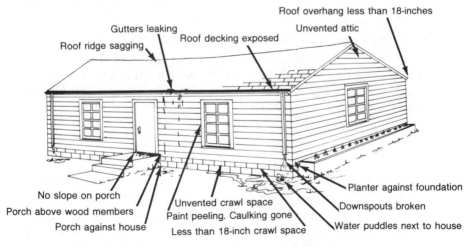

Roof overhang less than 18-inches

Gutters leaking

Unvented attic

Roof decking exposed

Roof ridge sagging

No slope on porch

Planter against foundation

Porch above wood members

Unvented crawl space

Downspouts broken

Paint peeling. Caulking gone

Porch against house

Less than 18-inch crawl space

Water puddles next to house

(b)

What to look for when inspecting a house. (a) Example of good house; (b) example of bad house. (*Source: U.S. Department of Agriculture–Forest Service.*)

Example of professional inspection report

3/19/84

Mr. John Smith
123 Fairfax Dr.
Arlington, VA 22209

Dear John:

Here is our inspection report on the property at 134 Main Street, Arlington, Virginia 22204.

Overall, this approximately 44-year-old brick colonial was structurally quite sound, solidly built, and in very good condition for its age. No major defects were noted. A more detailed report follows:

Structural

The construction of the house is brick, on blocks supported by poured concrete foundation. The roof and interior framing are of wood. The foundation, wall, floor, and roof systems were visually examined, as accessible, and found to have been without any significant structural defects. While we found no visual evidence of structural damage due to termite or other wood borers, we do recommend that you have a complete wood borer inspection and maintain a warranty protective contract from year to year.

Electrical

Electric service to the house was 125 amps through a fuse box distribution panel, with copper lower branch wiring, which is quite good. Its installation appeared to be normal. A large sampling of duplex outlets thoughout the house and in the garage were tested with a circuit tester for proper grounding and polarity; all were found to have been wired normally, with the exception of the garage duplex outlets. We were not able to determine the exact nature of this problem; however, it would appear that there was measurable voltage to ground. We would recommend that a licensed electrician repair this

244

situation as soon as possible, as it could present a shock hazard. The refrigerator duplex outlet was not tested. The 240-volt air-conditioning outlet at the second floor landing appeared to be inoperative, but it would only need to be activated should an air conditioner be installed in the window above. The overhead light fixture in the northeast corner's bedroom closet should be resecured to the ceiling. With the exception of the above discrepancies, we would consider the electric system for the house to be safe and adequate for your needs.

Heating

The house is heated by the original Columbia oil-fired forced air furnace. Statistically, oil-fired furnaces have a normal life expectancy of 20 to 30 years. In light of this, and also of the fact that this furnace is very inefficient compared to new furnaces, we would recommend that you budget for its replacement within the next 5 years. We have included a sheet on the maintenance of oil-fired heating appliances for your reference. Neither of the service disconnects on the furnace was operating, nor was the burner emergency switch at the top of the cellar stairs. All of these should be repaired. There is a loose wire within the thermostat that should be corrected, since arcing is currently occurring inside the thermostat. Air distribution throughout the forced-air system was adequate; however, the fan belt needs to be replaced and tightened. A considerable improvement in air distribution should be noticed, once this is done. The two replaceable air filters should be inspected monthly and changed as necessary. You should be able to install an electric central air-conditioning system in the house without an electrical overload. We would strongly recommend that you install the air-conditioning as part of the furnace replacement package, given the savings normally associated with such an installation as this. We would recommend that you consider a replacement gas furnace with an efficiency of 85 percent or better.

Plumbing

The house is served by public water and sewage systems. The freshwater supply and distribution system in the house is copper; this is excellent, given its long-enduring qualities. The waste drains are cast iron, which is also quite good. The water pressure in the house was adequate; however, there was a pressure drop when more than one second floor fixture was operated at the same time. We would suggest that this is a problem not of pipe clogging but of pipe sizing, and that what you are actually getting is a volume drop rather than a pressure drop. There is not too much that can be done about this. At any rate, the situation should not get significantly worse. Hot water is provided by an approximately 10-year-old 40-gallon gas-fired water heater, which was operating normally at the time of inspection. In light of its age, you should budget for its probable replacement within the next 5 years. The hot-water valve for the basement's bathroom sink should be repacked, and new faucet washers are needed in the laundry tub. The bathtub's compression seal was leaking and should be sealed with a bead of silicone sealer. We would recommend the installation of a bathroom exhaust fan in the second floor bathroom.

Basement

The basement was dry at the time of inspection and appears to have been so for a fairly prolonged period. This condition can be continued by maintaining good surface-water control around the foundation, with emphasis on grading and on downspout extensions (as discussed below). The keeper plate should be adjusted in the basement's exterior door.

Kitchen

The kitchen is in good overall condition. The gas range and refrigerator, which both appear to be less than 10 years old, were in normal operating condition. There was no disposal or dishwasher.

Interior

The interior of the house was also in good overall condition for its age. The floors were hardwood tongue-in-groove oak. The walls and ceilings were covered with plaster. The windows were steel casement. We would recommend the installation of storm windows—preferably interior storm windows, because these are normally quite less expensive. The attic's pull-down stairway needs repairing. A piece of furring strip or a two-by-four should be installed beneath the one roof deck board that does not meet with the roof rafter; to step on this area of the asphalt shingles could cause a hole in the shingles, due to the lack of support.

Exterior

The exterior of the house was in very good overall condition for its age. The roof on the house was asphalt shingle (a second layer over the original asphalt shingle) and appeared to be in sound condition. We would estimate that you will get at least another 5 years of life from this roof before replacement is necessary. The gutters and downspouts on the house were a combination of galvanized steel and aluminum. They were in generally good condition; however, we would recommend that you budget to replace the galvanized steel gutters within the next 5 years. The exterior brick veneer and wood clapboard were all in good condition. It would appear that the wood clapboard should be painted within the next 2 years. At the time of painting, loose paint should be scraped down, where applicable, to bare wood. The wood should be primed with an oil-based primer. Caulking should be done where necessary, and the wood should be painted with two coats of a good exterior acrylic latex house paint. The wood on the deck at the rear of the house appeared to be reasonably well constructed and was quite sound and firm when walked upon.

Weatherization

There is currently a 6-inch loose fill of Rockwell insulation in the attic. This gives you approximately an R–15 value in an area where R–30 is considered the standard for new construction. You may want to lay in an additional 6 inches of unfaced fiberglass bat insulation directly over the existing insulation to bring the R value up in excess of R–30. There are birds' nests in the gable vents, which should be cleared to allow for a better cross-flow ventilation. We would also encourage the installation of a roof-mounted, thermostatically controlled attic exhaust fan; this would help to keep the attic cooler during hot summer weather, thus helping to prolong the life of the asphalt shingle roof and to keep the living spaces below more comfortable.

The following is a list of expenses that you may expect to incur within the next 5 years (a) due to normal equipment and system life expectancies, (b) for normal maintenance activities, and (c) for upgrades:

Minor electrical repairs	$40–$60
Biennial gas furnace service	$60–$80
Gas furnace replacement	$1,400–$1,800
Install central air-conditioning	$2,300–$2,700
Probable water heater replacement	$350–$425
Minor plumbing repairs	$50–$70
Grading and downspout extension improvements if done by a landscape contractor	$500–$700
Laying in an additional 6 inches of fiberglass bat insulation in the attic (approx. cost, materials only)	$0.30/sq. ft.
Install thermostatic attic fan	$200–$300
Miscellaneous expenses involved in maintaining a house of this size, style, and age	$300–$500

If we may be of any further assistance, please feel free to call us at any time. It has been a pleasure having been of service to you.

Very truly yours,

G. Gilbert Engler

G. Gilbert Engler
HOME INSPECTOR

lc

ESTIMATED USEFUL LIFE OF HOUSE COMPONENTS AND APPLIANCES*

- Indefinitely: aluminum siding, ceramic tile, copper plumbing pipes, exterior wood, masonry envelope (brick, stone, block, or wood paneling)
- 50–60 years: galvanized iron pipe
- 20–30 years: furnace
- 20–25 years: range
- 15–20 years: freezer, refrigerator, roof (wood or asphalt shingles)
- 12–15 years: clothes dryer
- 10–30 years: air-conditioner
- 10–15 years: vinyl flooring
- 8–12 years: clothes washer, dishwasher, water heater
- 5–10 years: carpet
- 5–7 years: interior paint
- 4–5 years: exterior paint

* *Source:* American Society of Home Inspectors, as cited in *Changing Times,* January 1984 p. 46.

HOUSE INFORMATION SHEET

Address: _____ Zip _____ Start date _____

			Equipment	Yes	No
Basement	**1St Floor**	**2nd Floor**			
Size _____	L.R. _____	B.R. _____	Stove		
O.S.E. _____	D.R. _____	_____	Refrig.		
			Dishwasher		
Cr. Sp. _____	Kit. _____	_____	Disposer		
R.R. _____	B.R. _____	Bath_____	Ex. fan		
			Attic fan		
Bath _____	_____	3rd Level	A/C units		
B.R. _____	_____	B.R. _____	CAC		
			Washer		
	Bath _____	Bath _____	Dryer		
Heat _____	Fam. Rm. _____	Other _____	Storm wind		
Hot water _____	Other _____	_____	Porch _____		
Ut. Rm. _____	_____	_____	Garage _____		

Rents: B.R. 1 _____   B.R. 2 _____   B.R. 3 _____   B.R. 4 _____
Utility bills av. (   )   Split four ways (   )
   Gas _____   Oil _____   Elec. _____   Water and sew. _____
Public transportation:
   Bus/Subway no.? _____   How often? _____
   Distance? _____   How long to downtown? _____

Neighbors:

Name	Address	Phone Number

Additional information: _____
_____
_____

LIST OF CALLERS

Date	Person's name	Home tel.	Office tel.	Comments	Appointment

TENANT APPLICATION FORM

1. Name of prospective tenant _____
2. Home phone _____ Office phone _____
3. Present occupation _____
4. Name and address of firm _____
    _____
    _____
5. Name of supervisor _____
    Supervisor's phone _____
6. Previous occupation (if employed less than 6 months at present
    job) _____
7. Name of previous supervisor _____
    Previous supervisor's phone _____
8. Address(es) of applicant for last 2 years

Address	Dates	Landlord	Phone

9. Name, address, and phone number of nearest relative

    _____ _____ _____
         Name   Address   Phone
10. Name and phone number of two friends locally

    _____ _____ _____ _____
      Name   Phone No.   Name   Phone No.
Comments:

RENTAL AGREEMENT

THIS AGREEMENT HAS BEEN MADE between those parties named below, herinafter referred to as Tenant(s) and _____, hereinafter referred to as Owner.

The term "Tenant" refers to the individual signators of this Rental Agreement. The term "Tenants" denotes all tenants in the household. "Tenant(s)" means either "Tenant" or "Tenants" or both, as determined by the Owner. Responsibilities of a Tenant pertain only to that individual. Contractual obligations of Tenants are binding on each Tenant and denote both individual and joint responsibility of all Tenants.

In consideration of a monthly rent stated below, Tenant(s) are entitled to share the residence at _____ on a month-to-month basis.

The following points are agreeable to the Tenant(s) and the Owner, and are mutually binding:

1. Rent will be due the first day of every month.
2. Tenant, before occupancy will pay the first month's rent and an equal amount toward the last month's rent.
3. Tenant will pay a security deposit of $ _____ before occupying the premises. Within 30 days after departure, if all obligations have been paid, and if the premises have been maintained in satisfactory condition as determined by the Owner, the deposit will be returned to the Tenant. Any deductions will be itemized in writing and sent to the Tenant.
4. Tenant(s) will assume full responsibility for all gas, electricity, water, sewer, waste removal and telephone bills until the last day of legal tenancy.
5. In the event there are fewer than 3 tenants in the household, an individual Tenant will pay no more than one-third of the bills for gas and electricity, and the Owner agrees to pay the remaining share. If a Tenant has not paid his or her share of the utilities after terminating the agreement, Owner reserves the right to use part of the Tenant's security deposit to meet the Tenant's obligation to the household, if sufficient funds are available after other obligations have been paid. However, Owner does not assume any liability if a Tenant fails to pay his or her share of any utility bill.
6. Owner will assume expenses for the major maintenance, cleaning, and repair of the furnace, roof, water heater, central air-conditioning, gutters, and outside plumbing, and repairs to equipment and appliances (except for the lawn mower and disposer) when

RENTAL AGREEMENT *cont'd.*

required if they have been used in a proper manner. See attached "Inventory of Owner's Appliances and Equipment."

7. Owner will pay to exterminate carpenter ants, termites and other wood-boring insects, and waterbugs. The expense to eradicate all other insects, including cockroaches, will be borne by all Tenants.

8. Tenants will assume responsibility for minor maintenance such as replacement of fuses, filters, light bulbs, washers in faucets, and batteries in smoke alarms. In addition, Tenant(s) are responsible for changing screens and storm windows and for repairing screens and cracked window panes and door panes unless they can demonstrate that the damage was beyond their control. Tenant(s) are responsible for repairing any damage to the premises or the appliances which was caused by Tenant(s) misuse or negligence.

9. Tenant(s) will keep the premises, including all plumbing fixtures as clean and safe as condition permits and will unstop and keep clear all waste pipes and outdoor drains. Unless the cause is beyond their control, Tenant(s) are responsible for loss or damage from freezing of water pipes or plumbing fixtures or from the stopping of water closets and drains which will be repaired at the expense of the Tenant(s).

10. Tenants, at their own expense, will keep up and preserve in good condition the lawn and garden and will remove ice and snow as necessary to keep walkways clear. Tenants at their own expense will keep the premises neat and free from rubbish and/ or hazards, and maintain woodpiles, if any, at a distance from any structure. The Tenant occupying the lowest level of the house is responsible for clearing leaves and debris from the outdoor drain(s).

11. It is expressly understood and agreed by and between the parties of this agreement that, unless liable under law, Owner will not be liable for any damage or injury to any person or persons which may occur on the premises for the duration of this agreement; nor will the Owner be liable for any personal property which is stolen or damaged due to flooding, leaks, fire, malfunction of equipment, structural problems, or for any reason whatever. All persons and personal property in or on the premises will be at the sole risk and responsibility of the Tenant(s).

12. The premises will be used as a single-family household for no

254

RENTAL AGREEMENT *cont'd.*

more than 4 unrelated persons and for no other purpose or additional number of people whatever except for temporary guests. A temporary guest is herein defined as someone occupying the premises for no more than 10 days in the course of a year. Further, all Tenants are entitled to share all living areas, to have access to all outside doors, and to utilize a common cooking facility.

13. Tenant(s) cannot sublet the premises without the express consent of the Owner.

14. No pets are permitted on the premises without the express consent of the Owner.

15. No alterations, additions, or improvements may be made on the premises without the express consent of the Owner. Any alterations, additions, or improvements will become the property of the Owner when the Tenant(s) depart, unless the premises can be restored to its original condition.

16. Tenant(s) agree to allow the Owner at any reasonable hour, by appointment, to enter the premises to inspect the same, to make repairs, or to show the premises to any parties.

17. Tenant(s) and Owner will, by mutual consent screen and select new tenants to fill vacancies.

18. This agreement and the tenancy hereby granted to a Tenant may be terminated at any time by either party by giving the other party not less than 30 days prior notice in writing. Terminations initiated by the Tenant must end on the last day of a month.

All the undersigned parties have read this agreement, agree to abide by its terms, and each has a copy of this agreement.

Date	Monthly Rent	Amt. of Sec. Dep.	Date Occupancy Will Begin	Amount Attached	Date Termin.	Comments

_____ TENANT

_____ OWNER

Date	Monthly Rent	Amt. of Sec. Dep.	Date Occupancy Will Begin	Amount Attached	Date Termin.	Comments

_____ TENANT

_____ OWNER

Date	Monthly Rent	Amt. of Sec. Dep.	Date Occupancy Will Begin	Amount Attached	Date Termin.	Comments

_____ TENANT

_____ OWNER

Date	Monthly Rent	Amt. of Sec. Dep.	Date Occupancy Will Begin	Amount Attached	Date Termin.	Comments

TENANT   OWNER

Date	Monthly Rent	Amt. of Sec. Dep.	Date Occupancy Will Begin	Amount Attached	Date Termin.	Comments

TENANT   OWNER

INVENTORY OF OWNER'S APPLIANCES AND EQUIPMENT

Address _____

APPLIANCE/ EQUIPMENT	DESCRIPTION
Hot Water Heater (Capacity,)	
Heating/Cooling System	
Humidifier (Capacity:)	
Dehumidifier (Capacity:)	
A/C Unit(s) BTU's: (Voltage:)	

(BTU's   ) _____

(Voltage:)

(BTU's   ) _____

(Voltage:)

Washing Machine _____

Dryer _____

Stove _____

Refrigerator _____

Dishwasher _____

Disposer _____

Attic Fan _____

Lawn Mower _____

In signing this attachment, the Tenant agrees that the above mentioned appliances and equipment are in the household and are in operable condition when the Tenant moved into the premises.

PLEASE NOTE: disposer and lawn mower (if any) are for the convenience of the tenant(s) and repairs, if any, will be paid by tenant(s).

_____   _____

TENANT   DATE

APPLICATION FOR LEASE

(PLEASE PRINT)

Date _____

Application is made to lease premises known as _____

for _____ year(s), beginning on the _____ day of _____, 19 _____ for the monthly rent

of $ _____ payable in advance on the _____ day of each month. Rent commences on the _____ day of

19 _____.

It is understood the premises are to be used as a family residence occupied by not more than _____ persons; and that occupancy is contingent upon property being vacated by present occupant. All personal property placed in said premises shall be at tenant's risk. A deposit in the sum of $ _____ is made herewith to be held by _____, with a clear understanding that this application, including each prospective occupant, is subject to approval and acceptance. If this application is not approved and accepted by the owner or agent, the deposit will be refunded. CREDIT CHECK FEES ARE NON-REFUNDABLE. IF THIS APPLICATION IS APPROVED, A DEED OF LEASE MUST BE EXECUTED WITHIN _____ DAYS OTHERWISE APPLICANT WILL BE LIABLE FOR LIQUIDATED DAMAGES. ☐ CHECK ☐ CASH ☐ MONEY ORDER ☐ TRAVELER'S CHECKS

(Names of adults only to appear on lease. Names of both husband and wife to appear on lease.)

IT IS IMPORTANT THAT ALL OF THE FOLLOWING INFORMATION BE GIVEN:

1. Applicant's Name (print) _____

   (First) _____ (Middle) _____ (Last) _____ (Suffix) _____ Date of Birth _____

   a. If member of Armed Forces give Rank and Branch _____ Length of Service _____

   b. Social Security No. _____ Driver's License No. _____ State _____

   c. Where can you be reached prior to the lease term? (Home phone) (___) _____ (Office phone) (___) _____

2. Present Employment _____ How long? _____

   Business Address _____ Zip _____ Phone No. (___) _____ Ext. _____

   Position _____ Salary $ _____ (per ___) Supervisor _____ (Name and Title)

   Other Income $ _____ Source _____

3. Previous Employment _____ How long? _____

   Business Address _____ Zip _____ Phone No. (___) _____ Ext. _____

   Position _____ Salary $ _____ (per ___) Supervisor _____ (Name and Title)

260

4. Other Applicants: Ages _____ Names _____ Relationship _____
_____
_____
_____

Any pets _____ Describe _____

5. Present Address _____ Zip _____ How long? _____
   Name of Landlord _____ Landlord's Phone No. (_____) _____ (Day/Night) Rent/Month _____

   Reason for moving _____

6. Previous Address _____ Zip _____ How long? _____
   Name of Landlord _____ Landlord's Phone No. (_____) _____ (Day/Night) Rent/Month _____

7. Spouse's Name (print) _____ (First) _____ (Middle) _____ (Last) _____ Date of Birth _____
   Present Employment _____ How long? _____
   Business Address _____ Zip _____ Phone No. (_____) _____ Ext. _____
   Position _____ Salary $ _____ Per _____
   Supervisor's Name _____ Title _____

8. AUTOMOBILES, CAMPERS, VANS, TRAILERS, TRUCKS, COMMERCIAL VEHICLES, ETC.
   Make   Model   Year   Color   State   License Number
   _____ _____   _____ _____   _____   _____
   _____ _____   _____ _____   _____   _____
   _____ _____   _____ _____   _____   _____

   A. Do you own or plan to purchase a water bed? _____

9. HOBBIES: Applicant _____
            Spouse _____

NVBR FORM 1001, 8/83

Pg 1 of 2

261

10. **BANK REFERENCES**

Name _____ Acct. No. _____ Current Balance _____

Name _____ Acct. No. _____ Current Balance _____

Name _____ Acct. No. _____ Current Balance _____

11. **CREDIT CARD REFERENCES** (Print all digits)

Name _____ Acct. No. _____

Name _____ Acct. No. _____

Name _____ Acct. No. _____

Name _____ Acct. No. _____

12. **OTHER CREDIT REFERENCES** (Local if possible)

Name _____ Acct. No. _____

Address _____ Zip _____

Name _____ Acct. No. _____

Address _____ Zip _____

Name _____ Acct. No. _____

Address _____ Zip _____

Name _____ Acct. No. _____

Address _____ Zip _____

13. **PERSONAL REFERENCES**

Name _____ Phone No. ( ) _____

Address _____ Zip _____

Name _____ Phone No. ( ) _____

Address _____ Zip _____

14. **MONTHLY PAYMENTS** (Payments of 12 months or more duration)

Automobile: To _____ Amount $ _____ Balance _____

To _____ Amount $ _____ Balance _____

Other To _____ Amount $ _____ Balance _____

(Alimony, To _____ Amount $ _____ Balance _____

Dependent To _____ Amount $ _____ Balance _____

Support, To _____ Amount $ _____ Balance _____

Taxes, Garnishment)

15. **IN CASE OF EMERGENCY, NOTIFY:**

Name _____ Relationship _____

Address _____ Zip _____ Phone No. ( ) _____

16. **HAS APPLICANT EVER FILED FOR BANKRUPTCY?** _____

Date Filed _____ In what state filed? _____ Date Granted _____

17. Have you ever been evicted or had judgment issued against you? Yes _____ No _____

18. IF APPLICANT IS SELF-EMPLOYED, PLEASE ATTACH PHOTOSTATS FOR PAST TWO YEARS OF:

    a. Individual U.S. Tax Form 1040   b. Self-employment U.S. Tax Schedule C

19. IF APPLICANT IS PAID ON AN HOURLY OR WEEKLY BASIS, ATTACH FORM W-2 FOR THE PAST TWO YEARS WITH YOUR APPLICATION.

20. I HEREBY CERTIFY THAT THE ABOVE INFORMATION IS TRUE TO THE BEST OF MY KNOWLEDGE.

21. I HEREBY AUTHORIZE THE PERSON OR FIRM TO WHOM THIS APPLICATION IS MADE, ANY CREDIT BUREAU OR OTHER IN-VESTIGATIVE AGENCY EMPLOYED BY SUCH PERSON, TO INVESTIGATE THE REFERENCES HEREIN LISTED OR STATEMENTS OR OTHER DATA OBTAINED FROM ME OR FROM ANY OTHER PERSON PERTAINING TO MY CREDIT AND FINANCIAL RE-SPONSIBILITY.

PLEASE READ BEFORE SIGNING APPLICATION.

Leasing Agent _____   Applicant _____

Firm _____   Applicant _____

Agent to Verify Applicant's Identification   Applicant Acknowledges Receipt of Copy of this Application

Type of Identification _____

Agent attach Business Card

FOR OFFICE USE ONLY

Approved By _____ Date _____ Applicant Notified _____ Date _____

Lease Signed (Date) _____   Desired Occupancy Date _____

DEED OF LEASE

Tenant
Landlord
Agent

THIS DEED OF LEASE made this _____ day of _____, 19 _____, by and between _____, hereinafter referred to as Tenant, and _____, hereinafter referred to as Landlord, and _____, hereinafter referred to as REALTOR-Agent.

WITNESSETH

Address of Property
Term Rent

THAT IN CONSIDERATION of the premises, rents and covenants herein expressed, Landlord hereby leases to Tenant and Tenant rents from Landlord, upon the terms and conditions herein set forth, the certain property known as _____ for the term commencing _____, 19 _____, and ending _____, 19 _____, for the total sum of $ _____ payable as follows: the first installment of $ _____ covering the period _____ through _____, 19 _____, due before occupying the premises and subsequent installments of $ _____ due on the first day of each calendar month thereafter without notice, demand or deduction.

REALTOR-Agent is authorized to manage the property on behalf of Landlord, and REALTOR-Agent's address is _____. If Landlord is an individual not residing in Virginia and is required by Va. Code 55-218.1 to appoint an agent, the name and address of such agent are _____

Late Fee
Cost of
Returned
Checks

1. If any installment of rent is not received by REALTOR-Agent/Owner within _____ days from the due date, Tenant covenants and agrees to pay as additional rent the sum of $ _____. Tenant further agrees to pay REALTOR-Agent/Owner a handling charge of $ _____ for each check returned by the bank for insufficient funds or any other reason.

264

Default of Rent

In the event that Tenant fails to pay when due any installment of rent, or additional rent, and such rent, or additional rent, is not paid within five (5) days after written notice by Landlord or REALTOR-Agent of non-payment and of intention to terminate this lease, in addition to other remedies provided by law, Landlord may terminate this lease. Upon such termination Landlord shall be entitled to possession of the property, to any unpaid rent or additional rent, to any damages sustained and to such attorney's fees as may be recoverable by law. It is further covenanted and agreed between the parties hereto that if any installment of rent hereinbefore reserved be not paid at the time and place agreed upon, although no formal or legal demand shall have been made for the same, or if any of the covenants, conditions, or agreements herein contained shall not be performed or observed by the Tenant, according to their full tenor and effort, or in case the leased premises shall be deserted or vacated, then in either or any of said events the Landlord may proceed to recover possession of said premises in accordance with the law governing proceedings between Landlord and Tenant.

Security Deposit

2. Tenant has paid or before occupying the premises agrees to pay the sum equal to one months rent as security for the faithful performance by Tenant of his obligations hereunder. In the event of any breach or failure of Tenant hereunder, the Landlord shall have the right to use and apply the said security in the manner provided and permitted by law. Within seventy-two (72) hours following termination of the tenancy, Landlord or his Agent shall make a final inspection of the

Inspection and Condition of Property

premises. If Tenant had faithfully performed his obligations hereunder, paid all rent and other charges due Landlord, returned all keys and left the premises (including all fixtures, facilities and appliances) in the same condition as when premises were occupied except for reasonable wear and tear and normal depreciation, then Landlord shall within forty-five (45) days after the termination of tenancy and delivery of possession of premises return the amount of the security to Tenant with such interest as required by law. If Landlord has made any deductions from security deposit or accrued interest as permitted by law, all of said deductions shall be fully itemized in writing to Tenant within forty-five (45) days of termination of tenancy. No part of said security or any accrued interest as required by law shall be applied by Tenant as payment of any part of the rent or other obligations due hereunder and Tenant shall pay rent required each month as though no security were ever made. The Tenant further covenants and agrees that in the event of his default in any installment of rent, or in the event of his breach of any covenant or condition hereof, that he will reimburse the Landlord for any money expended for reasonable attorneys' fees or other costs which may be incurred, such reasonable attorneys' fees being 20% of any sums owed to Landlord by Tenant.

Renewal

3. This lease shall not be construed to be automatically renewed at the end of the term for which drawn. A new lease negotiation will be required.

Fixtures Provided

4. Landlord shall under this lease provide the following fixtures and appliances: _____

_____

Sublease

5. This lease shall shall not be assigned, nor any portion of the premises sublet without the prior written consent of the Landlord or REALTOR-Agent. Any sublease approved by the Landlord shall not in any way relieve Tenant from the obligations contained in this lease.

Use

6. Tenant will use said property as a _____ for _____ persons and for no other purpose or additional number of persons whatever, except children born hereafter and temporary guests, without prior written consent of Landlord or Agent.

NVBR 14277 PMe

Pets

7. Tenant shall not keep pets on premises without written consent of Landlord or REALTOR-Agent. If written consent is granted, the following pet(s) may be kept on the premises: _____ The Tenant agrees to pay the cost of having the house de-flead and de-ticked by a professional exterminator at the termination of occupancy, should the above consent be given. Tenant further agrees to assume all liability and to be responsible for any damage caused by said pet(s).

Health and Safety

8. Tenant shall comply with all obligations primarily imposed upon tenants by applicable provisions of building and housing codes materially affecting health and safety.

Plumbing and Appliances

9. Tenant shall keep the premises, including all plumbing fixtures, facilities and appliances as clean and safe as condition permits; and shall unstop and keep clear all waste pipes thereon. The Tenant expressly covenants and agrees that at the termination of the lease that all utilities will be in good working order and that the premises will be in good condition ordinary wear and tear excepted. The Tenant is responsible for loss or damage from freezing of water pipes or plumbing fixtures or from the stopping of water closets and drains which shall be repaired at the expent of the Tenant, unless cause is beyond his control.

Use and Repair of Facilities

10. Tenant shall use in a reasonable manner all electrical, plumbing, sanitary, heating, ventilating, air conditioning, and other fixtures, facilities and appliances in the premises, and Tenant shall be responsible to repair them at his expense for any damage caused by his failure to comply with this requirement.

Damaging Property

11. Tenant shall not deliberately or negligently destroy, deface, damage, impair or remove any part of the premises (including fixtures, facilities and appliances) or permit any person to do so whether known by the Tenant or not, and Tenant shall be responsible for any damage caused by his failure to comply with this requirement.

Notice of Defects or Malfunction

12. Tenant will give Landlord or REALTOR-Agent prompt notice of any known defect, breakage, malfunction or damage to or in the structure, equipment or fixtures in or on said property. This covenant, however, does not obligate, and is not to be understood, interpreted, construed, or in any way to imply that Landlord or Agent is obligated or expected to repair or correct such defect, breakage, malfunction, or damage.

Tenant Conduct

13. Tenant shall conduct himself and require other persons on the premises with his consent, whether known by the Tenant or not, to conduct themselves in a manner that he will not disturb his neighbors' peaceful enjoyment of their premises, and the Tenant further covenants and agrees that he will not use nor permit said premises to be used for any improper, illegal or immoral purposes, nor will he use, permit, or suffer the same to be used by any person or persons in any noisy, dangerous, offensive, illegal or improper manner.

Burglary Prevention

14. Tenant shall, if he installs for his safety new burglary prevention and fire detection devices, provide Landlord with a duplicate of all keys and instructions on how to operate all devices and shall, upon termination of tenancy if requested by Landlord, remove all such devices and repair all damages.

Redecorating

15. Tenant shall obtain written permission before redecorating and shall not, except for 14 above, make any alterations, additions, or improvements without first obtaining Landlord's written consent and such shall, at the option of Landlord, remain with the property or be removed by Tenant and premises returned to original condition at the expense of Tenant.

Maintenance of Lawn and Fences

16. Tenant shall, at his own expense, keep up and preserve in good condition the lawn and garden (including all trees and shrubs), if any, and keep the fences and walls, if any, in good repair, natural wear and tear excepted. Tenant shall also remove ice and snow as necessary and/or required by local ordinance.

Trash Removal

17. Tenant shall provide appropriate receptacles for the collection, storage and removal of garbage, rubbish and other waste and arrange for the removal of same.

Utility Charges

18. Tenant will pay all utility charges, including but not limited to gas, water, sewer fee, electricity, waste removal and telephone. Said utility charges will commence on _____, 19 _____.

Insurance Negligence

19. Tenant shall protect by insurance in the amount of $300,000 public liability and $50,000 property damage from whatever cause to his person or property and to the person or property of those on the premises with his consent, and Tenant shall indemnify and hold Landlord harmless from all claims arising from any such injury or damage. (Nothing herein shall be construed to relieve Landlord of any of his liability to Tenant rising under law.) The insurance policy shall name the Landlord as additional insured, and a certificate evidencing such inclusion shall be forwarded to the Landlord within ten (10) days after commencement of the lease.

Truthfulness of Rental Application

20. The Rental Application submitted by Tenant has been an inducement for Landlord to rent the premises to Tenant. If any material facts in the Rental Application are untrue or if the premises are occupied by anyone other than Tenant and his family as stated in the Rental Application, Landlord shall have the right to terminate this lease, to hold Tenant liable for any damage to the premises, to avail himself of all rights and remedies to which he may be entitled at law or in equity, and to recover reasonable attorneys' fees and costs as allowed by law.

Good Repair

21. Except as otherwise provided herein, Landlord will maintain the said property in good repair and tenantable condition and will be responsible for all repairs not due to the fault or negligence of the tenant during the continuance of this lease.

Possession of Premises

22. In the event that Landlord is unable to deliver possession of the premises at the commencement of the tenancy, the Landlord agrees to use whatever efforts are in his determination reasonable to secure possession of the premises for Tenant, including the recovery of possession as against a former occupant wrongfully holding over, but in no event, except for the willful and deliberate conduct of Landlord, shall be liable to Tenant for any delay in possession. Notwithstanding the provisions of the foregoing sentence, Tenant shall have no responsibility to pay rent for the time elapsing from the beginning of the term of this lease until the premises are available for occupancy by Tenant.

Subordination of Lease

23. This lease shall be subordinate to the lien of existing and future mortgages placed on the premises, and Tenant agrees to execute whatever additional agreements are required to so subordinate this lease. Landlord shall have the right to assign any of his rights under this agreement at any time.

Condemnation

24. Landlord shall have the right to terminate this lease if the premises, or any part thereof, are condemned or sold in lieu of condemnation.

Access to Property by Landlord, REALTOR-Agent and Their Duly Designated Representatives

25. Upon reasonable notice to Tenant and at reasonable times, Landlord, REALTOR-Agent and/or their duly designated representative may enter the premises in order to (a) inspect the property, (b) make necessary or agreed repairs, decorations, alterations or improvements, (c) supply necessary or agreed services, (d) exhibit the property to prospective or actual purchasers or tenants, mortgagees, workmen or contractors, and (e) in addition, one month proceding the expiration or termination of said term, Tenant will allow "for rent" or "for sale" signs to be placed on the property. In case of an emergency, Landlord, Agent, or their designated representative may enter the dwelling unit without consent of Tenant. During the last ten (10) days of this lease or any renewal period, if the premises have been vacated, Landlord or Agent shall have access to the premises in order to make repairs or decorate for an incoming tenant.

NVBR 14277 PMe

DEED OF LEASE—*Page 2*

267

Tenant's Refusal to Allow Access

26. If Tenant refuses to allow access to Landlord or REALTOR-Agent as provided in paragraph 25 of this lease, Landlord may obtain injunctive relief to compel access or may terminate this lease. In either case, Landlord may recover actual damages sustained and reasonable attorneys' fees. After termination of this lease, whether by expiration of the term or by termination by Landlord upon breach by Tenant, the property shall be promptly vacated by Tenant, all items of personal property of Tenant shall be removed, and the property shall be left in good and clean order, reasonable wear and tear excepted. If Tenant fails to so vacate the property, Landlord may bring an action for possession and damages against Tenant, including reasonable attorneys' fees.

Rights of Landlord Upon Breach of Lease by Tenant

27. If Tenant violates any of the provisions of this lease or any of the rules and regulations imposed by Landlord or the Agent, or if any bankruptcy or insolvency proceedings are filed by or against Tenant (or a receiver or trustee is appointed for his property), or if the premises are vacated or abandoned, Landlord shall be entitled to avail himself of all rights and remedies to which he may be entitled, either at law or in equity (including but not limited to, the right to terminate this lease and recover possession) and Landlord shall be also entitled to recover reasonable attorneys' fees and costs as allowed by law. Landlord's waiver of one default by Tenant shall not be considered to be a waiver of any subsequent default. Tenant waives the benefit of any exemption under the homestead, bankruptcy, and any other insolvency law as to his obligations in this lease.

Virginia Residential Landlord-Tenant Act

28. The rights and responsibilities of the persons signing this lease are governed by the Virginia Residential Landlord and Tenant Act (Chapter 13.2, Title 55 of the Code of Virginia as amended), and to the extent any provision of this lease is in conflict with the Virginia Residential Landlord and Tenant Act, the provisions of the Act will control.

Posting of Signs

29. No signs, advertisements or notices shall be painted or affixed upon any part of the building, outside or inside, nor shall any article be suspended outside the building, save with the consent in writing, of the Landlord.

Placement of Extra-Heavy Items

30. The Landlord reserves the right to prescribe the weight and proper position of iron safes, or other extra heavy articles, and the manner of placing them in position; and the Tenant shall be liable for all damages to the building caused by taking in, using or removing the same.

Equipment That Overloads A System

31. Tenant will not install or use, or permit to be installed or used, any equipment of any kind that will require any alteration or additions to, or create an overload on, any gas, water, heating, electrical, sewerage, drainage, or air conditioning systems of the said property, without prior written consent of the Landlord, and the permission of any governmental agency or public utility company, as and if required, and compliance with applicable public laws.

Explosives and Inflammables

32. The Tenant will not use or keep in the dwelling any explosives, or inflammable or combustible materials which would increase the rate of fire insurance on the premises.

Rental Fee

33. Landlord has agreed and does hereby agree that in consideration of REALTOR-Agent's management services, Landlord will pay REALTOR-Agent a commission of _____ per centum per month of the rental received from Tenant during the term of this lease and during any renewal and extension thereof or during the term of any new lease respecting the premises between Landlord and Tenant. No sale, transfer or assignment by Landlord shall affect REALTOR-Agent's right to receive commissions, provided that in the event Landlord sells the premises, then upon Landlord's furnishing REALTOR-Agent with an agreement signed by the purchaser assuming Landlord's obligations to the Agent under this lease, REALTOR-Agent will release the original Landlord from any further obligations to REALTOR-Agent hereunder. REALTOR-Agent is a party to this lease solely for the purpose of enforcing his rights under this paragraph, and it is understood by all parties hereto that REALTOR-Agent is acting solely in the capacity as agent for Landlord. Tenant agrees to look exclusively to Landlord with respect to the covenants and agreements to be performed by Landlord hereunder.

REALTOR'S Commission on Sale or Exchange

34. Should Tenant or Tenant's heirs or assigns purchase said property during the original term or any extension or renewal of this lease, or within three months following the termination thereof, REALTOR-Agent shall be paid in cash by Landlord a commission of _____ per centum of the purchase price at the time settlement or conveyance is made pursuant to such purchase. This paragraph is not to be construed, interpreted, or understood, however, as giving the Tenant a right, privilege or option to purchase said property.

Transfer Clause

35. It is further understood, agreed and covenanted that if Landlord is transferred back to the Washington Metropolitan area by his employer, he shall have the right to terminate this lease by giving Tenant at least _____ days notice in writing to that effect, whereupon Tenant will vacate and surrender possession of said property to Landlord within said termination period; and similarly, if Tenant is transferred from the Washington Metropolitan area by his employer, he shall have the right to terminate this lease by giving Landlord at least _____ days notice in writing to that effect, whereupon Tenant will vacate and surrender possession of said property to Landlord within said termination period. In the event of termination pursuant to this paragraph, then rent shall be adjusted to the termination date specified in notice given by party that gave termination notice. The terminating party shall be obliged to furnish the other party a copy or other official certification of the transfer orders.

Additions and Improvements

36. It is expressly covenanted and agreed that all alterations, additions to fixtures, and improvements in or on said property made by either party (except movable furniture or unattached and movable equipment put in at the expense of Tenant) shall immediately become the property of the Landlord and shall remain upon and be surrendered with the said property as a part thereof at the termination of this lease, unless prior to removing such alterations, additions, fixtures and improvements which were made or installed by Tenant, Tenant shall restore or fully compensate Landlord for the cost of restoring the property hereby leased to its original condition, that is, its condition before such alterations, et cetera, were made or installed.

Liens Upon Property

37. The Tenant has no authority to incur any debt or to make any charge against the Landlord and/or REALTOR-Agent or assign or create any lien upon the said leased property for any work or materials furnished the same.

Destruction by Casualty

38. If the said property shall be partially damaged by fire or other cause without the fault and neglect by Tenant, the damage shall be repaired by and at the expense of Landlord and the rent, according to the extent that the property is rendered untenantable, shall be suspended until such repairs are completed. If the said property is damaged by fire or other cause to such extent that Landlord shall decide not to restore the property to the former condition or Landlord shall decide to demolish the structures on said property, then and in either of such events, Landlord shall have the option to terminate this lease by written notice to Tenant, and the term of this lease shall terminate on the day such notice is given with the balance of the rent due hereunder adjusted to the date of such termination.

No Waiver

39. No waiver or oversight of any breach of any covenants, condition or agreement herein contained, or compromise or settlement relating to such a breach shall operate as a waiver of the covenant, condition or agreement itself, or any subsequent breach thereof.

Property Unfit for Habitation

40. If the whole, or any part, of said property should be declared, posted, or be the subject of formal notice, by or pursuant to any governmental authority or law, that it is unfit, unsafe, uninhabitable, unsuitable or not lawfully usable for the purpose or persons under this lease, Landlord shall have the option of eliminating or correcting the cause thereof, if such can be done, and Landlord elects to do so, or terminating this lease from the date Landlord gives notice to Tenant of such termination or from the date Landlord is compelled by law to terminate further occupancy or use of said property, whichever date is earlier, and the remaining rent due hereunder shall be proportionately adjusted to the effective date of such termination.

269

Condemnation

41. If the whole, or any part, of said property shall be taken or condemned pursuant to any governmental authority for any public or quasi-public use or purpose, the term of this lease shall cease and terminate from the date when the possession of the part so taken or condemned shall be required for such use or purpose, and the remaining rent due hereunder shall be proportionately adjusted to the effective date of such termination.

Landlord Without Liability

42. In no event shall Landlord or Agent be liable for damages or compensation to Tenant or Tenant's assigns, household, agents, or licensees, or any other person or entity, because of the events, conditions, actions, or terminations described in or arising from or connected with the provisions of paragraph 40 or 41.

Failure to Fulfill Covenants

43. It is specifically covenanted and agreed between the parties hereto that these presents are executed upon each and all of the conditions, covenants and agreements contained herein, and that if the Tenant, or his executors, administrators, family or invitees do or shall neglect, fail or refuse to perform or observe any of the covenants, conditions, agreements, or undertakings herein contained, or if said premises shall be deserted or vacated, then and in any of said cases, in addition to other remedies therefor provided by law, the Landlord or those having the estate in said premises, may lawfully forthwith or at any time thereafter, enter into and upon the said premises, or any part thereof, by force or otherwise and without being liable to any prosecution, suit or damages therefor, and repossess the same and expel the Tenant or those claiming under or through him and remove his or their effects without demand or notice, and without prejudice to any remedies which might otherwise be used for arrears of rents, or preceding breach of covenant, and this lease shall terminate and end, and the Tenant hereby specifically agrees that he will indemnify the Landlord, its successors or assigns, against all loss or deficiency of rent or other payments which he may incur by reason of such termination, and without further notice or consent of the Tenant may proceed to relet said premises. The Tenant also agrees that all property on the said premises and for thirty (30) days after removal, shall be liable to distress for rent, and waives the benefit of all laws exempting any of his property from levy and sale either on distress for said rent or on judgment obtained in a suit therefor.

Removal of Property

44. It is further provided and agreed between the parties hereto that said Tenant shall not remove, or attempt to remove any personal property or other properties so moved to the said premises while there shall yet remain due and owing, any portion of the rent reserved to be paid hereunder; and if the Tenant shall attempt to remove said property, then and in such event, the Landlord is hereby empowered to forthwith seize and detain the same until it shall be fully paid for or such rent as shall be due him under the term of this lease.

Tenant Neglect and Costs

45. If at any time during the term of this lease, or any renewal or extension thereof, Landlord should be required by any governmental authority to make repairs, alterations or additions to said property or its equipment, caused by the use or neglect thereof by Tenant, Tenant hereby agrees to have said repairs, alterations or additions made at Tenant's risk, cost and expense, and if Tenant fails to do so promptly, Landlord shall have the option of terminating this lease, or causing such repairs, alterations, or additions to be made, and the cost of same, plus 6% thereof, shall be considered as additional rent for said property and payable forthwith by Tenant. The provisions of this paragraph shall be in addition to, and shall not prevent the enforcement of, any claim Landlord or Agent may have against Tenant for any other breach or damages under this lease.

Death of Tenant or Landlord

46. If the Landlord or Tenant, husband or wife, should die during the term of this lease, the surviving spouse of the deceased may terminate this lease by giving thirty (30) days written notice to the other parties involved in the lease. This right of termination of lease must be exercised within ninety (90) days of death of party concerned.

47. All individual provisions, paragraphs, sentences, clauses, sections and words in this lease shall be severable and if any one or more such provision, section, paragraph, sentence, clause or word is determined by any court, administrative body, or tribunal, having proper jurisdiction, to be in any way unenforceable, or to be in any way violative of or in conflict with any law of any applicable jurisdiction such determination shall have no effect whatsoever on any of the remaining paragraphs, provisions, clauses, sections, sentences, or words of this lease.

THIS AGREEMENT is the entire agreement between the parties, and no modification or addition to it shall be binding unless signed by the parties hereto. The covenants, conditions and agreements contained herein are binding upon and shall inure to the benefit of the parties hereto and their respective heirs, executors, administrators, personal representatives, successors and assigns. Tenants signing this Agreement shall be jointly and severally liable. Wherever the context so requires, the singular number shall include the plural, the plural the singular, and the use of any gender shall include all other genders.

Witness the following signatures and seals:

_____ (SEAL)
Tenant

_____ (SEAL)
Tenant

_____ (SEAL)
Tenant

_____ (SEAL)
Tenant

_____ (SEAL)
Landlord

_____ (SEAL)
Landlord

_____ REALTOR

By: _____ (SEAL)

DEED OF LEASE—Page 4

NVBR 14277 PMe

271

MAINTENANCE SCHEDULE

Address: _____   Year: _____

Task	Scheduled	Performed	Person/Firm
1. Annual inspection	_____	_____	_____
2. Gutters cleaned	_____	_____	_____
3. Heating/cooling system serviced	_____	_____	_____
4. Water and sewage payment checked	_____	_____	_____
5. Termite inspection	_____	_____	_____
6. Christmas gift for tenants	_____	_____	_____
7. Other	_____	_____	_____
_____	_____	_____	_____
_____	_____	_____	_____
_____	_____	_____	_____
_____	_____	_____	_____
_____	_____	_____	_____
_____	_____	_____	_____
_____	_____	_____	_____
_____	_____	_____	_____
_____	_____	_____	_____

FINANCIAL RECORD-KEEPING FORMS

INCOME

Date	Source of Income	Item	Amount Paid	Security Deposit	Outstdg. Balance

EXPENSES

Advertising

Date	Item	Paid to	Amount

Cleaning and Maintenance

Date	Item	Paid to	Amount

Repairs

Date	Item	Paid to	Amount

Supplies

Date	Item	To Whom Paid	Amount

Other

Date	Item	To Whom Paid	Amount

CAPITAL EXPENDITURE

Date	Improvement	Cost	Recovery Period

END-OF-THE-YEAR EXPENSES

1. Auto and Travel   _____
2. Commissions   _____
3. Insurance   _____
4. Interest   _____
5. Legal and Other Professional Fees   _____
6. Taxes   _____
7. Other

INDEX